COLLECTED ECONOMIC PAPERS

VOLUME ONE

COLLECTED ECONOMIC PAPERS

JOAN ROBINSON

VOLUME ONE

The MIT Press
Cambridge, Massachusetts

First MIT Press edition, 1980
Published in Great Britain by Basil Blackwell, 1980

© Basil Blackwell Publisher 1951

Library of Congress Cataloging in Publication Data

Robinson, Joan, 1903–
   Collected economic papers.

   Includes bibliographical references and index.
   1.   Economics—Addresses, essays, lectures.
I.   Title.
HB33.R6 1980   330   79–24584
ISBN 0–262–18093–6 (v. 1)
         0–262–18094–4 (v. 2)
         0–262–18095–2 (v. 3)
         0–262–18096–0 (v. 4)
         0–262–18097–9 (v. 5)
         0–262–18098–7 (Index)
         0–262–18099–5 (v. 1–5 & Index)

Printed in Great Britain

TO MY PUPILS

INTRODUCTION

THIS volume of collected papers is dedicated to the pupils whom I have been trying to teach during the last twenty years at Cambridge, because any merit there may be in it is due to the continual effort that they have forced upon me to reconcile contradictions, remove obscurities and eliminate mysticism from the body of economic doctrine that I had to expound.

I do not add the usual reservation to my acknowledgement to my pupils, for I think they should be held responsible for any errors that they have allowed me to maintain.

When I came up to Cambridge, in 1922, and started reading economics, Marshall's *Principles* was the Bible, and we knew little beyond it. Jevons, Cournot, even Ricardo, were figures in the footnotes. We heard of 'Pareto's Law', but nothing of the general equilibrium system. Sweden was represented by Cassel, America by Irving Fisher, Austria and Germany were scarcely known. Marshall was economics.

There is a deep-seated conflict in the *Principles*, of which Marshall himself was uneasily aware,[1] between the analysis, which is purely static, and the conclusions drawn from it, which apply to an economy developing through time, with accumulation going on; but somehow we managed to swallow it all.

When I returned to Cambridge in 1929 and began teaching, Mr. Sraffa's lectures were penetrating our insularity. He was calmly committing the sacrilege of pointing out inconsistencies in Marshall (his article of 1926,[2] also, was still reverberating) and at the same time revealing that other schools existed (though they were no better). The elders reacted by defending Marshall as best they could,[3] but the younger generation were not convinced by them. The profound inconsistency between the static base and the dynamic superstructure had become too obvious.

At this point, it seems to me now that I took the wrong

[1] See, in particular, Appendix H.
[2] 'Laws of Returns under Competitive Conditions', *Economic Journal*, December, 1926.
[3] 'Symposium on Increasing Returns and the Representative Firm', *Economic Journal*, March, 1930.

turning. Professor Pigou had long since worked the hard core of Marshall's analysis into a logical system of static theory (to do so, he introduced the idea of the optimum size of firm, as a means of rescuing competition from internal economies). Instead of abandoning the static analysis and trying to come to terms with Marshall's theory of development, I followed Pigou and worked out the *Economics of Imperfect Competition* on static assumptions. The first group of pieces in this collection belong to that system of ideas, though the second already exposes the weakness of the analysis, and the third was intended only to show that static equilibrium theory could provide a distraction from the state of the news. The third group, which includes pieces on Marx and on books by Schumpeter and Harrod, deals with theories of development. It seems to me now that, if we had taken him in the right way, Marshall would belong there also.

In the monetary field, in 1922, the Quantity Theory was dominant, in spite of the fact the Keynes' *Tract on Monetary Reform* had thoroughly exposed its hollowness. Unemployment was an oppressive problem in the real world, but theory had little to say about it. (I remember, in my first year, asking my supervisor what was the objection to putting men to work on publicly financed schemes, and being told that, as the dole was less than the wage, it was more economical to leave them unemployed.)

In 1929 Keynes was lecturing from the proof-sheets of the *Treatise of Money*. When the book appeared at the end of 1930, a great rage of controversy and discussion began, from which the *General Theory of Employment, Interest and Money* emerged five years later. The first piece in the second part of this collection gives an outline of Keynes' theory as far as it had got in 1933. (This article was written for the first number of the *Review of Economic Studies*, a journal which was founded as part of a movement by some of the younger members of the London School of Economics and of the Cambridge faculty to get together behind the backs of their embattled seniors.)

There is a curious point connected with this article. The controversy which immediately succeeded the publication of the *Treatise* was largely occupied with what we used to call the 'buckets-in-the-well theory'—that is the theory that when the demand for consumption goods falls (thriftiness increases) the demand for capital goods (investment) rises by an equal amount,

I wrote an article (as far as I can recollect, in the summer of 1931) attempting to explain Keynes' answer to this argument (the article is somewhat tedious at this time of day, and is not included in this collection). It was accepted by *Economica* but (I never knew why) it did not appear until February, 1933, a few months before the first number of the *Review of Economic Studies* came out. After Keynes' death Professor Samuelson pointed out, in a jesting footnote,[1] that this pair of articles exhibits the transition from the *Treatise* to the *General Theory*, and Mr. Klein followed up his hint by an attempt to date the birth of the *General Theory* between February and October 1933.[2] I tell this tale as an awful warning to historians.

The pieces in the second section of this collection are various attempts to expound and defend the *General Theory*.

The third section, on dynamic theories, and the fourth, on international trade, are also deeply influenced by Keynes and consist mainly of applications of his method to problems which he did not deal with himself.

The last item in this collection owes nothing to Keynes, but everything to Marshall.

Articles and reviews from the *Economical Journal*, *Economica*, the *Review of Economic Studies*, the *Quarterly Journal of Economics*, *Nationaløkonomish Tidsskrift*, *Economia Internazionale*, *The Times*, and *Soviet Studies*, appear with the kind permission of the editors concerned. They are republished without alteration (except for a few excisions) but I have added short postscripts to several of them.

JOAN ROBINSON

CAMBRIDGE

---

[1] *Econometrica*, Vol. XIV, 1948, p. 200.   [2] *The Keynesian Revolution*, pp. 39–40.

CONTENTS

PART I

PART IV

PART V

PART I

EULER'S THEOREM AND THE PROBLEM OF DISTRIBUTION

I⊤ is characteristic of the development of economic theory that propositions which appear very simple when we have arrived at them should be first sighted through a haze of ambiguities and approached only by a labyrinth of devious controversy. Of this curious process the history of the famous 'adding-up problem' provides a striking example.[1]

As soon as it began to be asserted that factors of production are paid in accordance with their marginal products, the problem was posed: How do we know that, if each factor is paid its marginal product, the total product is disposed of without residue, positive or negative? Of course, it is obvious that in any case the total product is distributed among the factors of production. The real question is: Can it be true that each and every factor receives a rate of reward equal to its marginal product? To some writers the theory of marginal productivity appeared as a grand moral principle which showed that 'what a social class gets is, under natural law, what it contributes to the general output of industry'.[2] But others were beset by doubt. It appeared easy enough to show that the self-interest of employers will ensure that the rate of earnings of each employed factor is equated to its marginal product.[3] The difficulty lay with the entrepreneur. How can we be certain that, when the factors have been paid, the residue which is left over measures the contribution of the entrepreneur?

One answer, provided by J. B. Clark among others, was that in static conditions the entrepreneur makes no specific contribu-

[1] This question, first canvassed in about 1890, is still 'the subject of lively controversy'. Professor Robbins (Introduction to Wicksteed's *Common Sense of Political Economy and Selected Papers*, Vol. I, p. xi).

[2] J. B. Clark, 'Distribution as Determined by a Law of Rent', *Quarterly Journal of Economics*, April, 1891, p. 313. See also *Distribution of Wealth*, p. 3.

[3] A necessary assumption which often fails to be made clear is that the supply of each factor to an individual employer is perfectly elastic, so that the price of a factor represents its marginal cost to the employer.

tion, so that in fact the earnings of entrepreneurship are always tending to approach zero. Another was that since it is always open to an employer to take service as an employee, or for an employee to set up in business as an employer, the earnings of an individual cannot depart from what he would receive as an employee, and what he would receive as an employee is equal to his marginal product. This argument, used in a more or less ambiguous form by many writers, was explicitly stated by Edgeworth,[1] only to show that it is not perfectly satisfactory. A similar point of view is to be found in Marshall's application of the 'principle of substitution' to the problem.[2]

An entirely different line of attack was adopted by Wicksteed, in the *Co-ordination of the Laws of Distribution.* Using 'the mathematical form of statement . . . as a safeguard against unconscious assumptions, and as a reagent that will *precipitate* the assumptions held in solution in the verbiage of our ordinary disquisitions',[3] he set out the theorem derived from Euler that, where $P = f(a,b,c, \ldots)$ is a homogeneous function of the first degree, so that

$$mP = f(ma, mb, mc, \ldots),$$

then
$$P = a\frac{\partial P}{\partial a} + b\frac{\partial P}{\partial b} + c\frac{\partial P}{\partial c} + \ldots$$

Translated into economic language, this proposition states that the total product is equal to the sum of the amounts of the factors, each multiplied by its marginal product, provided that conditions of constant returns prevail, in the sense that a given proportional increase in the amount of every factor of production would lead to the same proportional increase in the product.

When confronted with the precision of Euler's theorem, the argument from the principle of substitution is seen to prove at once too much and too little. It amounts to saying that when the employing factor can take service as an employed factor without any loss of advantage, then the normal level of profits for employers is equal to their marginal productivity as employees. Therefore what they actually receive, when profits are normal, is their marginal product. Thus, on the one hand it makes no overt proviso that constant returns prevail, and so appears to be too

---

[1] *Papers Relating to Political Economy,* Vol. I, p. 30.
[2] *Principles of Economics,* Book VI, Chapter VII.
[3] *Co-ordination,* Prefatory Note, p. 4.

general. On the other hand, it leaves us in doubt as to what would happen in a case in which the employing factor has only inferior alternative occupations, and equally in a case in which profits are not normal. It was this vagueness which led Edgeworth to say that the theorem that the employer, as well as the employed factors, receives a reward equal to his marginal product 'is neither quite true nor very important'.[1]

Euler's theorem leaves us in no such doubt. If constant returns prevail, and if each employed factor is paid its marginal product, then the remnant which goes to the employing factor is equal to its marginal product, whether profits are normal or not.

But at the same time the solution by Euler's theorem did not appear to be perfectly satisfactory. It seemed to imply that we are not to be allowed to believe in the principle of marginal productivity unless conditions of constant return can be shown to prevail in the real world.[2] This gave rise to an appearance of conflict between the mathematical and the economic line of reasoning, which, as the sequel will show, was completely illusory.

Wicksteed himself regarded conditions of constant physical returns as universal,[3] but he was perplexed because the 'social product' of an industry in terms of satisfaction obviously does not increase proportionately to the factors of production employed by the industry; nor does the 'commercial product' of a firm increase proportionately to the factors employed by the firm. He suggested an ingenious method for surmounting the first difficulty. The consumers also might be regarded as a factor necessary for the production of satisfaction.[4] Then, if each factor in an industry, including consumers, is increased in a given proportion, the satisfaction produced will be increased in the same proportion, and the conditions of Euler's theorem will be fulfilled. But even this expedient will not serve to meet the second difficulty, and

---

[1] *Papers*, Vol. II, p. 338. See also Chapman, 'Remuneration of Employers', *Economic Journal*, December, 1906, p. 528.

[2] For most of the contemporaries of Wicksteed (though not, I think, for Marshall) the 'theory of marginal productivity' was a formulation of a somewhat mysterious law of nature. For the modern economist it is merely a series of self-evident propositions displaying the implications of the initial assumption that the individual employer acts in such a way as to maximize his profits. It is this fundamental difference in point of view which gives what appears to the modern reader such a perverse and fantastic character to the controversies surrounding the 'adding-up problem'.

[3] *Co-ordination*, p. 33.   [4] Ibid., p. 34.

Wicksteed realized that for a monopoly, or for a firm controlling an appreciable proportion of the output of a commodity, conditions of constant returns in value of product cannot obtain.[1]

He was therefore obliged to confine his discussion to conditions of perfect competition, and he asserted that, assuming competition to be perfect, constant returns to the individual concern must prevail universally 'equally in Robinson Crusoe's island, in an American religious commune, in an Indian village ruled by custom, and in the competitive centres of the typical modern industries'.[2] This solution of the problem was met by Edgeworth with mockery rather than argument,[3] and by Pareto with the objection that it is illegitimate to assume constant returns in terms of physical product.[4]

Wicksteed retreated in face of this criticism, withdrew the argument of the Co-ordination,[5] and substituted for its heroic precision a very cloudy passage in the Common Sense of Political Economy.[6] Professor Robbins has pointed out,[7] however, that at heart he was impenitent and continued to make use of the argument of the Co-ordination in his lectures to University Extension classes[8] some time after Pareto's criticisms had appeared.

Meanwhile Walras had published a 'Note sur la réfutation de la théorie anglaise du fermage de M. Wicksteed'.[9] While acclaiming him as a kindred spirit for his use of precise methods, and congratulating him on his refutation of the English theory of rent, Walras complained of Wicksteed's failure to take any notice of his own contribution to marginal productivity theory.[10] Following a suggestion by Barone, Walras criticized Wicksteed for postulating a homogeneous production function of the first degree, but showed that Wicksteed's result follows from the axiom that costs are at a minimum under perfect competition.[11]

[1] Co-ordination, pp. 35–6.   [2] Ibid., p. 42.   [3] Papers, Vol. I, p. 31.

[4] Cours d'économie politique (1897), Vol. II, p. 83 note, and 'Anwendung der Mathematik auf Nationalökonomie', Encyklopädie der Mathematischen Wissenschaften (1904), Vol. I, Part II, p. 1117 note.

[5] Common Sense, Vol. I, p. 373 note, and Review of Pareto's Manuale, Economic Journal, December, 1906, p. 554 note.

[6] Common Sense, Vol. I, pp. 370–73.   [7] Ibid., p. xi.   [8] Ibid., Vol. II, p. 862.

[9] Recueil publié par la Faculté de Droit, Université de Lausanne, 1896.

[10] The peevish egoism of Walras contrasts unfavourably with the modesty and single-mindedness of Wicksteed.

[11] Pareto accused Walras of the same error of which Walras accused Wicksteed. We have here started a hare which it would take too long to pursue. For the history

Walras (like Pareto and many subsequent critics) implies that Wicksteed had merely overlooked the possibility of increasing returns due to economies of large scale to the firm. In the present context 'increasing returns' means a state of affairs in which an equal proportional increase in each factor would give a more than proportional increase in the product. Clearly where economies of large scale are present, increasing returns in this sense will prevail. But Wicksteed had not forgotten this obvious fact. His error was far more subtle. He rejects 'the crude division of the factors of production into land, capital, and labour', and maintains that 'we must regard every kind and quality of labour that can be distinguished from other kinds and qualities as a separate factor. . . . Still more important is it to insist that instead of speaking of so many £ worth of capital we shall speak of so many ploughs, so many tons of manure, and so many horses, or foot-pounds of power'. 'On this understanding', he writes, 'it is of course obvious that a proportional increase of all the factors of production will secure a proportional increase of the product'.[1] Now, economies of large scale can only arise from the existence of an indivisible productive unit which is not being used to its full capacity.[2] On Wicksteed's plan such a unit would be regarded as a single factor of production. Thus a firm which is subject to economies must be employing the whole of at least one indivisible 'factor'. The smallest increase in output that can then be made without altering the proportions of the 'factors' is an increase of a hundred per cent, and the marginal productivity principle cannot be applied. In order to consider the effect upon output of a small change in the amount of a factor, it is necessary to define the factors in a manner at least sufficiently crude for each factor to be finely divisible.[3] Wicksteed had not gone astray

of this dispute, which contains some entertaining incidents, the reader is referred to Professor Schultz, 'Marginal Productivity and the General Pricing Process', *Journal of Political Economy*, October, 1929.

[1] *Co-ordination*, p. 33.

[2] Cf. E. A. G. Robinson, *Structure of Competitive Industry*, p. 25.

[3] It must, however, be conceded to Wicksteed that, strictly speaking, it is impossible to reduce a group of non-homogeneous productive units to a common term so that they can be treated as a single factor. Any statement about the marginal productivity of a 'factor' which is not perfectly homogeneous cannot be perfectly accurate. I should like to take this opportunity of pointing out that the device suggested in my *Economics of Imperfect Competition* (p. 332) for getting over the difficulty by constructing 'corrected natural units' is completely worthless.

because he had ignored the existence of economies of large scale, but because in his endeavour to define the factors in such a way as to eliminate the possibility of increasing physical returns he had accidentally eliminated the possibility of defining the marginal productivity of a factor. When the factors are divided on a plan which makes marginal analysis applicable to them, the possibility of increasing returns reappears.[1]

Mr. J. A. Hobson, some years later, made the existence of economies of large scale the basis of a grand attack upon the whole marginal productivity principle,[2] which was very inadequately answered by Marshall in the well-known footnote about shepherds.[3] Mr. Hobson constructs a numerical example in which there are increasing physical returns to the individual productive unit up to a certain output, and beyond that output diminishing physical returns. He shows that where increasing returns prevail, the marginal product multiplied by the amount of the factor[4] is greater than the total product, and declares that the notion that factors are paid their marginal products is therefore completely nonsensical. He goes on to argue that the individual concern will consist of such an amount of factors that average productivity is at a maximum, and points out that the earnings of the factor is equal to its average product.

Marshall dismisses this argument with the remark that 'he appears to be mistaken'. But clearly Mr. Hobson was right; with perfect competition and normal profits (these are postulated, though somewhat vaguely) the average net productivity of each factor is at a maximum, and is equal to the wage of the factor.[5] Where he went wrong was in denying that marginal productivity also is equal to the wage.[6] The reason why he overlooked this

[1] The reader will perceive that the above treatment of this problem is superficial, but I must beg him to let it pass, for if we were to turn aside now to explore this territory we should certainly be benighted before the end of our journey.

[2] *The Industrial System* (1909), pp. 112–20.

[3] *Principles*, p. 517 note.

[4] His analytical technique being somewhat primitive, he considers only one factor for the sake of simplicity.

[5] Cf. my *Economics of Imperfect Competition*, p. 249.

[6] In my opinion, Mr. Sraffa over-estimates Mr. Hobson's insight on this point. See 'Sulle relazioni fra costo e quantità prodotta', *Annali di Economia*, Vol. II, no. I (1925), p. 312 note.

fact is rather curious. The following is one of his arithmetical examples (labour is the only factor employed):

No. of Men	Total Product	Average Product	Marginal Product
1	10	10	—
2	22	11	12
3	37	$12\frac{1}{3}$	15
4	60	15	23
5	72	$14\frac{2}{5}$	12

From this he argues that production will be carried on by groups of four men, who will receive a wage, not of 23, which is the marginal product of a fourth man, but of 15, which is the average product. It is the crudity of his arithmetical example that has betrayed him.[1] If the average product of four men is 15, and the marginal product 23, average productivity must still be rising at the point where four men are employed. The true maximum of average productivity lies somewhere between four and five men, and, at the maximum, marginal and average productivity are equal.

Thus Marshall and Mr. Hobson are each right in what they assert, and wrong in what they deny,[2] and if Mr. Hobson had been more subtle in his use of arithmetic, or Marshall less unable to suffer fools gladly, the whole controversy would have been cleared up on the spot.

Meanwhile, Wicksell had expanded Walras' account of the problem.[3] He adopts the view that there is no specific economic function for the employer as such, and deduces from this that the supply price of enterprise or normal level of profits must be zero, for if at any moment a positive profit were being earned by employers, it would soon be reduced to zero by the competition of new entrants eager to share this painless method of earning a livelihood.[4] He proceeds to show, by a line of argument similar to that of Wicksteed, that when each employed factor is paid a

---

[1] Cf. Edgeworth on Prof. Seligman, *Papers*, Vol. II, p. 397.

[2] Marshall's example of the shepherds is not open to this objection if it is taken to apply to what I call the 'quasi-long period' (*Imperfect Competition*, p. 47). There is no tendency for normal profits to be established among his sheep-farmers.

[3] *Vorlesungen über Nationalökonomie*, Vol. I, pp. 186–91.   [4] Ibid., p. 187.

rate of reward equal to its marginal product to the firm, profits can only be zero if constant physical returns prevail.[1]

He then argues that at a position of competitive equilibrium constant physical returns will prevail. Up to a certain output of the firm there will be increasing returns due to economies of large scale, but if increasing returns to the firm prevail, average cost per unit of output will be falling and competitive equilibrium will be impossible. Beyond a certain output rising average cost may occur. This also is incompatible with equilibrium, because if the output of a firm is so large that average costs are rising, the firm must be earning a positive profit; consequently new firms will enter the industry, and the fall in price of the commodity will drive the old firms back to the output at which average cost is at a minimum.

The upshot of all this appeared to be that, so long as conditions of perfect competition[2] are postulated, there is no difficulty about constant physical returns to the firm. But it is necessary to be clear as to what exactly we mean by a firm. The problem of providing a formal treatment of the factor 'entrepreneurship', which is easy to handle analytically and at the same time is not too remote from actuality, has never been satisfactorily solved. Three possible methods may be considered, each more appropriate to some problems than to others, but none perfectly satisfactory for any.

First, we may postulate (following Wicksell) that there is no specific function of decision-taking for the entrepreneur to perform, and that the owners of one factor—for instance, capital— hire the services of the others. Capital, as well as the other factors, must be assumed to be employed up to the point at which its marginal productivity to an employing unit is equal to its cost

---

[1] Dr. W. L. Valk in criticizing Wicksell's argument on this point shows that he fails to mention the difference between the marginal product of the 100th man when 100 men are employed with 100 units of land, and the marginal product when 100 men are employed with 101 units of land. Dr. Valk appears to argue that the fact that marginal productivity analysis requires us to conceive changes in the factors so small that this difference is negligible, is sufficient to render marginal productivity analysis completely valueless. *Principles of Wages*, p. 74. Cf. Edgeworth on Mr. J. A. Hobson, *Papers*, Vol. I, p. 19, note 3.

[2] Throughout this essay I am using the phrase perfect competition to mean simply that the elasticities of demand and of supplies of factors for a single firm are infinite. This implies no reference to free entry into the trade or normal profits.

to that unit—that is, to what it can earn as an employed factor.[1] Capital is thus upon exactly the same footing as the other factors. A profit or loss to the employer is then a difference between total receipts and total costs, including the cost of capital. Second, we may postulate that each firm consists of a single indivisible unit of entrepreneurship whose supply price is independent of the amount of output it controls. Or, third, we may postulate that each entrepreneur is not a fixed unit, but performs more or less of his decision-taking function according to the reward which he can earn.

In the first two cases clearly there is no meaning to be attached to the notion of 'marginal product of entrepreneurship to the firm'. When either of these schemes of analysis is adopted, therefore, the employer must not be regarded as a specific factor of production from the point of view of the firm, and constant returns to the firm must be said to prevail when a given proportional increase of every factor except entrepreneurship would give the same proportional increase in output. In the third case the entrepreneur must be conceived to regulate the amount of effort he supplies to the firm by its marginal productivity to the firm, in just the same way as he regulates the amount of the factors he employs. The entrepreneur's effort is therefore upon exactly the same footing as an employed factor. Constant returns are then said to prevail when a given proportional increase of every factor, including the entrepreneur's effort, gives the same proportional increase in output, and profits are reckoned excluding the variable element in the reward of the entrepreneur.

Each of these methods of depicting entrepreneurship is highly unrealistic, but they are adopted merely in order to display the workings of the marginal productivity principle in various types of case, and are not put forward as an attempt to solve the problem of a realistic treatment of entrepreneurship as a factor of production.[2]

Whichever method is adopted, it is clear from Euler's theorem

---

[1] The case of imperfectly elastic supply of factors to an employing unit is considered later.

[2] A large part of the literature of the subject is devoted to debating the proper analytical treatment of entrepreneurship as a factor; see Edgeworth (*Papers*, Vol. I, 'Theory of Distribution') and the authors cited by him. The question has recently been revived by Mr. Kaldor: 'The Equilibrium of the Firm', *Economic Journal*, March, 1934.

that in conditions where physical returns, in the relevant sense, are constant, profits in the relevant sense must be zero. For when competition is perfect the wage of each factor is equal to the value of its marginal physical product and there is no residue for the employer.

It is now apparent that Wicksell's assumption of zero normal profits is an essential step in his argument. It is impossible to argue in general that because average cost to the firm is at a minimum in competitive equilibrium therefore constant physical returns to the firm prevail; for the cost which is at a minimum in competitive equilibrium is average cost including normal profits. If normal profits are positive the output at which average cost is a minimum is greater than the output at which net economies of large scale give way to net diseconomies, and constant physical returns do not prevail.

The history of the controversy up to this point is summarized in the Appendix to the *Theory of Wages* by Dr. Hicks.[1] He shows, in effect, that even when Wicksteed had taken the drastic step of confining his argument to cases of perfect competition, he was not yet out of the wood, for he had postulated constant physical returns as a universal technical necessity. This postulate is shown by Pareto and by Walras to be inadmissible, but Wicksell contends that, for the output which will be produced in competitive equilibrium, constant physical returns to the firm do prevail whatever the technical conditions. Thus it appeared that Wicksteed's assumption of perfect competition, required to get him out of a difficulty of which he was aware—diminishing returns in terms of value—incidentally saved him from a difficulty of which he was not aware—increasing returns in terms of physical product.

Wicksteed's problem was that the marginal productivities of the factors, multiplied by the amounts of the factors, absorb the whole product without residue only in conditions of constant returns. Wicksell's argument shows that constant physical returns will prevail under perfect competition. Thus it appears that, so long as we admit Wicksell's postulate of zero normal profits, there is really no problem at all. On the contrary, the result is exactly

[1] I should like to take this opportunity to make my acknowledgments to Dr. Hicks for the helpful guide-map which he provides to this else bewildering territory, and to Professor Robbins as the champion and editor of Wicksteed.

what we should expect, for it is only if competition is perfect that the earnings of the factors are equal to the value of their marginal physical products, and only when profits are zero that the earnings of the factors absorb the whole product. After all this long debate we reach a self-evident conclusion.

Nevertheless it is impossible to be satisfied with a solution which applies only to the case of zero profits. The condition that the employed factors receive the value of their marginal physical product to the firm under perfect competition must be fulfilled even when profits are positive or negative.[1] But it is an illusion to suppose that this presents any difficulty, for if profits are not zero, constant returns do not prevail. In the present context, increasing or diminishing returns must be said to prevail according as a given proportional increase in the amount of every factor would lead to a greater or smaller proportional increase in output. Now, the economist can prove that profits are negative or positive according as returns are increasing or diminishing for the individual firm. For, under perfect competition, marginal cost to the firm, for the output at which profits are a maximum, is equal to the price of the product. When a loss is being made by the employer, price is less than average cost. Therefore marginal cost is less than average cost. Therefore the average cost curve of output is falling, and physical returns are increasing. Conversely, when a profit is being made by the employer, physical returns are diminishing. While the mathematician has only to set out the generalized form of Euler's theorem in order to show[2] that

$$P \lesseqgtr a\,\frac{\partial P}{\partial a} + b\,\frac{\partial P}{\partial b} + \ldots$$

according as

$$mP \gtreqless +f\,(ma,\ mb,\ \ldots)$$

If the normal level of profits is positive, the number of firms will be so limited that diminishing physical returns to the firms prevail to just the extent which is compatible with the required profit. A positive profit of this level will fail to attract in new

[1] Dr. Hicks is content to confine himself to the case of zero profits since he holds that in conditions of equilibrium there is no function for the entrepreneur (*Theory of Wages*, p. 234). Beyond this point in our argument, therefore, Dr. Hicks' guidance is less helpful.

[2] Cf. Wicksell, loc. cit., p. 189, and Chapman, loc. cit., p. 526 note.

enterprise, and so fail to drive existing firms back towards the output at which constant physical returns prevail.

Thus it appears once more that there was really no problem, for it is obvious that the total product cannot be absorbed by the earnings of the employed factors when profits are positive, and we already knew that when profits are positive diminishing physical returns prevail.

But all this applies only to marginal productivity from the point of view of a firm under perfect competition. We have as yet thrown no light on the proposition, contested by Edgeworth, that the entrepreneur, as well as the employed factors, receives a reward equal to his marginal product. For the marginal product of the entrepreneur to the firm has no meaning. The question must therefore be whether the earnings of the entrepreneur are equal to the marginal productivity of entrepreneurship to the industry.[1] Our next task is to consider marginal productivity from the point of view of an industry, retaining the assumption of perfect competition.

From the point of view of an industry, enterprise must be treated on just the same footing as the other factors, for even if we take the view that there is no specific economic function of entrepreneurship, yet it remains true that the productivity of the other factors varies with the number of firms in which they are organized, and the difference which is made to their productivity by adding an entrepreneur is the marginal product of entrepreneurship.[2]

The proposition that, with constant physical returns to the industry, total output is equal to the sum of the amounts of the factors each multiplied by its marginal physical product to the industry, can be very simply proved by means of Euler's theorem. But the economist can supply his own demonstration of it. The self-interest of the entrepreneurs will ensure that, under conditions of perfect competition, the value of the marginal physical product to the firm of each employed factor is equal to its wage.

[1] The relationship of productivity to the industry with productivity to society is not here discussed.

[2] Anyone who rejects altogether the notion of diseconomies of large scale to a firm is at liberty to say that the marginal productivity of entrepreneurship to an industry may be zero or negative, but never positive. The argument which follows is purely formal, and begs no questions about the nature of entrepreneurship as a factor.

And under constant returns marginal physical product to the industry is equal to marginal physical product to the firm. It only remains to prove, therefore, that the reward of the entrepreneurs is equal to *their* marginal physical product to the industry. The marginal productivity to the industry of entrepreneurship is the difference which would be made to output if one entrepreneur were withdrawn.[1] That is, the output of one firm *minus* the output which the factors employed by that firm would produce if they were dispersed among the remaining firms. Thus, the value of the marginal physical product of entrepreneurship is the value of output of one firm *minus* the amounts of the employed factors each multiplied by the value of its marginal physical productivity. This is equal to the total receipts of the firm *minus* the total cost of the employed factors. And this is the reward of the entrepreneur.

It is to be observed that this proof contains no reference to normal profits. If we are considering Wicksell's case in which there is no supply price of entrepreneurship, so that the level of normal profits is zero, then in full equilibrium the entrepreneurs receive nothing, and their marginal productivity to the industry is zero. If the normal level of profits is positive, their marginal productivity in equilibrium is positive. If profits are more or less than normal, the marginal productivity of entrepreneurs to the industry is correspondingly high or low, owing to the temporary scarcity or superabundance of entrepreneurs which has caused profits to depart from the normal level.[2]

But what of economies of large-scale industry?[3] When there are economies of large scale, the sum of the amounts of the factors each multiplied by its marginal physical product is greater than the total output. But this causes no difficulty, for the simple reason that the rewards of the employed factors are not equal to

[1] The number of firms in the industry being n, it is necessary to assume that n is so large that the difference between the marginal physical productivities of the constant amount of other factors when they are working with n entrepreneurs and when they are working with $n - 1$ may be neglected. Cf. above, p. 8, note 1.

[2] When the entrepreneur's earnings vary with the amount of effort which he supplies to his firm, the unit of entrepreneurship from the piont of veiw of the industry is best regarded as a single entrepreneur doing that amount of work whose marginal cost to him is equal to its marginal product to the firm.

[3] It is here that we must finally dispense with the guidance of Dr. Hicks, for in this region his map contains nothing but a blank space marked *Terra Incognita*. Loc. cit., p. 240.

their marginal physical products to the industry. The marginal product of a factor to the industry is greater than to the firm by the extent of the economies induced by a unit increase in the amount of the factor employed. And it is the marginal product to the firm which is equal to the wage of the factor. Similarly, the marginal productivity of an entrepreneur to the industry is greater than his earnings by the amount of economies which accrue to the other firms when an increment is added to output whose value is equal to the value of his marginal physical product to the industry.[1] Thus once more the economist finds himself in complete accord with Euler. If the factors *were* paid the value of their marginal products to the industry, total cost would be greater than total receipts when increasing returns to the industry prevail. But actually each factor is paid less, and the total product is exactly disposed of among them.

Conversely, if there are diminishing returns to the industry, in the sense in which we have been using that term, that is, if there are real diseconomies of large-scale industry,[2] then the factors are paid more than their marginal product to the industry to a degree exactly corresponding to the extent of the diseconomies.[3]

All this while we have been dwelling in the world of perfect competition. It is time to return to Wicksteed's long-neglected difficulty, and consider the analysis of marginal productivity under

[1] This is upon the assumption that economies of large-scale industry depend solely upon the output of the commodity and not on the proportions of the factors, so that the production function is homogeneous, though of a higher degree than unity. If the economies vary with the amounts of particular factors employed (the production function is not homogeneous) then only those factors which give rise to economies receive less than their marginal physical products to the industry. Cf. Tarshis, *Review of Economic Studies*, February, 1934, p. 145.

[2] We are here concerned with the 'rare type' of diminishing returns (see *Imperfect Competition*, p. 348). The reader must guard against misleading associations with the 'common type' of diminishing returns.

[3] The above argument bears some resemblance to that of Sir Sydney Chapman in his article on the 'Remuneration of Employers' (*Economic Journal*, December, 1906). But his definition of 'increasing and diminishing returns' is somewhat obscure, and matters are not much improved by Edgeworth's comments (*Papers*, Vol. I, p. 99). Sir S. Chapman is quite correct in saying that the reward of the entrepreneur is less than the value of his marginal physical product to the industry when there are economies of large scale. What he evidently failed to realize was that his argument applies to the other factors just as much as to entrepreneurship (loc. cit., p. 527 note). His argument was somewhat grudgingly received by Edgeworth (*Papers*, Vol. II, pp. 331-9), who appears to have had a rooted objection to applying the marginal productivity analysis to the case of the entrepreneur.

imperfect competition. First consider the matter from the point of view of the individual firm, assuming that, while the market for the commodity is imperfect, the supplies of factors to the firm are perfectly elastic. Under imperfect competition, a firm which is earning zero profits must be producing at falling average cost.[1] Therefore conditions of increasing physical returns to the firm prevail. At a hasty glance it might appear that the provisions of Euler's thoerem are therefore violated. But this is not the case. For the earnings of a factor are not equal to the value of its marginal physical product, but to the marginal product in value to the firm; and are thus less than the value of the marginal physical product in the ratio of marginal revenue to price.[2] To satisfy the conditions of Euler's theorem it is necessary to show, not that constant returns in terms of physical output prevail when profits are zero, but that constant returns in terms of value prevail. That is to say, a given proportional increase in every factor employed must give the same proportional increase in the total value of the product.

Wicksteed regarded constant physical returns as a universal condition; therefore, since the price of the commodity produced by the firm falls as its output increases, it was impossible for him to conceive of constant returns in value under imperfect competition. For him diminishing returns in value must always rule. But as soon as we introduce economies of large scale to the firm into the picture Wicksteed's difficulty disappears. Constant returns in value will prevail at the output at which technical economies due to an increase of output just offset the accompanying fall in selling price. And it will be proved in a moment that constant returns in value do prevail when the firm is earning zero profits. Once more the methods of economic analysis will be found to lead to the conclusions of Euler's theorem.[3]

[1] See *Imperfect Competition*, p. 97. In that passage I am including normal profit in cost, whereas in the present context cost is reckoned excluding profit.

[2] Ibid., p. 237.

[3] The complete harmony between them is well illustrated by the case in which a firm selling in an imperfect market happens to be producing under conditions of constant physical returns. This will occur when, by a fluke, the marginal revenue curve cuts the marginal cost curve at the output at which it in turn cuts the average cost curve. Constant physical returns prevail, but the factors are receiving less than their marginal physical product; consequently there is a positive profit. The factors receive their marginal product in value, but diminishing returns in value prevail; consequently there is a positive profit. By either line of reasoning the conditions of Euler's theorem are seen to be fulfilled.

Before turning to the general proof let us consider the case in which competition in hiring the factors is not perfect, so that the supplies of factors to the firm are less than perfectly elastic. We know that in such a case the wage of a factor is less than its marginal product in value. For the marginal product must be equated to the marginal cost of the factor to the firm, and this *ex hypothesi* is greater than the wage.[1] Once more there appears at first sight to be a contradiction, but once more upon examination the difficulty disappears, for it is no longer appropriate to measure the factors in physical terms; they must be measured in terms of outlay.

The condition of constant returns may now be more generally defined. It obtains when a given proportional increase in the outlay upon every factor employed would lead to the same proportional increase in value of output. Hitherto we have considered cases in which the supplies of the factors to the firm are perfectly elastic, so that up to this point it has been indifferent whether the factors are measured in physical terms or in terms of outlay. But in the general case a given proportional increase in the outlay upon a factor gives a proportional increase in the amount of the factor which is less in the ratio of average to marginal cost of the factor to the firm.[2] Although the wage of a factor may be less than its marginal product in value per physical unit of the factor, it must be equal to the marginal product per unit of outlay. It follows at once from Euler's theorem that profits are zero, positive, or negative according as returns are constant, diminishing or increasing, measured in terms of value and of outlay.

The same proposition can be proved without resort to Euler's theorem. When profits are zero the average cost curve of the firm is tangential to the demand curve for its output.[3] For the output at which the curves are tangential, profits are at a maximum of zero; any greater or smaller output would yield a loss. Therefore a curve relating value of output to average outlay per unit of value of output would be at a minimum at this point, and

---

[1] See *Imperfect Competition*, p. 293.

[2] The above argument applies to the case of an entrepreneur who supplies units of effort to his firm at rising cost (see above, p. 9), a rising subjective cost of effort being reckoned in money terms. The entrepreneur will supply that amount of effort whose marginal cost to him is equal to his marginal product in value to the firm. Cf. Edgeworth on Mill (*Papers*, Vol. I, p. 17).

[3] Cf. *Imperfect Competition*, p. 94.

constant returns in terms of value and outlay prevail. If a positive profit is being made, the demand curve for the firm lies above its average cost curve. But for the most profitable output, marginal revenue and marginal cost are equal; therefore the demand curve, which is higher, must have a greater slope than the cost curve.[1] Therefore receipts per physical unit of output fall off faster than outlay as output increases, and conditions of diminishing returns in terms of value and outlay prevail. Conversely, when a loss is being made, increasing returns in terms of value and outlay prevail. The harmony between the economist and the mathematician is complete.

It only remains to consider the case of an industry with imperfect competition between the firms composing it. To isolate the effect of imperfect competition, assume constant physical returns to the industry.[2] Then the employed factors receive less than the value of their marginal physical products to the industry, these being equal to their marginal physical products to the firm. Thus it can be shown directly by appealing to Euler's theorem, that the entrepreneurs receive more than the value of their marginal physical product to the industry. Alternatively, adapting the argument developed above for the case of perfect competition, we may say: the marginal physical product of an entrepreneur is equal to the output of a firm *minus* the amounts of the factors employed by a firm each multiplied by its marginal physical product. But the factors are paid less than the value of

---

[1] Let x be output, y price, and z average cost.

Then $y + x \dfrac{dy}{dx} = z + x \dfrac{dz}{dx}$ (marginal revenue = marginal cost).

$\therefore$ if $y > z, \dfrac{dy}{dx} < \dfrac{dz}{dx}$.

$\therefore$ the negative slope of the demand curve is greater than that of the cost curve.

(In perfect competition—see p. 10 above—we have the special case in which $\dfrac{dy}{dx} = 0$.

$\therefore$ when $y > z, \dfrac{dz}{dx}$ must be positive. Since the prices of the factors are constant, this entails diminishing physical returns.)

[2] It is to be observed that the kind of falling supply price for an industry that occurs because competition becomes more perfect as the industry expands (*Imperfect Competition*, p. 101) is not due to increasing returns in the sense here relevant, but arises from the fact that the proportion of entrepreneurship to other factors becomes more favourable (that is, less) as the industry expands and the firms grow in size.

their marginal physical products; therefore the earnings of the entrepreneurs are greater than the value of the marginal physical product of entrepreneurship. This is a symptom of the fact that under imperfect competition the ratio of entrepreneurs to other factors is higher than that which would give minimum cost,[1] or, in other words, that the size of the firm is uneconomically small.[2]

The fact that under imperfect competition the entrepreneurs receive more than their marginal physical productivity to the industry was perceived by Wicksteed, but, shaken by Pareto's criticisms, he had not sufficient confidence to state it as a definite proposition. In 1905 he wrote that the 'general result of investigation so far as it has yet been carried is to make it seem probable that in proportion as we approximate to the state of things usually assumed in the Theory of Political Economy (i.e. free competition, in which each individual competitor does only a small fraction of the total business of his market) we approximate to the result indicated [total product equal to the sum of the factors each multiplied by its marginal product]. So far as we recede from these conditions (for instance, in a great monopoly or trust) we recede from this result, and give the persons who control the concern something more than their distributive share in the product as measured by their marginal industrial efficiency'.[3]

And already in 1894 he had caught a glimpse of it: 'The failure fully to confirm and generalize a property in the productive functions which would yield an admirably compact and complete co-ordination of the laws of distribution need not discourage us. Its suggestions as to the line of attack we must follow in dealing with monopolies, and with the true socialising of production, are so magnificent in their promise that we are more than consoled for the want of completeness in our immediate results'.[4] But, after forty years, economists are still debating the adding-up problem and neglecting to fulfil that magnificent promise.

[1] This is true even if the reward of the entrepreneur is zero, for in that case his marginal physical product to the industry must be negative.

[2] The analysis of the effects of increasing or diminishing physical returns to the industry can be superimposed on the analysis of imperfect competition. For instance, it can be seen that if increasing returns prevail, the employed factors will receive less than the value of their marginal products for two reasons, while the entrepreneurs will receive a reward which may be less or more than the value of their marginal product, according as the effect of increasing returns outweighs or is outweighed by the effect of imperfect competition.

[3] *Common Sense*, Vol. II, p. 862.   [4] *Co-ordination*, p. 38.

POSTSCRIPT

This paper was written in a satirical spirit, as a comment on those who believe that a proposition can be 'mathematically correct' and yet not true.

The last point seems to be wrongly stated. Monopoly secures high profits, not by raising the reward of the entrepreneur above his marginal product, but by keeping his marginal product artificially high.

WHAT IS PERFECT COMPETITION?

WHAT do we mean by 'perfect competition'? The phrase is made to cover so many separable ideas, and is used in so many distinct senses, that it has become almost valueless as a means of communication. It seems best, therefore, to begin with a definition. By perfect competition I propose to mean a state of affairs in which the demand for the output of an individual seller is perfectly elastic.

This is a far more restricted definition than that which is to be found in many modern writings. To Professor Knight, for instance, perfect competition entails rational conduct on the part of buyers and sellers, full knowledge, absence of frictions, perfect mobility and perfect divisibility of factors of production, and completely static conditions.[1] This definition is unusually wide. More commonly these various strands of thought are separated from each other, and the term 'perfect competition' applied only to some of them. There are, however, two notions which seem to be very closely linked in many minds and lumped together as 'perfect competition'. These are, first, a situation in which a single seller cannot influence price (that is perfect competition in my terminology), and second, a situation in which a single seller cannot make more than normal profits. Leaving all the rest on one side, I wish to confine myself to discussing only these two meanings of the phrase 'perfect competition'.

Mr. Sraffa, whose article[2] of 1926 took such an important part in the work of emancipating economic analysis from the tyranny of the assumption of perfect competition, was not himself completely aware of the freedom that he was winning for us. He was content to say that when competition is imperfect there is no need to consider the problem of normal profits and the entry of new firms into an industry, since the entry of new firms into an imperfect market must necessarily be difficult.[3] But it is a simple

---

[1] *Risk, Uncertainty, and Profit*, pp. 76–80.
[2] 'The Laws of Returns under Competitive Conditions', *Economic Journal*, December, 1926.
[3] Ibid., p. 549.

step to carry Mr. Sraffa's own argument to its logical conclusion. He had shown that in the real world almost every market is imperfect, and it would be impossible to contend that in the real world new firms hardly ever enter any industry. In 1930, Mr. Shove[1] was still adopting a somewhat ambiguous attitude to the question and failed to snap completely the connection between the notion of perfect competition and the notion of free entry into an industry.

Professor Chamberlin in 1933 performed a useful service in categorically separating the two ideas. He distinguishes between 'pure competition' and 'perfect competition'.[2] *Pure* competition is a state of affairs in which the demand for the output of each firm is perfectly elastic,[3] while *perfect* competition may be conceived to require the further conditions of 'an ideal fluidity or mobility of factors', 'absence of uncertainty',[4] or 'such further "perfection" as the particular theorist finds convenient and useful to his problem'. Here the issue is clearly stated. But Professor Chamberlin's terminology is somewhat misleading, and pays a verbal tribute to the old confusion. It seems better boldly to define *perfect* competition in the terms which he confines to *pure* competition and so to force the particular theorist to state specifically what further conditions he finds it useful to assume for the purposes of each problem.

In his article on 'Doctrines of Imperfect Competition'[5] Mr. Harrod appears at first sight to follow this procedure, and his definition of 'perfect competition' is the same as my own. But in the course of his argument it becomes clear that even for him 'perfect competition' implies free entry.[6] It therefore seems desirable, before discussing the conception of a perfectly elastic demand for the output of an individual seller, to say something

---

[1] 'Symposium on Increasing Returns and the Representative Firm', *Economic Journal*, March, 1930.

[2] *The Theory of Monopolistic Competition*, p. 6.

[3] Professor Chamberlin does not give quite this account of 'pure competition'. He says, 'Purity requires only the absence of monopoly, which is realized when there are many buyers and sellers of the *same* (perfectly standardized) product' (op. cit., p. 25). These conditions, as we shall find, are unnecessarily severe, but by 'absence of monopoly' he appears to mean a state of affairs in which no one firm can raise its price without sacrificing the whole of its sales, and this is the essential point.

[4] Professor Chamberlin is here referring to Professor Knight, loc. cit.

[5] *Quarterly Journal of Economics*, May, 1934, p. 443. [6] Loc. cit., p. 460.

about the other strand of thought which has been entangled with it—the notion of normal profits.

The idea of normal profits in its most naïve form is the idea of a single general level of profits. Profits in any one industry, on this view, are normal when they are the same as profits in the generality of other industries. But there is obviously no more reason to expect a uniform level of profit for enterprise than there is to expect a uniform level of rent for land. In the world depicted in the well-known beginners' question, in which all land is alike in respect of fertility and site value, there is a uniform rate of rent per acre in the long period. In a world in which all entrepreneurs are alike there would be a uniform rate of profit in all industries in the long period. In the real world entrepreneurship is no more homogeneous than land in the real world. This view of uniform normal profits may therefore be dismissed as a beginner's simplification. The idea that there is one level of profits which obtains in competitive industries, and that when competition is not perfect profits must exceed this level, is clearly untenable.

Indeed, this is one of those problems in which the main difficulty is to see what the difficulty is. Normal profits are simply the supply price of entrepreneurship to a particular industry. The essence of the notion of normal profits is that when profits are more than normal, new firms will enter the trade, and normal profits are simply the profits which prevail when there is no tendency for the number of firms to alter. It is possible, of course, that the number of firms may be arbitrarily restricted. The firms may require a licence from some controlling authority, or the existing firms may be so strong that they are able to fend off fresh competition by the threat of a price war. They may even resort to violence to prevent fresh rivals from appearing on the scene. In such cases no level of profits, however high, will be great enough to tempt new firms into the trade, and the supply of enterprise to that trade is perfectly inelastic at the existing amount. For such an industry any level of profits is normal, and the term ceases to have a useful application.

In all less extreme cases there will be some elasticity of supply of new enterprise, which may be small or great according to the circumstances of the trade. The normal level of profits will be different in different industries and different at different scales of the same industry, and the level of normal profits will depend upon the conditions of supply of enterprise. Trades which require unusual personal ability or special qualifications, such as the power to command a large amount of capital for the initial investment, will tend to have a high level of normal profits; trades which are easy to enter will have a lower level.

Now there is nothing in all this which is connected with the notion of perfect competition, in the sense in which I use that phrase. It is true that a high level of normal profits will often be found where competition is imperfect. The fact that an old-established firm enjoys 'goodwill' has the effect both of giving it a hold upon the market, which enables it to influence the price of the commodity which it sells, and of increasing the cost of entry to new rivals. And the powerful firm which uses the methods of 'unfair competition' to strangle rivals is highly unlikely to be selling in a perfect market. But this association of high normal profits (not abnormally high profits) with imperfect competition is a purely empirical one. The two conceptions are analytically quite distinct, and we shall have made a considerable advance towards clear analysis when we have learned habitually to distinguish them.

But quite apart from this gratuitous confusion the whole notion of normal profits is beset with difficulties. Mr. Shove[1] has pointed out that there is not one level of normal profits, but two. The level of profits which will attract new enterprise into an industry is usually higher than the level which is just sufficient to retain existing enterprise. Entry into a trade is likely to involve considerable initial expense, and often involves, as Marshall was fond of pointing out, a lean period of low profits before the name of the firm becomes known. To move out of this trade into another would involve fresh sacrifice. 'When you are in you are in', and if demand falls after you are established you will prefer to stay where you are at a level of reward that would not have tempted you to enter the trade if you had the choice still to make.

This notion of a gap between the two levels of normal profits is associated by Mr. Harrod with imperfect competition.[2] And it

[1] *Economic Journal*, March, 1933, pp. 119–21.

[2] See Harrod, *Economic Journal*, June, 1933, p. 337, and *Quarterly Journal of Economics*, May, 1934, p. 457. In the latter article Mr. Harrod, if I understand him aright, uses the phrase 'excess profit' to describe any surplus above the lower normal level.

must be conceded that a gap is likely to occur wherever goodwill is important, so that in fact the phenomenon is likely to be found in many industries where the market is imperfect. But it is important to realize that there is no necessary connection between the two ideas. The existence of the gap depends upon costs of movement from one industry to another, and these may very well occur when competition is perfect. Moreover, competition may be imperfect, for instance, from differential transport charges, when there are no costs of movement. A gap between the upper level of reward, necessary to tempt new resources into an industry, and the lower level, necessary to drive old resources out, will exist wherever there is cost of movement between one trade and another, and the double level of normal profits is merely one example of a phenomenon which may affect every factor of production equally.

A general discussion of the phenomenon of the gap would lead us far afield, and in the present paper I propose only to inquire whether the existence of the gap destroys the usefulness of the notion of normal profits. Before tackling this question it is necessary to make a digression upon the manner in which equilibrium is attained. When we are considering discontinuous changes in the number of firms in an industry, the existence of the gap between the two levels of profits is a very serious matter. When profits are more than normal in a certain industry, a number of fresh entrepreneurs (each in ignorance of the others' action) come into the trade. With this new competition actual profits are depressed much below the level that tempted in the new entrepreneurs, but they are not, perhaps, low enough to drive out any existing firms. The industry will continue at this swollen size, and it will be in equilibrium in the sense that no new enterprise tends to enter it or old enterprise to leave it. Yet the actual size of the industry, the price of the commodity, and the level of profits ruling, are determined by the number of firms, which is determined by the excessive optimism of the latest entrants. In such a case the supply price of any amount of output depends to a large extent upon the immediate past history of the industry. If fewer firms had happened to enter in the period of high profits, the present price of a given output would have been higher; if more had entered, it would have been lower. The whole notion of a unique long-period supply curve breaks down, and with the notion of a supply curve the notion of normal profits goes by the board.

In order, therefore, to justify the notion of a supply curve at all we must make the artificial assumption that equilibrium is attained by a gradual and continuous movement. When profits are more than normal a few firms enter. Profits decline; if they are still more than normal, a new firm comes in, and another, and another, until profits are just reduced to the upper normal level and there is no incentive for one fresh firm to enter. Equilibrium is thus reached without oscillation. Similarly, when profits fall below the lower normal level, first one then another decides to abandon the struggle, and profits for those that remain are gradually raised till each of the remaining firms is contented with its lot, and no more find it worth while to leave.

This account of the matter is obviously extremely unrealistic if we have to do with large erratic movements of demand. But if demand is expanding or contracting continuously, it is plausible to suppose that firms enter or leave the industry one by one. I think, therefore, that in order to retain the idea of a long-period supply curve we may permit ourselves to take this view of the process of reaching equilibrium. And then the existence of two levels of profits introduces only a minor complication into the analysis.

There are two supply curves, one above the other. The upper one applies only to expansions of the industry, and the lower one applies only to contractions.

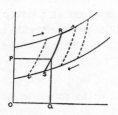

Each point on the upper curve is joined to that point on the lower curve at which the number of firms is the same by what I call a 'quasi-long-period supply curve'[1]—the supply curve of a

---

[1] *Economics of Imperfect Competition*, p. 47.

fixed number of firms. This is determined under perfect competition by the marginal cost curves of the given number of firms. Suppose we are considering an expansion of demand, and we start from a position in which price is OP and output OQ. Then, as demand is raised, supply price climbs up the quasi-long-period supply curve to R, and then proceeds (for further increases of demand) along the upper long-period supply curve to the right. Now suppose that we start from the same point and consider a contraction of demand. Then supply price slides down the quasi-long-period curve to S and for further contractions of demand supply price follows the lower long-period curve to the left.

The quasi-long-period position does, of course, depend upon past history. There is a continuous series of quasi-long-period curves, and which curve we are on at any moment depends upon the number of firms in existence at that moment, just as the familiar short-period curve depends upon the amount of fixed plant that there happens to be in the industry. But the pair of long-period curves is as much uniquely determined as the old-style single long-period curve ever was.[1] By making an admittedly unrealistic assumption about the way in which equilibrium is attained, we can rescue the long-period supply curve from the perils of the gap between the upper and lower levels of normal profits.

So much for normal profits. Leaving all this on one side, let us return to the main question. What is perfect competition? Let us take our stand boldly on the formal definition and see what it requires of us.

Competition is perfect when the demand for the output of any one firm individually is perfectly elastic. In what conditions can this be true? We are accustomed to say that there are two conditions:

1. That the market must be perfect.
2. That the number of firms must be large.

Let us examine these two conditions in turn.

---

[1] The width of the gap depends upon the length of the period in respect to which the curves are drawn. For some industries, in a sufficiently long period, there will be no gap at all; for others a considerable gap would be found even if an indefinitely long period were taken into account. The familiar short-period supply curve bridges the gap at its widest point.

The first condition, that the market must be perfect, was dealt with by Mr. Sraffa. Marshall writes: 'The more nearly perfect a market is, the stronger is the tendency for the same price to be paid for the same thing at the same time in all parts of the market; but, of course, if the market is large, allowance must be made for the expense of delivering the goods to different purchasers'.[1] Mr. Sraffa pointed out[2] that absence of frictions is not sufficient to make a market perfect, since buyers may have good and permanent reasons for preferring the output of one firm to that of another, while the presence of differential transport costs may be sufficient by itself to make the market imperfect. Moreover, he showed that the condition that the same price shall rule throughout the market is not adequate to define perfection, for if all the firms in an industry are alike in respect both to the costs and the conditions of demand, the same price will rule throughout the market no matter how imperfect it may be.

Professor Chamberlin's attitude to the perfection of the market is not quite clear. He seems to associate imperfection simply with differentiation of the product.[3] But the relationship between differentiation of the commodity and imperfection of the market is somewhat complicated. Physical differentiation is not a *necessary* condition for market imperfection. Two commodities may be alike in every respect except the names of the firms producing them, and yet the market in which they are sold will be imperfect if different buyers have different scales of preference as between the two firms. Nor is differentiation a *sufficient* condition for market imperfection. Two firms may be producing two distinct commodities, and yet these two commodities may be sold against each other in a perfect market. Suppose that every individual buyer will pay 6*d*. more for *A* than for *B*, and that everyone buys either *A* or *B*, never some of each. Then when *B* is selling at 1*s*., the smallest rise in the price of *A* above 1*s*. 6*d*. will cause every buyer to transfer his custom to *B*, and the sales of *A* will cease; and the smallest fall in the price of *A* below 1*s*. 6*d*. will increase its sales by an amount equal to the whole output of *B*. The demand for either *A* or *B*, given the price of the other, is perfectly elastic, although they are two distinct commodities.

---

[1] *Principles of Economics*, p. 325.   [2] Loc. cit., p. 542.
[3] Op. cit., Chapter IV. Mr. Harrod adopts the same view, *Quarterly Journal of Economics*, May, 1934, p. 445.

On the other hand, the market will not necessarily be perfect if all buyers have the same scale of preferences as between A and B. Suppose that when the price of A rises, each buyer purchases somewhat less of A, and somewhat more of B, but does not forsake A entirely. Then the market as between A and B would not be perfect, even though all buyers were alike. Similarity of buyers is a necessary but not a sufficient condition for the market to be perfect. For the market to be perfect it is necessary, first, that all buyers should be alike in respect to preferences, and second, that each buyer should deal with only one firm at any one time. When these conditions are fulfilled, a rise in the price charged by any one firm would, if other prices remained the same, lead to a complete cessation of its sales. And this is the criterion of a perfect market.

The definition of a commodity is completely arbitrary, and the definition of a market depends upon the definition of a commodity. Suppose that we start with a single quality of a certain perfectly homogeneous product, offered for sale by a firm at a single place and time, and group with it all other products which satisfy the condition of market perfection. In most cases we shall reach the boundary of the perfect market even before we have reached the boundary of the output of a single firm. Now let us agree upon a certain degree of imperfection in the market and group together all products in respect to which the imperfection has less than the agreed value. This group of products may be described as a single commodity. Often we can fix a convenient boundary by obvious natural landmarks, so that within it we have products which are all obviously in an everyday sense a single commodity (steam-coal, or chewing-gum), and all products outside the boundary are other commodities. But at best there must be some arbitrary element in drawing the boundary, and all products must be regarded as a continuous series in more or less close rivalry with each other. Thus the first prerequisite of perfect competition is a 'commodity' clearly demarcated from others by a boundary of natural gaps in the chain of substitutes, within which the market is perfect.

The second condition required for perfect competition is that the number of firms selling within the market is such that when any one firm alters its price there is no consequent alteration in the prices charged by the others. It is this condition that we must now examine.

First, it is necessary to stop up a blind alley that might lead us astray. It is sometimes supposed that for competition to be perfect it is necessary that the number of buyers should be large.[1] But this is the reverse of the truth. If there is only one buyer, the market for each firm must be perfect, since a relative lowering of the price by any firm would cause the single buyer to prefer its output to that of the others. And if there is more than one buyer it is necessary for perfection of the market that the buyers should all be exactly alike in respect of their preferences. The larger the number of buyers who are potential customers of any one firm, the more likely is the market to be imperfect, since the more likely are differences of preference to occur.[2]

To return to the main argument—the number of sellers necessary to secure perfect competition in a perfect market. On this point there seems to be a considerable amount of confusion. Cournot stated[3] that competition will be perfect if each seller provides so small a part of the total output of a commodity that his removal from production would make no appreciable difference to price. On this view the number of firms required for even approximately perfect competition must be extremely great. Now there is nothing unrealistic in the notion of a firm so small that its total disappearance would leave price unaffected. A certain farmer may very well root up his three acres of strawberries without producing any effect upon the price of strawberries in Covent Garden market. But is this not because, in the real world, demand curves always contain small but perceptible discontinuities? Until amount is reduced enough to put, say, a halfpenny on to price, no one will notice that anything has

[1] E.g., Chamberlin, see above, p. 21, note 3.

[2] Similarly, the larger the number of sellers supplying any one buyer, the more likely is the market to be imperfect from the point of view of buyers. The fact that the market must be perfect, from the point of view of sellers, if there is only one buyer, and is likely to be imperfect from the point of view of a buyer if there are many sellers, throws some light upon the question of 'bargaining strength' between employers and workers. In the ordinary case a single buyer, that is, one employer, will be buying from a fairly large number of sellers—the workers. Thus the workers are necessarily in the weak position of selling in a perfect market, whereas the employer is very likely to be in the strong position of buying in an imperfect market. For the employer there will be some element of what I call 'monopsony' in the situation, whereas for unorganized workers there is no element of monopoly. Cf. Harrod, loc. cit., p. 460.

[3] *Mathematical Principles of the Theory of Wealth* (Bacon's translation), p. 90.

happened. But if we assume (as we must do at this level of abstraction) a perfectly continuous demand curve, the conception of a number of firms so great that each produces a negligibly small proportion of the output of an industry, is a somewhat uncomfortable one. But it is clear that Cournot's condition is much too severe.

More commonly it is said to be sufficient for perfect competition that an increase in the output of any one firm should produce a negligible effect upon price. But this way of stating the matter is extremely unsatisfactory. How exactly does the number of firms come into the picture? Is the individual firm conceived to increase its output by a certain definite amount (one ton of coal)? In that case the effect upon price (given the elasticity of the total demand curve) depends upon the ratio of this amount (one ton) to the total output of the industry, and the number of firms has nothing to do with the case. Or is the firm conceived to increase its output by a certain proportion, say 5 per cent? Then certainly the smaller is the share of this firm in the total output, the less will be the effect upon price; but why should we be concerned with a *proportionate* change in the output of a firm? The apparent simple statement dissolves into a haze of ambiguities as soon as it is closely examined.

From this fog we emerge when the condition is stated in a third way. A small increase in output made by a single firm, the output of other firms remaining the same, will produce a perceptible effect upon the price of the commodity. But if the total output of the firm is sufficiently small, the price-cut upon its whole output, when a unit is added to the output of the industry, will be negligible. Marginal revenue is equal to price *minus* the fall in value of the old output when output is increased by one unit. If the output of the firm is very small the difference between marginal revenue and price will be very small. Marginal revenue will be almost equal to price, and the demand curve for the firm will have an elasticity sufficiently near to infinity for us to say that competition is almost perfect. The point is, not that the change in price due to a change in output is negligible when the number of firms is large, but that the effect of the change of price upon any one firm is negligible. Competition will be more perfect the smaller is the ratio of the output of one firm to the output of the industry, and more perfect the greater is the elasticity of the total demand curve. At first sight it may appear strange that the degree of competition *within* an industry should be affected by the elasticity of the total demand curve. But, after all, it is natural that this should be so. For the form of the demand curve represents the degree of competition between the product of this industry and other commodities. The stronger the competition from substitutes for this commodity, the smaller the degree of competition within the industry necessary to secure any given elasticity of demand for each separate producer.

This third statement appears to give a far more reasonable account of the matter than the account given in the first two statements. It was at this stage I had arrived when I wrote my book on the *Economics of Imperfect Competition*. I was then too much under the influence of tradition to imagine that there was anything more to be said about the matter, but I now feel that the argument must be pushed a stage further.

The difficulty lies in the assumption that when one firm in a competitive industry adds a unit to output, the output of the other firms remains unchanged. Clearly, if we take the continuity of the demand curve and of the marginal cost curves seriously this assumption is unwarranted. A small increase in the output of the industry will produce a small but perceptible fall in price. The fall in price will lead all other firms to reduce output by some fraction of a unit, since each equates marginal cost to price. We thus reach the conclusion that an increase in the output of one firm by one unit will *not* increase the output of the industry by a whole unit, but by something less. If competition is absolutely perfectly perfect, an increase in the output of one firm by one unit would leave the output of the industry unchanged, and there would be no change in price at all. Competition will be near enough to perfection for practical purposes if an increase in the output of one firm by one unit increases the output of the industry by so much less than one unit that the effect upon price is negligible.

This argument is different from the argument of the third stage. At the third stage we said that an increase in the output of a firm by one unit *would* produce a perceptible effect upon price, but the share of the firm in the loss due to the price cut would be so small as not to affect its conduct. At the stage where

I now stand we say that a unit increase in the output of one firm will not produce a perceptible effect upon price at all.

If we adopt this position it remains to inquire what effect will be produced upon the output of the other firms when one firm increases its output. This will clearly depend upon the slopes of the marginal cost curves of the other firms. The proposition to which my lengthy preamble leads up is this—it is impossible to discuss the number of firms required to ensure perfect competition without discussing the marginal cost curves of the firms composing the industry.[1]

First consider the case in which the firms have falling marginal costs for all outputs. Then, so long as the market is perfect it is impossible for two firms to survive in the industry. If there are two firms, each will be anxious to increase its output at the expense of the other, and any cut in price made by one of them will be answered by an equal cut by the other. Price will be driven down to the point at which one or other of the firms is forced out of the industry, and when only one firm is left in possession of the field it is impossible that competition should be perfect. Of course, both firms may survive if each is afraid to begin the war. The price may then be at any level, but the situation cannot be regarded as an equilibrium position, since any accidental increase in output by either firm would precipitate price-cutting.

Next, consider the case in which marginal costs are constant. Then if there are two firms competition will be perfect. Either by lowering its price to a level infinitesimally less than the marginal cost of the other can drive it from the field, and either by raising its price infinitesimally above the marginal cost of the other will lose its whole market. Here, then, we have perfect competition. But this situation cannot persist in the long period. For a firm with constant marginal costs, long-period average costs must be falling, since there must always be some fixed element in the cost of a firm, if only the minimum income of the entrepreneur. Thus when price is equal to marginal cost it is less than average cost and one or other of the firms must ultimately disappear.

We are brought back, therefore, to the familiar conclusion that marginal costs must be rising if more than one firm is to survive in a perfect market. Consider, then, an industry consisting of

[1] Cf. Harrod, *Economic Journal*, December, 1933, p. 664.

several firms for each of which marginal costs are rising. For each firm marginal cost will be equal to price. Suppose that one of these firms makes a unit increase in output. In the first instance the price of the commodity will fall to an extent depending upon the slope of the total demand curve. This fall in price will lead the remaining firms to contract output to an extent determined by the slope of their marginal cost curves. In the new position the output of one firm is greater by a unit, the output of each other firm is less by a fraction of a unit, and the price is lower than before. It follows that the cut in price associated with a unit increase in the output of one firm will be smaller, given the number of firms, the less is the slope of the marginal cost curves of the other firms. And it will be smaller, given the slopes of the marginal cost curves, the greater is the number of firms. Competition can only be absolutely perfect, given rising marginal costs, if the number of firms is infinite. Absolute perfection of competition is therefore an impossibility. Let us agree to call competition perfect if the price-cut associated with a unit increase of output by one firm is less than a certain small finite value. Then for any given slope of the marginal cost curves there is a certain number of firms which will make competition perfect. This number will be smaller the smaller the slope of the marginal cost curves, and greater the greater the slope of the marginal cost curves.

In the limiting case, where the marginal cost curves are rising vertically, we revert to our third account of the matter in which it was assumed that the output of the other firms was fixed. We are thus led to the conclusion that when supply for each firm is completely inelastic the number of firms required to give even a reasonable approximation to perfect competition must be indefinitely great.

At first sight this conclusion appears rather strange. If we are really required to believe that in the well-known case of the fish market on Saturday night there is not quite perfect competition, must we conclude that the competitive output is not sold? That some of the fish is always allowed to rot? This would certainly be hard to accept. But here another proposition comes to our rescue. When supply is perfectly inelastic it makes no difference whether competition is perfect or not. Marginal revenue is equal to marginal cost at the same output as price is equal to marginal cost, provided that the elasticity of the individual demand curve is greater than unity. Therefore price and output are the same whatever the individual elasticity of demand. Thus, although there is not, strictly speaking, perfect competition among the fishmongers on Saturday night, yet the competitive output will be sold at the competitive price unless the demand curve for fish is highly inelastic.[1]

We have thus reached the conclusion that there is not one universal value for the 'large number of firms' which ensures perfect competition. In each particular case, with given slopes of the marginal cost curves, there is a certain definite number of firms which will produce competition of an agreed degree of perfection, and this number, in some cases, may be quite small.

[1] The elasticity of the demand for one seller will be less than unity if the elasticity of the total demand falls short of unity to a sufficient extent.

RISING SUPPLY PRICE

It may seem strange at this time of day to reopen the old familiar subject of diminishing returns and rising supply price. My purpose is frankly escapist, and what follows has no relevance to any problem of importance in the real world.

Confusion in the discussion of the law of diminishing returns has mainly arisen from a failure to make clear what question is being discussed. When that has been decided the rest of the argument follows without difficulty. The classical analysis, which gave rise to the Ricardian theory of rent, dealt with the question of what happens when the supplies of labour and capital increase, and land remains fixed. This clearly has nothing to do with rising supply price for a particular commodity.[1] It belongs to the department of output as a whole. Then there is diminishing returns as it appears in the theory of employment. This is essentially a short-period problem—what happens to the prices of commodities in general when effective demand increases, organization and capital resources being given, and the amount of employment being free to increase. This also belongs to the analysis of output as a whole.

The problem of the long-period supply curve of a particular commodity belongs to the department of the theory of value, which treats of relative prices of commodities. Marshall's analysis appears to be a cross between the theory of value and the theory of output as a whole. For he seems most often to be discussing the problem of the change in the supply of a particular commodity which occurs in response to a *net* increase in demand. The demand for one commodity increases, but the demand for the rest does not decline. The additional factors, apart from land, employed in increasing the supply of the commodity are called into existence by the increase in demand. 'While the supplies of all other agents of production respond in various degrees and various ways to the

[1] Cf. Sraffa, 'The Laws of Returns under Competitive Conditions', *Economic Journal*, December, 1926.

demand for their services, land makes no such response. Thus an exceptional rise in the earnings of any class of labour tends to increase its numbers, or efficiency, or both. . . . And the same is true as regards capital'.[1]

'The building an additional floor on one factory or putting an extra plough on one farm does not generally take a floor from another factory or a plough from another farm; the nation adds a floor or a plough to its business as the individual does to his. There is thus a larger national dividend which is to be shared out. . . . In contrast to this, the stock of land (in an old country) at any time is the stock for *all* time; and when a manufacturer decides to take in a little more land to his business, he decides in effect to take it away from someone else's business'.[2]

Marshall's supply curve therefore relates to rather a queer problem. The demand for one commodity, say boots, is increased, the demand for all others remaining the same, so that there is an increase in total expenditure, devoted entirely to boots. The problem is too artificial to be interesting. But supposing we do want to discuss the problem, it is putting the cart before the horse to look at it in this way. Full employment of resources is always assumed, therefore a net increase in demand presupposes an increase in resources. And we cannot begin to discuss whether there will be diminishing returns or not until we know what factors of production have increased in supply.

The problem which belongs properly to the theory of value is the problem of how supply reacts to a transfer of demand. And when we are considering a transfer of demand, say, to boots from commodities in general, it is not at all obvious that Marshall's distinction between land and other factors has any relevance. Factors are released by the decline in demand for things in general, which are available to be employed in making boots, and land will be released as well as labour, capital, and entrepreneurship.

Professor Hicks comes nearer to discussing the proper problem.[3] But he also presents it in a peculiar form. There is an increase in the demand for commodity X at the expense of commodity Y. The price of X, according to Professor Hicks, must rise. But to this there is an obvious objection. Before we know what happens to the price of X we must know what factors are released from

---

[1] *Principles* (7th ed.), p. 534.   [2] Ibid., pp. 535–6.   [3] *Value and Capital*, p. 73.

the industry producing Y.[1] Professor Hicks merely relies upon the assumption of perfect competition.[2] Under perfect competition, it is true, marginal cost to the firm must be rising. But this is nothing to do with the case. We are discussing the supply of a particular commodity in long-period equilibrium, and it is both unnatural to assume that the number of firms producing that commodity is fixed, and unfair not to inform the reader that that assumption has been made. Further, we must notice that Professor Hicks's view that a rise in the general level of prices must accompany the rise in price of X is the result of an optical illusion, due to the fact that Y has been chosen as the *numéraire*. In a later passage Y is imperceptibly transmuted into money, and the increase in demand for X comes about through dis-hoarding.[3] The problem has thus become the issue of a cross between the theory of value and the theory of employment, comparable to that produced by Marshall's cross between the theory of value and the classical theory of output as a whole.

Let us now turn to the problem of a transfer of demand to one commodity, from commodities in general. We will assume (1) full employment, (2) perfect competition, (3) no economies of large-scale industry. The discussion is confined to conditions of full long-period equilibrium. In assuming perfect competition we have already begged the question of the definition of a commodity, for universal perfect competition is possible only in a world in which all consumption goods can be divided into groups (each group being called a commodity) such that within each group there is perfect substitutability, from the consumer's point of view, between any unit of the commodity and any other, while between commodities substitutability is less than perfect. Each group must be large enough to cover the output of a great number of firms. If the world were such that perfect competition were possible, it would be such that the demarcation of commodities would present no difficulty.

At the first stage of our argument we will further assume fixed supplies of all factors. In the real world the demarcation of factors is just as teasing a problem as the demarcation of com-

---

[1] Production has not yet been introduced at this stage of Professor Hicks's argument, but in later chapters its conclusions are taken to be valid for a system with production.
[2] *Value and Capital*, p. 83.   [3] Ibid., p. 108.

modities. But since we are assuming perfect competition, we may as well be hung for a sheep as a lamb, and assume that productive resources, as well as consumers' goods, exist in nature in groups (each group being called a factor) such that within each group the elasticity of substitution between units is infinite, while between factors it is finite or zero. By assuming no economies of large scale we have postulated that factors are divisible into units which are small relative to the supply of each factor.

Now to tackle our problem: the demand for a certain commodity, say alpha, increases while the demand for other commodities is reduced, the reduction in demand for any one commodity other than alpha being very small in relation to the increase in demand for alpha. Factors of production are transferred from industry in general to the alpha industry. If alpha employs factors in the same proportions as factors are released, the increase in output of alpha is produced under constant returns, and there is no change in relative prices.

But industries are idiosyncratic, and it is natural to suppose that alpha requires factors, not in the proportions in which they are employed in the average of all industries, but in proportions peculiar to itself. A relative increase in demand for alpha therefore entails an increase in the total demand for those factors which it employs in more than the average proportions, and a decline in demand for those factors it employs in less than the average proportions. The relative prices of factors therefore alter.

We are then confronted with the question: in what terms are we to measure the resources employed in alpha? We cannot say whether or not the supply price of alpha rises with an increase in its output until we know how prices are to be reckoned.[1] The obvious solution is to measure prices in terms of a composite unit of resources, the factors being weighted by the proportions in which they are found in industry as a whole. So long as we are assuming a fixed supply of each factor this measurement is quite unambiguous.

Now, the factors which alpha requires, or requires most, have risen in price in terms of the composite unit, while the factors which it does not require, or requires least, have fallen in price. Thus the supply price of alpha rises in terms of the composite

---

[1] Cf. Pigou, 'Laws of Diminishing and Increasing Cost', *Economic Journal*, June, 1927.

unit, while the supply price of all other commodities falls, each a little.[1] Thus, for any commodity considered separately there is rising supply price, because an increase in the output of any commodity turns the relative factor prices against itself.[2]

The strength of the tendency to rising supply price will depend upon three considerations.

1. The larger the proportion of all factors absorbed by alpha, the greater will be the effect upon relative factor prices of a given proportionate increase in the output of alpha. This expresses the familiar proposition that a widely defined industry is more likely to show rising supply price than a narrow one—there is more likely to be rising supply price for the products of engineering in general than for drawing-pins, and for agricultural produce than for brussels sprouts.

2. The more idiosyncratic alpha is in respect to the factors which it requires, the further will it be from employing factors in the average proportions, and the more will it raise the price of the factors which it requires in terms of the composite unit. This also is familiar; indeed, the whole theory of diminishing returns in particular industries has developed round the case of the industry employing a rare factor, such as special soil, a particular mineral, or an unusual human skill. In such a case the industry employs the whole of a factor which is not used in other industries at all, so that its selection of factors is very far from the average.

3. The more obstinately alpha adheres to a special selection of factors, that is, the more rigid the technical conditions, and the lower the elasticity of substitution between the factors which it employs, and between those other factors which it might employ, the greater will be the change in relative factor prices when alpha expands. For if the elasticity of substitution is high, alpha will alter its employment of factors in the direction of the average employment of all factors, in response to a rise in the relative price of the factors it happened to be employing in the first

---

[1] Cf. Robbins, 'Certain Aspects of the Theory of Costs', *Economic Journal*, March, 1934, p. 5, note.

[2] It is curious to observe that it is not necessary that there should be any change in the proportions in which factors are employed in alpha. It might happen that all the factors employed in alpha rose equally in terms of the composite unit, so that their prices relative to each other were unchanged. Thus rising supply price might occur without any appearance of diminishing returns in the ordinary sense.

position, and the change in relative factor prices will thus be kept in check.

A markedly unaverage selection of factors and a low elasticity of substitution between factors are necessary conditions for an appreciable degree of rising supply price. Even a very large industry will show a small rise in supply price if its selection of factors is near the average, or if it is nearly indifferent as to what factors it employs. On the other hand, a very small industry may enjoy sharply rising supply price if it has very specialized requirements.

Let us now remove the assumption that the supply of each factor is fixed. Within the conditions of the problem total primary resources—for instance, the population—must be assumed constant, but the supply of any particular factor—for instance, a special type of skill—may be assumed to vary in response to its price. On this assumption, when alpha expands and all other industries contract there is an increase in the supply of the factors which alpha employs in more than the average proportions, and a contraction in supply of factors which it does not employ, or employs in less than the average proportions. Our unit of measurement is no longer unambiguous, since the proportions of factors in industry as a whole are now altered. We may measure price either in terms of the composite unit appropriate to the first position, or in terms of the composite unit after the change has taken place. In either terms, the prices of the factors employed by alpha rise by less than they would have done if all supplies of factors were fixed. The change alters the composite unit in such a way as to bring it closer to the proportions of factors employed in the alpha industry; the rise in the price of the alpha factors is therefore less in terms of the new unit than of the old.

We must now add a fourth to the influences governing rising supply price. The tendency to rising supply price will be stronger the less elastic the total supplies of those factors required by the expanding industry.

When a change in the total supplies of factors is admitted, it is no longer a universal rule that each industry (unless it employs factors in the average proportions) is working in conditions of rising supply price. Falling supply price may also occur, quite apart from economies of large scale industry. To take the extreme case—suppose that all the factors which alpha employs in more than the average proportions are in perfectly elastic supply, while others, which it employs, but employs in less than the average proportions, are in perfectly inelastic supply. Then an expansion in alpha leads to a fall in the price of the bundle of factors which it employs, in whichever composite unit the price is measured.[1] In less extreme cases there may be a fall in terms of the new composite unit, when there is a rise in terms of the original composite unit. This type of falling supply price, due solely to changes in relative factor prices, is Professor Pigou's case of 'decreasing supply price *simpliciter*' which is not 'decreasing supply price from the standpoint of the community'.[2] Where falling supply price occurs, it will work more strongly the larger is the industry; for, the bigger the industry, the greater the effect of a given proportionate increase in its output in altering the supplies of factors favourably to its own requirements.

On the above analysis it is possible to support Marshall's contention that rising supply price is more likely to be found in agriculture and mining than in manufacturing industry. The primary industries are highly idiosyncratic in the factors which they require, elasticity of substitution is often zero between certain factors which they employ and any possible alternative, and the total supply of their factors is highly inelastic. Marshall's distinction between the natural factors, which give rise to diminishing returns, and man-made factors, which do not, can therefore be justified. The logical distinction is not between natural and man-made factors, but between rare and common factors, between cranky and adaptable factors, and between factors in less or more elastic supply. But when the distinctions are drawn on this basis the natural factors are clearly more likely to qualify,

---

[1] If each factor is in perfectly elastic supply constant returns must always prevail, for relative factor prices cannot alter. The departure from constant supply price, in either direction, will be greater (other things equal) the greater the difference between the elasticities of supply of those factors which the expanding industry uses in more than the average proportions and of those factors which it employs in less than the average proportions.

[2] *Economics of Welfare*, 3rd ed., p. 224. Professor Hicks must surely be in error in supposing that the 'stability conditions' cannot survive the faintest appearance of falling supply price, *Value and Capital*, p. 83. If he had provided himself with stability conditions of tougher morale he would not have been so appalled by the problem of monopoly.

in respect of rarity, crankiness, and inelastic supply, than human factors. For the general run of manufactured commodities, on the other hand, in the perfectly competitive world postulated by our assumptions, almost constant supply price would be the general rule.

The question which we have chosen to discuss is of very limited interest. No actual change in demand comes about in the form of an increase in demand for one commodity accompanied by a small reduction in demand at the margin for each other commodity. In reality the same causes which produce an increase in taste for one thing will reduce the taste for some particular other things. Thus even granted the extreme assumptions of perfect competition and full equilibrium, the question which we have been discussing is an unnatural one. When the increase in demand for alpha comes about at the expense, not of things in general, but of other particular commodities, say beta and gamma, we must know what factors are employed by beta and gamma before we can say what happens to the supply price of alpha. And we must know how the changes in price of beta and gamma react on the demands for delta and omega. The analysis can be extended to any degree of refinement, but the more complicated the question the more cumbersome the analysis. In order to know anything it is necessary to know everything, but in order to talk about anything it is necessary to neglect a great deal.

POSTSCRIPT

Keynes, who, characteristically, found time for a 'half-hour of escapism' in reading this article on April 20th, 1941 (just after Budget Day), raised this objection to point (3) on p. 39:

> I should have thought that the elasticity of substitution between the factors which a employs was merely a particular case of the much more important question of the elasticity of substitution between the factors which β, γ, etc., employ. If there is easy substitution between the factors employed by the other commodities, so that a small change in their relative prices releases the factor which a requires, a will not rise much in price, however particular it may be in its choice of factors. Generally speaking, much the biggest influence

on price is, I should have thought, the question of the ease with which the *other* commodities can be persuaded to substitute one factor for another.

This criticism is undoubtedly correct, but it does not apply to cases where the whole supply of the scarce factor is already employed by alpha.

'THE THEORY OF CONSUMER'S DEMAND'

By Ruby Turner Norris

THE theory of demand has long been due for an overhaul. Professor Hicks' reformulations, for all their elegance, make no important advance upon those of Marshall, for they are based on the same unreal view of consumers' behaviour, a view at variance not only with the teachings of modern psychology, but also with the simplest everyday observation. Dr. Norris sets out on the track of an anthropological approach: 'Something very like the hedonistic calculus is, I think, definitely a feature of our society. It occurs in somewhat different terms than are ordinarily discussed and it has much narrower applications than is commonly supposed. . . . But regardless of its extent and importance in our society it is vital for logical clarity to perceive that it is but a culture trait and therefore unstable, and is not to be supposed to characterize other societies and to be somehow inherent in our nature or ultimately more rational than other methods of exchange' (p. 67). 'The typical adult's consumption pattern is an accretion of pieces of consumption patterns he has put together like a jigsaw puzzle. Groups of pieces he has accumulated from different sources, but the majority usually come from his basic domestic economy' (p. 73). 'Let us move towards comprehensibility in terminology, realism in assumptions, and simplicity in exposition' (p. 58).

These resolutions are admirable, but unfortunately Dr. Norris is still entangled in the notions and the apparatus of utility theory, and tries to force her common-sense observations into the mould of indifference maps and marginal utility curves. This produces results of the greatest absurdity, as in the example (p. 12) where ten hats and no shoes are credited with the same total utility as five pairs of shoes and no hat, or the story (p. 131) of the girl who plays tennis, drives a car and climbs mountains, although her income is so low that she can possess only one pair of shoes.

In spite of this, some points of great interest are discussed, particularly the theory of complementary substitutes and its relation to differentiation of products (Chapter VIII). The analysis is somewhat clouded by failure to distinguish sharply enough between the demand curve of an individual consumer and the demand curve confronting an individual producer, and a related confusion between the questions which are interesting in connection with the economics of welfare and those which are connected with problems of price policy.

Latter-day experience of the restriction of consumption has brought into a clear light one great weakness of the traditional analysis of demand, which Dr. Norris does not touch upon, that is, the erroneous assumption of individualism. When a given cut in consumption has to be made, traditional theory teaches that the minimum sacrifice is imposed on consumers if the requisite amount of general purchasing power is taken away, and each consumer is left free to economize on what he feels that he can best spare. In reality, it is obvious that less sacrifice is caused by a total disappearance from the market of certain commodities, such as silk stockings, which are bought by each consumer mainly because other people have them. (Hats are an obvious example of this principle, though, at the time of writing, their production, for some reason, has not yet been prohibited). Perhaps the spread of Austerity to the United States will soon be suggesting to Dr. Norris a still more radical reconsideration of traditional theory.

In the process of reconsideration it is necessary to distil out of the conception of utility the common-sense element which it contains. The view that a second shirt adds more to satisfaction when only one is owned than a fourth when three are owned is in accordance with common sense, for it is a very great inconvenience to have no shirt to wear on washing day. But probably it would be better (as the incomplete success of Dr. Norris' treatment shows) to discard utility theory completely to start with, and to follow out the anthropological treatment of demand in a thorough-going way. When this has been done, utility theory can be credited with whatever validity the new treatment shows it to deserve.

POSTSCRIPT

It has been objected to the above that wearing silk stockings is not a matter of convention but a direct sensual pleasure. However, even if my example was ill-chosen, I stand by the main point.

'THE ECONOMIC EFFECTS OF ADVERTISING'

By Neil H. Borden

ADVERTISING has never been very well digested into the body of economic analysis. It cannot be fitted into a theory of demand in which consumers with 'given tastes' are depicted equalizing marginal satisfactions or climbing to the optimum position on an indifference surface. It is no less disturbing to the picture of producers maximizing their profits, for not only are innumerable combinations of price and advertising policy open to them in a given situation, but the yield in terms of profit of any one policy are excessively difficult to discover. The notion of a unique position of competitive equilibrium is a drastic abstraction, and the system of prices which obtains in reality is what economists call indeterminate—that is to say, it depends upon an intricate complexity of factors which economists have not succeeded in reducing to any simple formula. It seems vain to hope for much progress by traditional methods of *a priori* analysis, and factual study is therefore all the more to be welcomed.

Professor Borden has carried out a valuable piece of work in his survey of the advertisement of consumers' goods in the United States. Detailed case histories are given of advertisement of a number of commodities, from automatic refrigerators to walnuts, and every aspect of the economics of advertisement is discussed in the light of these studies and of other evidence culled from a wide field. Though written in the peculiarly dreary style which business schools seem to foster, the book is unusually well arranged, clear, and packed with fascinating detail.

All conclusions about the effects of advertisement must be tentative because of the impossibility of separating advertisement from the other influences upon demand and upon costs which are constantly changing along with it, but some broad generalizations it is possible to make.

Professor Borden comes to the conclusion that advertisement has, on the whole, little effect in moulding the general pattern of consumption. Demand for some commodities expands without

Economica, August, 1942.

any help from advertisement—he provides the example of lettuces; for others, advertisement is powerless to stem a contraction—he gives the example of men's shoes after the spread of motoring. Advertisement is important, not in expanding demand for commodities, but for particular brands. An important exception must be made for new commodities, such as refrigerators, where the unassisted growth of demand would probably have been very slow.

Another point of great interest which emerges from the discussion is the rhythmical interchange of price and non-price competition. 'The evidence indicates that when product differentiation is important in the mind of the consumer, and motives other than price are weighty in guiding consumer purchase, competition tends to turn from price to advertising and other non-price forms. Moreover, the more competition employs non-price forms, the greater is the spread between manufacturing cost and the price which consumers pay'. But 'there are strong forces to counterbalance any tendency for competition to turn solely to non-price forms. In most fields, in the course of time organizations and sellers appear who elect to offer consumers opportunity to buy merchandise on a price basis' (p. 605). A striking example of this process is provided by the history of the 10-cent cigarettes.

There is some evidence that price competition becomes more prevalent when incomes are declining. This supports Mr. Harrod's view that competition becomes more perfect after the onset of a slump.

The safeguard against excessive profit margins provided by actual or potential price competition does not operate for all commodities. For instance, in the case of tooth-paste the cheap, unadvertised brand can make little headway. With cigarettes, the consumer has only to try a packet to find what they are like, but with tooth-paste he has very little idea of what he is buying, and the reputation of the advertised brands (however mythical its foundations) makes him fear that if he buys cheap he may buy something inferior or even deleterious.

Non-price competition is particularly likely to prevail where a small number of firms dominate a market so that conditions of oligopoly obtain. A price cut is something definite, which rivals will have to follow, but it is possible to steal a march upon them by advertising. Sooner or later, however, they will counter by increasing their advertising, and so competition proceeds like an armaments race between nations. The cost is thrown upon the consumer, but the producers, as a group, do not gain, since their high profit margins are largely absorbed by marketing expenses, which in many cases amount to more than 50 per cent of gross receipts.

A large part of Professor Borden's argument is concerned with the question of whether advertising is a good thing. But it is hard to come to grips with this question, for it is impossible to separate advertising from other forms of 'aggressive selling', or to separate 'aggressive selling' from the economic system of which it is an integral part. His discussion of the ethics of advertisement, though full of interesting side-issues, is therefore somewhat superficial. The question is bound up with the question of the ethics of the profit system, which his terms of reference forbid him to discuss.

AN INHERENT DEFECT IN *LAISSEZ-FAIRE*

THE presumption in favour of *laissez-faire* arises from the view that a given total of productive resources will yield under free conditions the maximum of social benefit, measured by the aggregated utilities to consumers of the commodities produced. There are serious objections to the notion of aggregating utilities and to the notion of utility itself, but a very serious, though very simple, objection to the presumption in favour of *laissez-faire* arises after the notion of utility has been accepted.

To rule out the well-known exceptions, let us consider an economic system in which each market is perfect, in which there is free mobility of resources, and no 'external diseconomies' such as the smoke nuisance. In such a system, if price is everywhere equal to marginal cost, the optimum amount of each commodity is produced. Price is taken to measure marginal utility, and where marginal utility and marginal cost are equal, satisfaction is at a maximum. But the marginal principle only serves to show how much of each given commodity should be produced. It cannot throw light upon the question of what commodities should be produced. In order to decide whether a certain commodity ought to be produced at all, it is necessary to know whether its total utility exceeds its total cost. This condition must be satisfied by all those commodities which are in fact produced. Their average cost cannot be greater than their price, which measures their marginal utility, and *a fortiori* cannot be greater than their average utility. And the case in favour of *laissez-faire* rests upon the assumption that all commodities which it is profitable to produce will be produced. But this condition, though *necessary* for the maximization of aggregate utility, is not *sufficient*. There are a large number of commodities which it is not in fact profitable to produce, of which the average utility would exceed the average cost.

The choice of what commodities to produce should be made, not by applying the criterion of marginal utility (price), which only serves to regulate the ideal amounts of output, but by

---

Economic Journal, September, 1935. The title has been slightly altered.

49

applying the criterion of total utility. An all-wise dictator, to whom every utility function was known, could increase the social benefit derived from given resources by revising the constitution of the set of commodities produced under perfectly *laissez-faire* conditions.

The contention that *laissez-faire* fails to maximize total utility, by failing to provide the ideal selection of commodities, is by no means new. It is implicit in the admission of a well-known exception to the presumption in favour of *laissez-faire*. It has always been held that in certain conditions a commodity which could not be produced by a monopolist charging a single price, will be produced, to the social benefit, if a sufficient degree of discrimination happens to be possible. A doctor in a sparsely populated district could not practise unless he were able to charge high fees to his richer patients and low fees to his poorer patients. If he were compelled to work at a flat rate, and were therefore obliged to give up his practice, there would clearly be a social loss. The well-known argument runs thus: Even when discrimination obtains, the receipts of a monopolist cannot at greatest exceed the total of utility due to his product. If his total costs are not greater than his total receipts it is desirable that his commodity should be produced. For if he were to withdraw from business, the factors of production released from his product would be added at the margin to all other commodities, so that the total of additional utility from other commodities could not exceed the loss of utility from the commodity which had disappeared. This familiar case is an illustration of the presumption that (unless perfect discrimination is everywhere possible) *laissez-faire* will fail to provide the ideal selection of commodities.

The objection may be raised that this criticism upon a *laissez-faire* system is not, after all, of much importance, since it applies only to cases in which average costs are falling. A commodity which it is not profitable to sell at a single price, but which it is in the interests of society to produce, must be such that its average cost curve everywhere lies above its marginal utility curve, but somewhere lies below its average utility curve. On the assumption that the average utility of commodities always falls as the amount consumed increases, this condition can be fulfilled only if average costs are also falling. It follows that for no commodity of which average costs are constant or rising for all outputs will production fail to be profitable if it is socially desirable to produce it at all. But every commodity must have falling average costs for small outputs. There must therefore be a large number of non-existent commodities which would be introduced under an ideal distribution of social resources, and it does not follow, because the ideal output of each would be small, that in the aggregate they would be unimportant. The service of a doctor is only one example of innumerable commodities which, in an ideal economy, would be introduced, each to a small extent, wherever population is sparse, or incomes, tastes, and habits are diversified. The fact that the new commodities must necessarily each be produced under conditions of monopoly would merely create fresh examples of an already well-known class of cases in which interference with *laissez-faire* is necessary to produce ideal conditions.

This discussion is conducted without prejudice to the question whether maximum social utility is a legitimate conception.

POSTSCRIPT

This argument suggests that an individual with the same tastes as the majority of his fellow consumers will enjoy, in some sense, a larger real income, for a given money income, than an eccentric. On the other hand, if he is subject to the passion for keeping up with the Joneses, he will suffer the full blast of external diseconomies of other people's consumption, which the eccentric is likely to be spared.

PART II

THE THEORY OF MONEY AND THE ANALYSIS OF OUTPUT

THE plain man has always found the Theory of Money a bewildering subject, but at the present time many academic economists are as much bewildered by it as the plain man. The reason for this state of affairs is that the Theory of Money has recently undergone a violent revolution. It has ceased to be the Theory of Money, and become the Analysis of Output.

The conclusions and methods of economic analysis are naturally much influenced by the technique of thought employed by the economists, and in almost every case where a divergence between 'schools of thought' is to be found in economics the difference between one 'school' and another arises from a difference in the mental tools which their members employ. Now the orthodox Theory of Money may be generally described as an attempt to apply the supply-and-demand tool to the analysis of the purchasing power of money. Just as, in the Theory of Value, the supply-and-demand mechanism is used to analyse the forces determining the value of a single commodity, so in the traditional Theory of Money the supply-and-demand mechanism, with some necessary modifications, is used to analyse the forces determining the value of money. The entity with which this analysis is mainly concerned is therefore the price level.

It has always been admitted that the chief justification for a study of the price level lies in the fact that changes in the price level may affect the volume of output, that is to say, they may affect the amount of employment and the wealth of the community. But until recently no economist appears to have considered the possibility of tackling this problem directly, and setting the supply-and-demand apparatus to work on the question in which he was really interested—the forces determining the volume of output.

The apparatus used to analyse the determination of the price level were tautological statements known as Quantity Equations. The 'Cambridge' equation was consciously designed to deal with the value of money in terms of supply and demand. In its simplest form the 'Cambridge' equation was as follows:

$$\pi = \frac{kR}{M}$$

where π is the purchasing power of money, R the real national income, k the proportion of real income held in the form of money (cash and bank balances), and M the quantity of money. kR then represents the demand for money in terms of real wealth, and M the supply of money. The equation leads naturally to the simple argument that the greater the supply of money (M), the smaller is its value (π), and the greater the demand for money (kR), the greater is its value.

The Fisher equation was not cast in so definitely supply-and-demand a form, but it was essentially of the same nature.

$MV = PT$ or $P = \frac{MV}{T}$, where P is the price level, M the quantity of money, V its velocity of circulation (V varies roughly inversely with k), and T the volume of transaction. MV represents the effective supply of money, and PT the amount of work that money is required to do. The price-level, P (which is roughly equivalent to $\frac{1}{\pi}$) is then regarded as the resultant of T, which without straining our terms too much may be regarded as the demand for money, and MV the supply of it. An increase in M or V is equivalent to an increase in the supply of money, and leads to a fall in its value, that is, to a rise in P; while an increase in T is equivalent to a rise in the demand for money, and leads to a rise in its value, that is, to a fall in P.

An imposing theoretical structure was built up on these simple tautologies. The exponents of the Theory of Money were never satisfied with their apparatus, and were always finding themselves led into paradoxical positions. The necessity to adapt the equations to the analysis of observed events led to greater and greater refinements and complications, but in essence the apparatus of thought remained the same.

The nature of the equations, the fact that they were tautologies, devoid of causal significance, was recognized by the experts. But in the hands of the inexpert they were very misleading. Any student of economics who was set the beginner's question—'Describe the manner in which the price level is determined upon an island in which the currency consists of shell picked up on the beach', would glibly reply, 'The price level on this island is determined by the number of shells and their velocity of circulation', and nine times out of ten would omit to mention that it was equally true to say that the number of shells in circulation was determined by the price level. And economists who had ceased to be students were prone to say that the rise of prices in Germany in the great inflation was caused by the increase in the note issue and aggravated by the increase in the velocity of circulation due to the 'flight into real values' induced by the rise of prices.

It was in protest against this naïve view of the theory of money that Mr. Kahn set out the Quantity Equation for hairpins. Let P be the proportion of women with long hair, and T the total number of women. Let $\frac{1}{V}$ be the daily loss of hairpins by each woman with long hair, and M the daily output of hairpins. Then $M = \frac{PT}{V}$, and $MV = PT$. Now suppose that the Pope, regarding bobbed hair as contrary to good morals, wishes to increase the proportion of long-haired women in the population, and asks a student of economics what he had best do. The student sets out Mr. Kahn's equation, and explains it to the Pope. 'All you need do', he says, 'is to increase M, the daily output of hairpins (for instance, you might give a subsidy to the factories) and the number of long-haired women is bound to increase'. The Pope is not quite convinced. 'Or, of course', the student adds, 'if you could persuade the long-haired women to be less careless, V would increase, and the effect would be the same as though the output of hairpins had increased'.

Now, the experts in the Theory of Money certainly avoided these crude errors, but when they recognized that their equations were tautologies without causal significance they were beset by an uneasy feeling that their theory only provided them with wisdom after the event. Anything that had happened could always be explained in terms of their truisms, but they were never very confident in predicting what would happen next. Moreover, their methods condemned them to discuss the price level, when what they had really at heart was the volume of employment.

Now, once Mr. Keynes has shown us how to crack the egg, it appears the most natural thing in the world to attack the interesting part of the problem directly, instead of through the devious route of the Quantity Theory of Money. If we are interested in the volume of output, why should we not try what progress can be made by thinking in terms of the demand for output as a whole, and its cost of production, just as we have been taught to think of the demand and cost of a single commodity? But though the altered line of approach appears, once it has been seen, to be the obvious one to adopt, the sudden change of angle has caused a great deal of bewilderment. The new analysis still masquerades under the name of the Theory of Money; Mr. Keynes published his book on the subject under the title of a *Treatise on Money*. Moreover, Mr. Keynes, when he published the *Treatise*, had no very clear perception of the fact that the subject with which he was dealing was the Analysis of Output. This can be illustrated from several of the conceptions in the Treatise. For instance, consider the Widow's Cruse of profits.[1] Mr. Keynes' analysis may be summarized thus: When prices are in excess of costs, windfall profits are earned by entrepreneurs, and however much of these profits the entrepreneurs spend, the total of profits remains unchanged, since spending by one entrepreneur only serves to increase the windfall profits of others. This argument is valid upon the assumption that an increase in demand for consumption goods leads to no increase in their supply. Now, to assume that the supply of goods is perfectly inelastic is a natural simplification to make, at the first step in the argument, if we are primarily interested in the price-level, but to make such an assumption when we are primarily interested in the volume of output is to assume away the whole point of the argument.

A second example of Mr. Keynes' failure to realize the nature of the revolution that he was carrying through is to be found in the emphasis which he lays upon relationship of the quantity of investment to the quantity of saving.[2] He points out that if

---

[1] *Treatise on Money*, p. 139.
[2] Using 'saving' as it is defined in the *Treatise on Money*.

savings exceed investment, consumption goods can only be sold at a loss. Their output will consequently decline until the real income of the population is reduced to such a low level that savings are perforce reduced to equality with investment.[1] But he completely overlooks the significance of this discovery, and throws it out in the most casual way without pausing to remark that he has proved that output may be in equilibrium at any number of different levels, and that while there is a natural tendency towards equilibrium between savings and investment (in a very long run), there is no natural tendency towards full employment of the factors of production. The mechanism of thought involved in the equations of saving and investment compels its exponent to talk only of short-period disequilibrium positions. And it was only with disequilibrium positions that Mr. Keynes was consciously concerned when he wrote the *Treatise*. He failed to notice that he had incidentally evolved a new theory of the long-period analysis of output.

Moreover, Mr. Keynes, like the exponents of the Quantity Theory of Money, was apt to fall into the hairpins fallacy, and attribute a causal significance to his tautologies. The price level will only be in equilibrium when savings are equal to investment. Well and good. But suppose that over a certain range the supply of goods is perfectly elastic? Then, whatever happens, prices cannot rise or fall. Since Mr. Keynes' truisms must be true, a rise or fall in demand for goods, which will be met by an increase or decrease of output without any change in prices, must necessarily be accompanied by changes in savings and investment which keep the two in equality. When an increase in output is brought about by an increase in investment, if prices do not alter, the increase in output must bring about an increase in savings (as defined by Mr. Keynes) equal to the initial increase in investment, for Mr. Keynes' truisms must be true. Or, as Mr. Hawtrey[2] points out, in face of a very-short-period decline in demand, the supply of goods is perfectly elastic because shopkeepers do not immediately lower prices, but allow stocks to accumulate on their shelves. This also can be explained in terms of Mr. Keynes' equations. The demand for consumption goods falls off, say, because of an increase in savings. This leads to an accumulation of stocks, that is to say, an increase in investment, exactly equal to the increase

[1] Op. cit., p. 178.   [2] *Art of Central Banking*, p. 341.

in saving, and prices do not fall. But to say that prices do not fall *because* investment has increased is merely to argue that women bob their hair because the output of the hairpin factories has fallen off.

The case of a perfectly elastic supply of output as a whole presents an interesting analogy with the traditional Theory of Value. Marshall's analysis is described by him as showing how the price of a commodity is determined by utility and by cost of production. He himself shows that when cost of production is constant for all amounts of output, the price of a commodity will not be altered by a change in demand, but he complains that it is idle to argue that price is determined more by cost than by demand. This violent contradiction can be resolved by substituting the word 'output' for the word 'price'. It is true that the output of single commodities is determined by the interaction of supply and demand even when the price is uniquely determined by cost. It was this earlier misapprehension of the subject-matter of the so-called Theory of Value which misled the economists into supposing that the proper subject-matter of the so-called Theory of Money was the level of prices, and not the volume of output.

A further example of Mr. Keynes' initial failure to understand the significance of his new analysis is to be found in the emphasis which he lays upon profits as the 'mainspring of action' determining output. Here, again, there is an analogy with the traditional Theory of Value. When profits are more than normal in a certain industry, we are taught, new firms will enter the industry, and output will expand. Now it is sufficiently obvious that entrepreneurs who are deciding whether to set up in a certain industry are not guided merely, or even mainly, by the level of profits being earned by existing firms. They will take a general view of the conditions in the market, and of future prospects, and make their choice accordingly. It is idle to say that the abnormal profits *cause* the new investment. At the same time, it is true that if the new entrepreneur decides to set up in the industry, then (if he expects that his cost will be about the same as those of existing firms) it must be the case that abnormal profits are being earned by the existing firms, for unless the price of the commodity is greater than their costs (including normal profits) it will not be worth while for additional entrepreneurs to enter the trade. Thus the abnormal profits are a symptom of a situation in which new investment in the industry will take place. But to speak of them as a cause of new investment is only legitimate as an artificial device adopted to simplify the exposition of what is happening. In the same way profits as defined by Mr. Keynes are a symptom of a situation in which output will tend to increase. Output tends to increase when the price of commodities exceeds their cost of production because, in that situation, it is profitable for entrepreneurs to increase their sales. To regard the profits as a direct cause of the increase in output is apt to be misleading, and since in long-period equilibrium there are no profits in Mr. Keynes' sense, a theory which regards profits as the mainspring of action is incapable of dealing with long-period analysis.

When Mr. Keynes himself overlooked the fact that he was writing the analysis of output, as these examples show, it is small wonder that the change in the Theory of Money should have caused bewilderment. But once it becomes clear what has happened the confusion disappears. The Theory of Money, relieved of its too-heavy task, can be confined to its proper sphere, and become indeed a theory of money, while the Analysis of Output can continue to develop an analysis of output.

'THE TRADE CYCLE'

By R. F. Harrod

Mr. Harrod's *Essay* is to be welcomed as the first advance into the territories opened up by the *General Theory of Employment, Interest and Money*. Using and developing Mr. Keynes' system of analysis, he has made a considerable addition to the theory of the trade cycle.

Mr. Harrod makes two main innovations. The first is subsidiary and may be separately discussed. This is the 'Law of Diminishing Elasticity of Demand'. Mr. Harrod suggests that there is a strong tendency for markets to grow more imperfect as income increases, because it becomes progressively less worth while for the ordinary consumer to take trouble in searching for bargains as his standard of life improves. This principle has both a long-run and a short-run application. A secular rise of income causes consumers to become progressively less careful in marketing, while a sudden fall in income, which in any case requires a revision in the consumer's habits, will provoke him to a spurt of activity in comparing and discriminating between rival sellers. The importance of this principle for the theory of employment lies in the fact that it enhances the tendency of profits to rise relatively to wages as activity increases. A change in distribution favourable to profits increases the propensity of the community to save. Thus the Law of Diminishing Elasticity of Demand may have an important influence in causing the value of the Multiplier to fall as activity increases.

Mr. Harrod rests more weight upon the assumption that profits are always strictly maximized than it is calculated to bear, but so far as theoretical reasoning can go, he makes out a good case for his Law. There is, however, a powerful influence tending in the opposite direction which he omits to mention. The degree of monopoly does not depend only on the imperfection of the market for a commodity, but also on the number of separate units of control engaged in selling it, and, since the fear of loss is more powerful than the hope of gain, the tendency towards restrictive combinations is stronger in a slump than in a boom. This is a factor tending to amplify the swings of activity, and works against the operation of Mr. Harrod's Law.

Mr. Harrod's main contribution to the theory of the trade cycle lies in his combination of the principle of the Multiplier, which governs the manner in which an increase in investment increases consumption, with the principle of the Relation between the demand for consumption goods and the demand for instruments to produce them, which governs the manner in which an increase in consumption leads to investment.

When the ratio of capital to output is given, an increase in the stock of capital is required only when consumption is increasing, and a constant rate of net investment will not be maintained unless consumption is increasing progressively. Any decline in the rate of increase of consumption will therefore entail a decline in the rate of investment. But a decline in investment will lead to a decline in consumption, and a decline in consumption, in the simplified case where the ratio of capital to output is constant, will lead in turn to a complete cessation of net investment. Even when capital per unit of output is increasing, the rate of net investment will fall very low. Therefore, as soon as consumption ceases to increase at the rate required to maintain a constant level of investment, investment (and with it consumption) must suffer a violent decline. Now, since the value of the Multiplier falls as output increases, it is impossible for consumption to continue expanding at the required rate. A steady rate of expansion can therefore never be achieved. This conception is an important addition to the theory of employment; for Mr. Keynes has somewhat neglected the Relation, and in the main takes notice of it only in connection with the increase in working capital which accompanies an increase in consumption.

Mr. Harrod elaborates this central idea, with many modifications and qualifications, into an analysis of the trade cycle which conforms to the broad outlines of the observed facts and provides an explanation of the violence of recession compared to the mild and gradual nature of recovery—a feat which he wittily argues has not hitherto been performed by any theory of the trade cycle. But his analysis does not cover the whole ground. His treatment of recovery from the bottom of a slump is confined to a paragraph of six lines, and his argument hardly seems to provide any sufficient reason for expecting recovery to take place at all. He does, indeed, discuss a state of 'steady advance', but this has no bearing on the trade cycle. It is based on unnatural assumptions, which entail that saving does not cease to be positive unless total income falls to zero, and its sole purpose in Mr. Harrod's scheme is to show that a steady advance cannot occur. Again, the essential part which is played by the accumulation of capital in curtailing the inducement to invest is not given its due prominence in Mr. Harrod's analysis. It is contained, so to speak, in solution in Mr. Harrod's argument, but the reader's closest attention is required to distil it out. The chief merit of this *Essay* lies in the light which it throws upon the turning point from expansion to contraction, with which, indeed, it is mainly concerned.

Mr. Harrod's controversial excursions will be helpful to many readers. He exposes the very simple but very prevalent fallacy that a difference between saving and investment is caused by an increase in bank credit, and gives an entertaining account of its origin. He shows how the Quantity Theory truism is fulfilled, when effective demand alters, by induced changes in the velocity of circulation, and gives a painstaking analysis of the effects of time lags on Mr. D. H. Robertson's assumption that each week's expenditure is governed by last week's income. On all these points he is only elaborating suggestions made by Mr. Keynes, but the elaborations are extremely useful.

THE CONCEPT OF HOARDING

THE term 'hoarding' is used in current literature in a number of distinct senses.

1. 'An increase in hoarding' may mean an increase in the desire to hold money as opposed to securities. This may occur (*a*) as a result of a change in sentiment, as is implied in the phrase 'hoarding due to decline in confidence' or 'to financial panic'. It may occur (*b*) as a result of an increase in the total of wealth, for as wealth increases the demand for money as 'a store of value' normally increases, though by less than the total increase in wealth. The demand for money may also increase (*c*) as a result of an increase in the requirements of the active circulation.

If the total quantity of money is kept constant, an increase in the actual amount of money held by the community as a whole cannot occur, but an increase in the desire to hold money brings about a rise in the rate of interest (a fall in security prices). If an individual owner of wealth desires to increase his holding of money, he is free to do so, either by selling out securities or by holding new savings in the form of money. His action then raises the rate of interest to the point at which other individuals are prepared to part with the money which he acquires.

The rise in the rate of interest leads, after a certain time has elapsed, to a decline in the rate of investment, and a fall in incomes and trade activity.

It is in this sense of the word, particularly sense (1*a*), that the substantial meaning of 'hoarding' agrees with the aura of associations that the word carries with it in literary use.

2. 'An increase in hoarding' may mean an increase in the actual amount of money held by the public. This can only come about if the quantity of money is increased. An increase in the quantity of money, other things equal, leads to a fall in the rate of interest, and, after a time, to an increase in investment, incomes and trade activity.

In this sense 'hoarding' does not come about from the initiative of the public, but is induced by the action of the banking system.

These two senses of hoarding are combined in the cases where an increased desire to hold money is met by an increase in the quantity of money, which prevents the rate of interest from rising, or an increase in the quantity of money is offset by an increase in the desire to hold money, which prevents the rate of interest from falling.

3. 'Hoards' may be used to mean not the total quantity of money, but the total *minus* the active circulation ('idle balances'). 'An increase in hoarding', when the total quantity of money is constant, is then brought about by a decline in incomes and trade activity, which releases money from the active circulation, and is another name for a fall in the average velocity of circulation of money.

A fall in the velocity of the active circulation (such as may be due to lengthening customary intervals of income payments) causes an increase in the demand for money, and, if the quantity of money is constant, the rate of interest will rise to the point at which the additional money required by the active circulation is drawn away from 'idle balances'. In this case 'an increase of hoarding' sense (1c) causes a 'decrease of hoarding' sense (3).

'An increase in hoarding' in sense (1) is a cause of a rise in the rate of interest, but 'an increase of hoarding' in sense (3) is associated with a fall in the rate of interest. This fall acts as a brake upon the decline in activity, but cannot be sufficient to restore incomes (and consequently the demand for money in the active circulation) to the former level.

In this sense 'hoarding' is an automatic consequence of a decline in incomes, no matter what the cause of the decline may be. 'An increase of hoarding' in sense (1a) may lead to an increase in sense (3), since an increase in the demand for money, by driving up the rate of interest, tends to bring about a decline in incomes, and consequently a release of money from the active circulation. Such a combination of sense (1a) with sense (3) probably provides the most reasonable interpretation of the complex of ideas connected with the word 'hoarding'.

4. 'Hoards' may be measured not in money, but in real terms. In this sense 'an increase in hoarding' means an increase in the real value of the total stock of money. It is an automatic consequence of a fall in prices, no matter what the cause of the fall may be.

'An increase in hoarding' in sense (3) need not be associated with an increase in sense (4) (though commonly both occur together), for a decline in activity and incomes may come about without a fall in prices, though it is unusual for it to do so.

5. Senses (3) and (4) are combined when by 'hoards' is meant the real value of 'idle balances'—that is, the real value of the total quantity of money *minus* the real value of the active circulation.

It appears that an 'increase in hoarding' in sense (1) may be an independent causal factor acting upon trade activity, incomes and prices *via* the rate of interest, while 'an increase in hoarding' in sense (2), (3), (4) or (5) is a consequence of changes in banking policy, in activity, or in prices, which occur for other reasons.

6. An individual is sometimes said to 'hoard part of his income'. This is a portmanteau phrase containing the conception of saving as well as the conception of acquiring money. The individual in question is saving and using the increment of his wealth to acquire money. The amount of money which he holds is then increasing continuously through time. This sense of hoarding must be distinguished from sense (1*b*), for there 'an increase in hoarding' (demand for money) is the consequence of saving, while here the word 'hoarding' is used actually to *mean* 'saving'.

Terminological confusions about the meaning of the word 'hoarding', like the cognate confusions about the word 'saving', have formed a smoke-screen which conceals important points of substance.

It is sometimes suggested that the savings of individuals fail to 'get invested' in real capital because they somehow 'run to waste in hoards' or 'get held up in the banking system'. Such phrases may imply merely 'an increase in hoarding' in sense (1*b*). Investment is going on at a certain rate, individuals, taken one with another, are adding to their wealth at a rate equal to the rate of net investment, and they wish to hold a part of the increment of their wealth in the form of money. Thus the demand for money is rising gradually through time, and, if the quantity of money is constant, there is a gradually increasing upward pressure on the rate of interest. Here the significance of the desire of individuals to hold an increment of wealth in the form of money does not lie in any tendency for investment to fall short of savings, but in a tendency for the rate of interest to move up gradually through time, exercising an increasing discouragement to entrepreneurs carrying out investment in real capital.

More often these phrases have a tincture of 'hoarding' sense (6), and introduce tacitly an increase in thriftiness into the story. An increase in thriftiness, showing itself in a decline in the rate of spending for consumption, leads to an all-round decline in activity and incomes. Some individuals may now be saving at a greater rate than before, while other individuals, owing to the decline in their incomes, are saving correspondingly less. Now, if those whose rate of saving has increased have the same desire to hold money as those who are saving less, there is no net effect upon the demand for money, except a once-and-for-all decline due to the contraction of the active circulation ('decrease in hoarding' sense (1c) and 'increase in hoarding' sense (3)). If, however, it happens that those individuals who save have more than the average desire to hold money, then the demand for money will increase gradually through time, and there will be a gradual upward pressure on the rate of interest. In short, an increase in thriftiness which happens to be accompanied by 'an increase in hoarding' in sense (1) will have a greater effect in reducing activity than one which is not accompanied by 'hoarding'. But the decline in activity is mainly to be attributed to the increase in thriftiness, not to any 'increase in hoarding' which happens to accompany it.

Another idea is also concealed behind the terminological smoke-screen. It is sometimes suggested that an increase in bank credit is somehow 'added to the supply of investible funds', so that the demand for funds represented by the current rate of investment in real capital is met by the savings of the public *plus* newly-created money. It is impossible to add the *stock* of money to the *flow* of saving. These phrases therefore imply that with a given rate of investment there is a given *rate of increase* in the quantity of money. And this is a phenomenon which is never likely to occur in practice.[1] But, for the sake of argument, let us

---

[1] An increase in the quantity of money due to (a) goldmining and (b) a budget deficit financed by borrowing from the central bank is discussed by Mr. Keynes, *General Theory*, p. 200, and by me, *Introduction to the Theory of Employment*, Chapter X. We are here concerned with an increase in money due to the action of the banking system increasing its loans to entrepreneurs.

contrast an increase in investment financed by bank credit with one financed by the issue of securities to the public.

There are two points to be considered. First, an increase in the rate of investment leads, so long as the investment continues, to an increased demand for money, both for the active circulation and for 'finance' ('an increase in hoarding' sense ($1c$)). Where there is no increase in the quantity of money, and no falling off in the demand for money for other reasons, an increase in the rate of investment therefore promotes a rise in the rate of interest, which acts as a brake upon the increase in investment. If, however, the stock of money is increased each week by an amount equal to the increase in the weekly rate of investment, the once-and-for-all rise in the demand for money will be outbalanced after a certain time by the increase in its total stock, and a decline in the rate of interest will set in, giving a further stimulus to investment.

Second, when a certain amount of investment has been completed, there is an equal increment in the total of wealth owned by individuals, and consequently an increase in the demand for money ('hoarding' sense ($1b$)). If the investment has been financed by securities and the quantity of money is constant, there is then an upward pressure on the rate of interest. If it is financed by bank loans, then after a certain amount of investment has been completed the banks are left with an equivalent increase in both their assets (loans) and their liabilities (deposits), while the public are left with an equivalent increase in their wealth and in their bank deposits. The increase in demand for money generated by an increase in wealth ('hoarding' sense ($1b$)) is less than the increase in wealth. The supply of money has therefore increased more than the demand for it, and there is a tendency for the rate of interest to fall. The difference between the two methods of finance shows itself in the behaviour of the rate of interest, not in a difference in the behaviour of savings.

These two conceptions, 'savings lost in the banking system' and 'an inflationary supplement to saving', cancel each other. For, over any interval of time, the 'excess savings added to hoards' are represented by the increment of bank deposits held by individual savers, while the 'credits supplementing saving' are represented by the increased loans of the banks. Since the increase in deposits is necessarily equal to the increase in bank assets, the 'excess of saving over investment' is equal to the 'excess of investment over saving'. The two notions have only to be confronted with each other for both to disappear.

It appears that some readers of Mr. Keynes' *General Theory*, themselves believing that the 'wastage of savings due to hoarding' and the 'inflationary supplement to savings' are of prime importance, find themselves at a loss to understand why there is no place for 'hoarding' and 'excess investment' in Mr. Keynes' terminology, and attribute their absence to wanton perversity in the definitions. They are unable to conceive that the disappearance of these conceptions (to them all-important) from the analysis can be due to anything but verbal jugglery. But the reason why these notions have no place in the *General Theory* is not because Mr. Keynes has concealed a vital factor under a mask of unnatural terminology, but because, in his view, 'hoarding', except in sense (1), which is covered by the conception of 'liquidity preference', has no causal force, while the notions of 'savings lying idle in the banks' and of 'banks' loans as a supplement to current saving' are purely mythical conceptions. Mr. Keynes' repeated protestations that he regards the complex of ideas connected with these two conceptions as simply an error, a confusion of thought, have failed to take effect, and his critics continue to complain of his definitions instead of denying (or accepting) the substance of his analysis. The issue involved is a substantial one, not a question of terminology.

POSTSCRIPT

Professor Robertson's conception of hoarding does not fit in anywhere in the above classification, for he uses the word in a special sense: 'A man is said to be *hoarding* if he takes steps to raise the proportion which he finds to exist at the beginning of any day between his money stock and his disposable income'.[1] Thus *hoarding* is an act which takes place at a moment of time. It is clear that if a man whose income is running at a steady rate owns a hoard of money, he is not *hoarding* in this sense. If his income falls, but his hoard is kept intact, the ratio of his money stock to

_____
[1] *Essays in Monetary Theory*, p. 67.

his income has risen, but he has taken no steps, and so done no act of *hoarding*.[1]

If national income falls, for whatever reason, and the quantity of money remains the same, it is clear that some individuals are likely, at some stage in the process of adjustment, to perform acts of *hoarding*, but there does not seem to be any simple relation between the *hoarding* which occurs and the rise in the ratio of money to income for the economy as a whole.

Nor is it possible, in Professor Robertson's language, to distinguish between an increase in the desire to hold money which has a causal influence in raising the rate of interest, and an increase which is a consequence of a fall in the rate of interest.

---

[1] This may sound strange, but I am told by Professor Robertson that it is the correct reading of his definition.

THE ECONOMICS OF HYPER-INFLATION

THEORETICAL discussion of the great German inflation was for a long time clouded by political prejudices. The German writers regarded reparations payments as the primary source of the trouble, and consequently argued that the collapse of the mark exchange was the cause of the inflation (*inflation* is used in this article in a purely descriptive sense, to mean an inordinately great rise in prices, without any question-begging theoretical significance as to whether the rise in prices is 'the fault of money'[1]); while the spokesmen of the Allies blamed the budget deficit, and consequently argued that the inflation was primarily caused by creation of money. Professor Bresciani-Turroni, whose valuable book is now made available to English readers in an excellent translation, is a strong adherent of the Allied or Quantity Theory school.

At a first glance, as the author freely admits, the facts appear to tell strongly in favour of the German view. There is no dispute as to the fact that the transition from the relatively moderate and fluctuating movements in exchange and prices of the immediate post-war years to the violent inflation which set in in the second half of 1921 was inaugurated by a sudden fall in the mark exchange (May, 1921, 15 marks = 1 gold mark; November, 1921, 63 marks = 1 gold mark). This fall is generally attributed to the commencement of cash payments of reparations. In this period payment of one milliard gold marks was carried out, while the total of exports was of the order of six milliard gold marks per annum. It is therefore plausible to attribute the fall of the mark to the sudden demand for foreign exchange in respect of reparations. The author, anxious to exonerate reparations, attributes it rather to the shock to confidence caused by the partition of Upper Silesia (p. 96). But this is immaterial to the main theoretical question—whatever the cause of the collapse of the exchange, it seems clear that it was the collapse of the exchange which

Pigou, *Economics in Practice*, p. 81.

A review of: *The Economics of Inflation* by Bresciani-Turroni. *Economic Journal*, September, 1938, in a shorter version.

inaugurated the great inflation. Both the magnitude and the temporal order of price changes in 1921 and 1922 support the argument. If the impulse comes from the side of the exchange we should expect the fall in exchange to run ahead of the rise in prices, and the prices of traded goods to run ahead of home prices. This is precisely what occurred, the magnitude and speed of change being in this order: exchange, import prices, export prices, home prices, cost-of-living, wages. Moreover, the geographical diffusion of prices supports the argument, the movement spreading from the great ports and commercial centres to the interior of the country (p. 135).

To all this the author opposes a theoretical argument. If home incomes do not rise, exchange depreciation cannot continue indefinitely, but must somewhere come to rest (p. 84). The stimulus to exports and check to imports must wipe out an unfavourable balance of payments and establish a new equilibrium with a constant exchange rate. The author admits that, over a certain range, a fall in exchange rate may reduce the gold value of exports, owing to inelastic foreign demand, and so make the balance of trade still more unfavourable. But, he points out (p. 91), a *sufficient* rise in the home price of imported goods will choke off demand, so that there is always some level of the exchange rate at which the balance of trade will right itself and depreciation come to an end. For this reason he dismisses the view that the depreciation of the mark was the primary cause of the inflation, in spite of the evidence which he admits in its favour, and adheres to an alternative explanation.

His explanation is that the German budget deficit, financed by borrowing from the Reichsbank, led to a continuous increase in the volume of money. From this, in his view, all the rest followed. But this account of the matter must be more closely examined before it can be accepted, or even understood.

The influence of a budget deficit upon prices can be divided into two parts. The *direct* effect of a deficit is to increase incomes and therefore to increase expenditure and business activity, no matter how the deficit is financed. Even if the government is borrowing at long term from the public, an excess of expenditure over revenue must tend to increase incomes and activity. But this influence is not cumulative. A given rate of deficit is required, other things equal, to maintain a given level of income. The *indirect* effect of a deficit financed by borrowing from the Central Bank is to bring about an increase in the quantity of money, which continues cumulatively as long as the deficit persists.

Now, so far as the direct effect of the deficit is concerned, its influence was becoming weaker in the early stages of the inflation. In 1920 the deficit was 6 milliard gold marks; 1921, 3.7 milliard; in 1922, 2.4 milliard. (p. 438.)[1]

It is true that in 1923 compensation to the passive resisters in the Ruhr caused an increase in the deficit. Indeed, the German inflation can be divided into two distinct phases, separated by the pause which occurred in March, 1923. At that date the Reichsbank stepped into the exchange market and succeeded in raising the mark from 6,600 marks to the gold mark to 5,000, and holding it almost at that level for two months. Prices fell correspondingly, and for a time the inflation appeared to be checked. But this effort was frustrated by a sudden increase in the deficit, which rose to 600 million gold marks in March, 1923. This precipitated a fresh bout of rising prices, which sent the mark crashing to one million marks to the gold mark in August, 1923, and one billion in November. In this phase it is possible to say that the direct effect of the deficit was the initiating cause of inflation, but in the earlier phase from the summer of 1921 to March, 1923, the direct influence of the deficit was declining, and if no other cause had been at work, activity and prices would have been falling. If the deficit is to be blamed for the first phase of the inflation, it can only be because of its indirect effect—the increase in the quantity of money.

The author assumes, rather than argues, that an increase in the quantity of money was the root cause of the inflation. But this view is impossible to accept. An increase in the quantity of money no doubt has a tendency to raise prices, for it leads to a reduction in the rate of interest, which stimulates investment, and discourages saving, and so leads to an increase in activity. But

[1] These figures apply to *financial* years. The deficit for 1922 therefore includes the large deficit of March, 1923. A calculation in terms of gold marks does not give a perfectly accurate measure of the deficit, for the power of a deficit to increase activity depends upon its magnitude in terms of home prices and costs, not in terms of the exchange rate. Thus the figure in gold marks somewhat underestimates the deficit in 1921 and 1922, when the exchange rate was falling faster than home prices were rising.

there is no evidence whatever that events in Germany followed this sequence.

It is true that a very high rate of investment prevailed during the inflation (p. 291). And it is true that there was a drastic decline in thriftiness. Saving by the ordinary public ceased almost completely, investment being financed entirely from profits. Moreover, there was considerable dissaving by individuals who consumed their past accumulations of wealth. Both the high rate of investment and the low propensity to save played a large part in maintaining activity at a high level during the inflation, but all these effects spring from the expectation of rising prices— they reinforced an inflation which was already under way—not from excessively low interest rates.

The increase in velocity of circulation, which is held to be a subsidiary cause of inflation, operates in the same way as an increase in the quantity of money. It represents a fall in the demand for money, so that a lower rate of interest corresponds to a given quantity of money. And if the inflation was not due to a fall in the rate of interest, the velocity of circulation can have played no part in causing the inflation.

It may be of interest, however, to make a digression upon the subject of velocity of circulation. The fall in demand for money, which shows itself in increased velocity, can be divided into three parts. First, there was great economy in the active circulation. When prices were rising rapidly it was foolish to hold money for a day, or even an hour, longer than necessary, and balances in the hands of the public, the dealers and the manufacturers were reduced to the minimum. This economy of money was enhanced when the intervals of income-payments were shortened. In Germany, before the end, wages and even salaries were paid daily, and cash balances fell to the point below which it was impossible to reduce them further.

Secondly, the demand for money to hold completely disappeared. Dissaving by the public led to a corresponding accumulation out of profits, so that wealth was transferred from those who normally held it largely in money to those who held it in the form of real capital. And members of the public who did not dissipate their wealth used it whenever possible to acquire foreign exchange.[1] No one held money when the value of money was dwindling day by day.

Thirdly, the cessation of private saving abolished the demand for money which arises in normal times because the individual saver holds newly-acquired wealth temporarily in the form of money before he buys securities with it.

All this led to so great a fall in the quantity of money corresponding to a given level of money income that the real value of note circulation in Germany in 1922 was reduced to half its value in 1913 (p. 156).

Movements in the demand for money (and consequently in the velocity of circulation) provide a criterion which can be used to distinguish 'hyper-inflation' from a relatively mild inflation such as occurred in Great Britain or in France after the war. It is well known that in the early stages of inflation the velocity of circulation falls. Prices are rising, but the public expects that they will soon fall again. Thus consumers refrain from any expenditure which can be conveniently postponed, and the savings thus made, since they are designed to be temporary, are held in the form of money. The demand for money increases and the velocity of circulation falls. If the rise of prices continues, however, the reverse expectation is set up, further rises are anticipated, the temporary savings are disbursed, and incomes begin to be spent as soon as they are received. At the first stage the real value of the outstanding quantity of money is raised (since prices rise more slowly than the quantity of money is increased), and at the second stage it falls. A mild inflation does not proceed beyond the first stage. Thus in Italy, France, Holland, and Switzerland the real value of the note issue was higher in 1921 than in 1913, while in countries which suffered 'hyper-inflation', Russia, Austria, and Germany, it fell sharply after a certain point (pp. 160–5). In Germany the phase of 'hyper-inflation' set in in July, 1921.

All this brings us no nearer to an understanding of the causes of inflation. The author rejects the view that exchange depreciation caused the inflation. But we have found just as much objection to his own explanation. Neither the budget deficit nor

[1] When foreign exchange was hard to obtain the public bought German securities (p. 271). But one of the most surprising features of the inflation is the low price of ordinary shares throughout the period, particularly in 1922 when activity was at its height.

the increase in quantity and velocity of circulation of money can produce the effects attributed to them. Clearly in each explanation some essential item is missing.

The missing item is not far to seek. It is the rise in money wages. Neither exchange depreciation nor a budget deficit can account for inflation by itself. But if the rise in money wages is brought into the story, the part which each plays can be clearly seen. With the collapse of the mark in 1921, import prices rose abruptly, dragging home prices after them. The sudden rise in the cost of living led to urgent demands for higher wages. Unemployment was low (2 per cent of members of Trade Unions were unemployed August, 1921; 0.7 per cent in 1922), profits were rising with prices, and the German workers were faced with starvation. Wage rises had to be granted. Rising wages, increasing both home costs and home money incomes, counteracted the effect of exchange depreciation in stimulating exports and restricting imports. Each rise in wages, therefore, precipitated a further fall in the exchange rate, and each fall in the exchange rate called forth a further rise in wages. Thus the author's contention that the collapse of the mark cannot have caused the inflation, because the exchange rate will always find an equilibrium level, is deprived of all force as soon as the rise of money wages is allotted its proper role.

But though the German theory that depreciation causes inflation can be justified, the Allied theory is not thereby ruled out. A sufficiently great budget deficit, when unemployment is sufficiently low, will raise prices and increase the demand for labour to the point at which the pressure for higher wages becomes irresistible. Each rise in wages raises prices, and so the vicious circle revolves. Meanwhile a collapse of the exchange adds fuel to the fire.

We have already seen that in 1923 it was the budget deficit due to passive resistance in the Ruhr, which inaugurated the final downfall of the mark. It appears, then, that either exchange depreciation or a budget deficit may initiate inflation, and that the German history provides examples of both cases. But the essence of inflation is a rapid and continuous rise of money wages. Without rising money wages, inflation cannot occur, and whatever starts a violent rise in money wages starts inflation. It is even possible that an increase in the quantity of money might start an inflation. A sufficient fall in the rate of interest might conceivably lead to such an increase in investment that unemployment disappeared, and money wages and prices started their spiral rise. But this is merely a theoretical possibility, not an account of the course of events in Germany.

Actually the quantity of money was important, not because it caused inflation, but because it allowed it to continue. As we have seen, the amount of money required for a given level of income was enormously reduced, but the level of money income rose with wages and prices, and the actual quantity of money required for transactions increased correspondingly. If the quantity of money had not expanded it may be supposed that the rate of interest would have been driven up, investment impeded, and saving encouraged, so that unemployment would have appeared again and the rise in money wages would have been brought to an end. But, in fact, the budget deficit, the policy of the Reichsbank in 'meeting the needs of trade' and the various official and unofficial supplementary currencies which were improvised, combined to meet the demand for money, the short rate of interest did not begin to rise appreciably till July, 1922, and no obstacle was put in the way of the inflation. It is true that in 1923 the short rate of interest rose to such heights that loans were taken at 20 per cent *per diem* (though the maximum reached by the Reichsbank discount rate was only 90 per cent *per annum*). But by this time the expectation of a continued rise in prices was so strong that it was impossible for high interest rates to discourage entrepreneurs from investment or to restore the motive for saving to the ordinary public. Thus the fact that high rates did not stop the inflation in 1923 cannot prove that they would have been equally powerless in 1921. The champions of the quantity theory, therefore, may reasonably contend that it was the increase in the quantity of money which permitted the inflation to take place.

In his Conclusion the author claims no more than that an increase in the quantity of money is a necessary condition for inflation. A clear grasp of the distinction between a necessary and a sufficient condition seems to be all that is required to settle the controversy. It is true that a train cannot move when the brake is on, but it would be foolish to say that the cause of motion in a train is that the brake is removed. It is no less, but no more, sensible to say that an increase in the quantity of money is the cause of inflation. The analogy can be pressed further. If the engine is powerful and is working at full steam, application of the brake may fail to bring the train to rest. Similarly, once an expectation of rising prices has been set up, a mere refusal to increase the quantity of money may be insufficient to curb activity.

It is sometimes argued that the stabilization of the mark in November, 1923, indicates that inflation can be stopped at any moment if the quantity of money is strictly controlled. In spite of himself, the author advances evidence for an entirely different interpretation of the facts. Before the stabilization took place, inflation had reached such a pitch as to bring itself to an end. The stabilization occurred only when the mark had in effect almost completely ceased to function as money (p. 342). The mark lost the characteristics of money in three stages. By the autumn of 1921 it had ceased to function as a 'store of value'. The demand for money to hold disappeared when the expectation of a continuous rise in prices became general. This is one aspect of the increase in velocity of circulation, and marks, as I have suggested, the transition from moderate inflation to hyper-inflation. In the late part of 1922 the mark ceased to function as a 'unit of account'. It became more and more common to reckon all prices, and to fix wage rates, with reference to the exchange rate, so that, in effect, the dollar was the unit of account. The mark note never ceased altogether to function as a 'medium of exchange', but it was to a large extent displaced by foreign currency and the 'stable value' instruments of various kinds which were improvised. Finally, in the great slide of 1923 the mark had begun to lose the character of a 'standard of deferred payments' for loans began to be contracted in terms of dollars, copper, kilowatt hours, and what-not. As the process developed, the expectation of rising prices lost its power to stimulate investment and expenditure, for there was no expectation that prices in terms of dollars, or particular commodities, would rise. The force of inflation in stimulating activity was all but spent, and it is significant that unemployment rose sharply in August, 1923. The dislocation caused by the invasion of the Ruhr raised unemployment among Trade Unionists to 7 per cent in April, but the stimulus of inflation reduced it again to 3·5 per cent in July. In the final slide, the stimulus of inflation was exhausted and unemployment rose to 19 per cent in September (p. 449).

The Rentenmark was, in effect, no more than an official version of the 'stable value' currencies that were already in use (p. 347). The stabilization was no doubt a firm and courageous act of policy, but it provides no argument to support the view that inflation, at an advanced stage, can be checked by limiting the quantity of money.

POSTSCRIPT

The hypothesis, that the reappearance of unemployment in Germany in September, 1923, was due to the fact that the inflation had blown itself to pieces, has not, as far as I know, been further examined. An alternative hypothesis is that unemployment was due to the hoarding of materials and to the total disorganization and demoralization of the economy in the great slide of the mark. Perhaps there is some truth in each explanation.

'MONETARY EQUILIBRIUM'

By GUNNAR MYRDAL

AFTER the confluence of the 'Cambridge' and the 'Swedish' traditions of monetary theory, it is interesting to look back and see how the two streams were flowing while they were still divided by contours of language. Professor Myrdal's *Monetary Equilibrium* was published in Swedish in 1931, soon after the appearance of Mr. Keynes' *Treatise on Money*. The present translation provides English readers with a welcome opportunity to compare notes with their Swedish colleagues, and to pay tribute to the health and vigour of the Swedish tradition. Professor Myrdal remarks upon 'the attractive Anglo-Saxon kind of unnecessary originality' of Mr. Keynes and Mr. Robertson, who discovered for themselves many ideas already worked out by Wicksell, and this book provides much evidence of the advantages which the Swedish economists enjoyed in the freedom that Wicksell won for them from the tyranny of Say's Law and the Quantity Theory of Money. They enjoyed another advantage. Professor Pigou has suggested that among Marshall's pupils reverence for the master checked enterprise and initiative. But Wicksell succeeded in raising a generation of pupils who regarded criticism of the master as their first duty. Professor Myrdal makes no apology for pointing out errors, confusions, and ambiguities in Wicksell's theory in the course of his endeavour to expand it from within and develop from it a consistent and useful system of analysis.

He shows, first of all, that to make sense of Wicksell's 'natural rate of interest' it is necessary to interpret it as the expected rate of profit (the 'marginal efficiency of capital' of Mr. Keynes' *General Theory*), and he shows how the inducement to invest can be treated in terms of a difference between the price and the cost of capital goods. He then introduces what he regards as his own most important original contribution to the debate—the distinction between saving and investment *ex ante* and *ex post*. This is essentially a device to explain the fact that the rate of saving and the rate of investment for the community as a whole are necessarily equal, while decisions of individuals to save and to invest are not bound together, and produce opposite consequences. In this respect it is clearly superior to the device evolved by Mr. Keynes for the same purpose—the peculiar definition of savings in the *Treatise*. But in itself it is by no means ideal. Professor Myrdal shows how a decline in the rate of investment reduces incomes, increases dole payments and alters distribution, in such a way as to cause savings *ex post* to decline to an equal extent; and how an increase in savings *ex ante*, due to increased thriftiness, reduces incomes so that saving *ex post* fails to increase, while it reduces the incentive to invest and so leads in the end to an actual decline in the rate of saving *ex post*. Now, a difference between saving *ex ante* and *ex post* only occurs when there is an unforeseen change in the incomes of individuals. As soon as the system has settled down to a new level of activity the difference disappears. An excess of savings *ex ante* over savings *ex post* is thus nothing but a symptom of declining activity, and it befogs rather than illuminates the discussion of the causes of the decline.

The whole *ex ante* method is bound up with the conception of 'monetary equilibrium', which is defined as a position in which saving and investment, *ex ante*, are equal. Professor Myrdal shows that 'monetary equilibrium' can be attained at any level of activity, and certainly prevails at the bottom of a slump. His own argument, therefore, shows it to be a matter of secondary importance. Just as Wicksell deposed the Quantity Theory, while believing himself to adhere to it, so Professor Myrdal deposed the conception of 'monetary equilibrium' in the course of expounding it. The successive skins of the serpent are sloughed one by one.

Professor Myrdal solved several other questions with which the attractive Anglo-Saxons were still wrestling some time after his book was first published. For instance, he resolved the controversy between Wicksell and Davidson as to how equilibrium can be maintained in face of an increase in productivity, by showing that a constant rate of investment (and a given position of 'monetary equilibrium') is compatible equally with constant money wages combined with a fall in prices proportionate to the increase in productivity, and with constant prices combined with a proportionate rise in wage rates. And he showed how a rise in bank rate preserves the exchanges by creating slump conditions in the home country and so reducing the demand for imports.

His treatment of unemployment is less satisfactory. He regards a certain amount of unemployment as necessary and desirable in order to prevent the continuous rise of money wages and prices which comes about when the 'monopoly position' of the workers is too strong. But this is not at all the same thing as to say that a rise in money wages directly causes unemployment, and he appears to hold both that a rise in money wages which is not expected to be reversed will not reduce employment and that a fall in money wages will increase it.

There are vestigial traces of the fallacy that investable funds are provided by the 'creation of purchasing power' by the banks, and of the curious view of Wicksell's 'Austrian' disciples that a change in the rate of investment entails a change in the 'time structure of production', but these notions do not vitiate the main argument, which in no way depends upon them.

PLANNING FULL EMPLOYMENT

I

THE Government have promised that, after this war, mass unemployment will not be allowed to recur; but, beyond vague allusions to public-works policy, there has been very little official discussion of the means necessary to implement that promise. It is not long since the 'Treasury view' that public expenditure could not increase employment still dominated official opinion, and the abandonment of that view appears to have left a vacuum in its place. For ten years economists, under the leadership of Mr. J. M. Keynes, carried out a campaign against the Treasury view of 1929. The campaign, on the plane of argument, was almost completely victorious; and now war-time experience seems to indicate that public expenditure and public control on a sufficient scale can remove unemployment. The onus of proof is at any rate upon those who argue that it cannot. But it is not enough to win victories in argument. A constructive approach to the problem is now required.

It is widely agreed that the fundamental cause of mass unemployment lies in the failure of consuming power to keep pace with productive power in an unregulated economy. A Beveridge plan (or a super-Beveridge plan), combined with minimum wage legislation, would put purchasing power into the hands of those who need it most, and so ensure an enlarged and stabilized home market for consumption goods. But the demand for investment goods continually fluctuates with the prospect of profit, and this is the prime mover in the general fluctuations of trade. If the authorities had control over a sufficient proportion of the demand for new capital equipment, these fluctuations could be damped down, if not completely eliminated. By these means a higher and more stable level of useful productive activity could be maintained for the community as a whole.

The first obstacle lies in the difficulties which such a policy involves for the balance of trade. A continuous high level of activity in this country must increase the demand for imported goods. But our means to pay for even our pre-war level of imports have been seriously impaired by the loss of foreign assets, the earnings of which formerly brought us tribute from the world, and the outlook for our export industries, including shipping services, is unsettled. Under the old system the balance of trade was forcibly maintained by the high level of unemployment. A sufficiently low rate of industrial activity, and a sufficiently large proportion of the population living in penury, automatically cuts down the consumption of imports to the measure of exports. But if this is the only solution which *laissez-faire* has to offer, it can scarcely be doubted that the answer of the British people will be: 'So much the worse for *laissez-faire*'.

If full employment is sought, the balance of trade must be maintained, on the one hand, by a controlled direction and stimulation of exports, and, on the other hand, by a system of priorities for imports which will give precedence to the more over the less necessary. If imports are controlled, the stimulation of productive activity at home, through public investment or any other means, leads to an increased home consumption of home-produced goods, and constitutes no threat to the balance of trade. The controls at present operating over the foreign exchanges and over imported raw materials provide the foundation for a system which can at one and the same time regulate the balance of trade and allow home activity to rule at a level which would make it possible to fulfil the promise to abolish mass unemployment. A corollary is continued control over international capital movements so that home policy is not at the mercy of the sudden flights of 'hot money' which wrecked many national experiments in the last ten years before the war.

On the purely technical economic level a solution can thus be found for the problem of unemployment. But the fact must be faced that formidable difficulties on another level are bound to arise. In economic matters it is a good wind that blows nobody ill, and it is impossible to find any policy which does not damage some sectional interest within the community.

Public-works policy is a case in point. The leaders of industry, represented by the report of the Federation of British Industries on Reconstruction, and by the 120 industrialists who signed 'A National Policy for Industry', have accepted the principle of public works, and rely upon them to rescue industry from a threatening slump. But (to quote the latter document) they must be 'confined to "public" works, i.e. new roads, water supplies, housing, and the like'. That is to say, Government investment must be confined to spheres which in no way compete with profit-seeking capital. These spheres are narrow. It is possible to imagine a point beyond which road-building and the like might become an even less advantageous method of curing unemployment than the famous expedient of digging holes in the ground and filling them up again. This method at least leaves no traces behind, while unnecessary roads occupy space that might be better used.

If a sufficient volume of useful investment cannot be found in purely 'public' works, the industrialists suggest that private investment should be subsidized:

'For alleviating unemployment the State might be called upon to take, on suitable terms as to interest and repayment, a share of what would be an uneconomic risk for private industry'.

Even if there were no objection on general grounds to subsidizing private investments, it would be an extremely weak defence against the onset of a slump. For the characteristic of a slump is the disappearance of prospective profits, and no practicable reduction in the cost of borrowing can induce firms to embark upon capital expansion when the prospects of profit are nil. It seems, then, that the proposals of the industrialists may lead to an impasse. There may be a large mass of labour which they are unable to employ at a profit, but they may be reluctant to allow the State to embark on enterprises on a broad enough scale to employ it.

There are a number of spheres of activity in which operation through public corporations, on a non-profit basis, can be justified on its own merits, quite apart from the employment problem. If these were taken out of the hands of private enterprise, long vistas of useful investment would be opened up. A national medical service, such as Sir William Beveridge foreshadows, would require a large volume of investment, not only in the bricks and mortar of health centres and sanatoria, but in training medical and nursing staff on a scheme of State bursaries. House-building is conceded, at least in part, by the industrialists to be a proper sphere for public investment, and this opens up a huge field. Public operation of transport opens another, fuel and power a third.

If such large spheres of investment were under control the whole setting of public-works policy would be altered. Hitherto public works have been advocated as a makeshift device for stabilizing the trade cycle. The suggestion has been that private industry should always have the first pick, and that the State should find work on something or other to occupy the unemployed until private industry wants them once more. But if the main spheres of investment were under public control, operating within the framework of a general plan, the emphasis would be altered. The investment considered on general grounds the most advantageous would take precedence, and investment in private industry would be rationed under a system of priorities. A combination of stability with rapid progress in capital accumulation could then be achieved.

But even if the problem of mass unemployment were thus solved, a fresh crop of problems would spring up; for it is by no means a simple matter to remove unemployment and leave everything else the same.

II

Full employment is an ambiguous concept. No one, at the most optimistic, expects a complete disappearance of unemployment, and no one desires the continuance in peace-time of the super-full employment which we are enduring now with all the social stresses it implies. Occasional and temporary unemployment, provided that social services are adequate, is not a grave evil, and we may suppose that the objective of the policies discussed in the preceding article is to reduce unemployment to a moderate amount. Supposing the policies are successful, fresh problems arise. Unemployment is not a mere accidental blemish in a private-enterprise economy. On the contrary, it is part of the essential mechanism of the system, and has a definite function to fulfil.

The first function of unemployment (which has always existed in open or disguised forms) is that it maintains the authority of master over man. The master has normally been in a position to say: 'If you don't want the job, there are plenty of others who do'. When the man can say: 'If you don't want to employ me, there are plenty of others who will', the situation is radically altered. One effect of such a change might be to remove a number of abuses to which the workers have been compelled to submit in the past, and this is a development which many employers would welcome. But the absence of fear of unemployment might go farther and have a disruptive effect upon factory discipline. Some troubles of this nature are being encountered to-day, but in war-time the overriding appeal of patriotism keeps them within bounds. In peace-time, with full employment, the worker would have no counterweight against feeling that he is employed merely to make profits for the firm, and that he is under no moral obligation to refrain from using his new-found freedom from fear to snatch every advantage that he can. Payment by results might overcome these difficulties to some extent, but would be unlikely to remove them altogether.

The change in the workers' bargaining position which would follow from the abolition of unemployment would show itself in another and more subtle way. Unemployment in a private-enterprise economy has not only the functions of preserving discipline in industry, but also indirectly the function of preserving the value of money. If free wage-bargaining, as we have known it hitherto, is continued in conditions of full employment, there would be a constant upward pressure upon money wage-rates. This phenomenon also exists at the present time, and is also kept within bounds by the appeal of patriotism. In peace-time the vicious spiral of wages and prices might become chronic. This would bring a variety of evils in its train. It would greatly complicate the problem of controlling international trade, since it would require offsetting movements in exchange rates. It would make hay of the social security programme. It would bring about an arbitrary redistribution of real income within the country, *rentiers*, salary-earners, and ill-organized workers losing relatively to the members of the strong trade unions, who would secure the greatest wage advances, and to the industrialists, who could recoup themselves for rising costs by raising prices. Finally, if it moved too fast, it might precipitate a violent inflation.

Two solutions of the dilemma presented by full employment are offered to the modern world. Under Fascism, the trade unions are broken; direct terror, supplemented by a mystical propaganda appeal, is substituted as a means of discipline for the fear of unemployment, wages and prices are controlled, and full employment, mainly directed to building armaments, is thus made possible. Socialism presupposes the opposite solution. The long and bitter antagonism between capital and labour is to be brought to an end when capital becomes the property of the community as a whole. An appeal, similar to the appeal of patriotism which saves us in war-time from the perils attendant on full employment, is to cement discipline and make State wage-regulations acceptable.

Is there a third course? Sir William Beveridge has spoken of a 'British revolution'. It was argued in the preceding article that to control employment it would be necessary to remove certain substantial spheres of activity from the hands of private enterprise. In the remaining sphere price control, limitation of profits, and full publicity in respect of costs (as advocated by the 120 industrialists in 'A National Policy for Industry'), combined with a social security programme at least as generous as that proposed by Sir William Beveridge, and with an extension of works councils which would give the workers a voice in the day-to-day affairs of the factory, might produce a situation in which the workers would be prepared to accept discipline to the necessary and reasonable extent, and to accept an over-all wage treaty which would prevent the vicious spiral from setting in.

A state of full employment would require a further modification of the status of the workers. No national plan, however skilfully devised, can guarantee everyone work in his own trade, and, even if it were possible, it would be highly undesirable to allow the distribution of labour which happened to exist at the outset of planning to exercise a permanent influence in distorting the pattern of production. If stability is to be combined with progress, obstruction from whatever source to the introduction of new techniques cannot be tolerated. And a high degree of flexibility, conflicting in many ways with rigid trade-union rules, is a necessary condition for running industry at a continuous high level of activity.

Many practices which trade unionists themselves admit to be restrictive have their historical justification in the fear of unemployment. It is the right of a man to his trade which is defended by them, and the elaborate system of taboos which prevent one man doing another man's job has its justification in reluctance to take the bread out of someone else's mouth. Restrictive regulations upon employment are not confined to industrial trade unions. It is scarcely to be doubted that the difficulties placed in the way of women medical students have their roots in fear of increased competition in a limited market. National protectionism and monopoly restrictions of all kinds are based upon the same fear.

If a full-employment policy were successfully carried out, the *raison d'être* of trade-union obstructions to flexibility would disappear, and machinery could be set up for solving the problems involved, in a reasonable manner and in consultation with the workers themselves. Sir William Beveridge advocates retraining on a maintenance allowance as part of his scheme of unemployment relief. Greater flexibility of hours of work could be used to deal with minor fluctuations in activity, in place of the present brutal system of standing men off when trade is slack. These problems can all be solved. But they can only be solved after the problem of unemployment has been dealt with, since fear of unemployment lies at the root of them all. It is of no use to demand flexibility first. The trade unions will not give up their hard-won defensive positions in exchange for a mere pious hope that unemployment will not recur.

The foregoing discussion has brought to the surface a disagreeable dilemma, which must be squarely met if intellectual confusion and economic and social disaster are not to ensue. The fact that unregulated private enterprise and continuous full employment are incompatible must be frankly faced, if we are not to drift blindly in the fog. The existing system is nowadays usually defended on two grounds. The first is that our existing Civil Service, so admirably adapted to *laissez-faire*, is often inept in handling industrial problems. This may well be true but it is irrelevant, since it is obvious that a wholly different type of organization would have to be created in order to carry through a positive economic policy. The second is that unregulated private enterprise has, over two centuries, brought about magnificent achievements of technical progress. This argument is also irrelevant; for whatever the past achievements of private enterprise, regulation is now required to ensure further progress. Once it is clear that mass unemployment is the price that must be paid, probably at an increasing rate, for the unregulated economy of the past, further argument becomes unnecessary—even if there were no other reasons why unregulated private enterprise is inadequate to deal with the problems of modern industry.

WAR-TIME INFLATION

INFLATION is a word which is used in many senses, and first of all it is necessary to be clear what we mean by it. We are always told that the English are not logical and dislike clear-cut categories. In the conduct of affairs I think that there is a great deal to be said for the English way, but in the conduct of a lecture it is best to aim at precision. It is possible to distinguish three stages of inflation. First, a sharp rise of prices relatively to costs of production. Second, progressive inflation of the 'vicious spiral', when money-wage rates are raised to compensate the workers for the rise of prices. The rise of wages raises prices further, and so sets up a need for a further rise of wages, and so on and on. Third, the stage of hyper-inflation, when continuously rising prices set up an expectation of further rises, so that a scramble for goods sets in which ends in a complete collapse of the currency.

For Great Britain the problem has been to prevent the first stage from developing into the second, and on the whole it has been fairly successfully solved. In France, as I understand it, the problem is to prevent the second stage from developing into the third. The great inflations after 1918 were connected with a collapse of the foreign exchanges, but fortunately, so far, both our countries have been saved from that complication (except for an initial depreciation and consequent rise of prices in 1939) and we need not concern ourselves with it to-day.

The primary cause of the type of inflation which we have been experiencing in war-time Britain is an excess of money demand over the supply of goods. In war-time more work is done than in peace-time. There is no unemployment, hours of work are longer, and holidays shorter. Many people who did not earn before, such as married women, the retired, and *rentiers* who in peace-time lived on their *rente*, are working in war-time. Incomes therefore go up, and people have more money to spend. But goods to buy are reduced in quantity. The incomes are being earned in the Forces and in the munition factories, not in making goods for civilians to spend their income on. Thus demand exceeds supply,

---

This paper is the basis of a lecture delivered in Paris in January, 1945.

and prices tend to be pushed up. This is the essence of war-time inflation.

Why is inflation a bad thing? Why do we seek to avoid it? This may seem a strange question to ask. It is obviously bad, and it may seem a waste of time to analyse its evils. But I think it is necessary to ask exactly why inflation is undesirable, in order to understand the means to combat it.

From one point of view, inflation of the first stage is an ideal way of financing a war. It is necessary that there should be a reduced output of civilian goods, because all resources that can possibly be used for the war must be used for the war. If prices rise to the point where civilian income can only just buy what is available, the goods are, so to say, rationed amongst the public by the high prices. The excess profits which arise from high prices relatively to costs can be taxed, and so provide for the finance of war expenditure without increasing the National Debt. The capitalists act as the tax collectors, and high prices take over the function of rationing consumers. As a means of solving the financial problem of war economics it is a perfect system. But no sooner is it described than the objection to it becomes obvious. It *would* be a perfect system of war finance for a community with equal incomes. But when we start with very unequal incomes, it is an intolerable system. The rich would not be obliged to reduce their standard of life, and the whole of the reduction in civilian consumption would be at the expense of the poorest part of the community. Moreover, when a large part of the population is living in peace-time near the edge of extreme poverty, the rise of prices would plunge them into actual starvation.

This, then, is the first evil of inflation—that it exaggerates to an insupportable extent the inequalities which exist in peace-time, and that it presses down the standard of life of the mass of the workers to a level at which they cannot maintain efficiency.

The second evil of inflation (in the sense of a sharp rise of prices relative to costs) is that it encourages unnecessary consumption. In principle it is possible to tax away inflationary profits, but in practice it is never possible for the tax-collector's net to catch them all, and if super-profits are being made, there is a strong temptation for the profiteers to indulge in luxury consumption, so as further to enhance the mal-distribution of the available goods among the civilian population.

The third evil of inflation is that it makes the civilian market highly profitable. In Great Britain the authorities have relied to only a minor extent upon normal peace-time economic incentives to direct resources out of civilian production into the war effort. In the main, industry has been told what it has to produce, and labour has been directed by decree, not by the offer of high wages. But direct controls work far more easily if they are not swimming against the tide of economic incentives. If an employer can make large profits from producing ladies' hats, it is hard to force him to shut down. If he is already near to ruin because ladies have given up wearing hats, he is glad to go. If he could pay his workers high wages, it causes discontent to direct them into shell-filling at lower rates. If a market gardener can get high prices for daffodils, it is not easy to make him grow potatoes. Those who willingly accept direction, out of patriotism, feel aggrieved if the less virtuous are making money out of their lack of virtue. The high profits of an inflationary market clog the machinery of controls and the system works more easily if inflationary profits are not being made.

Finally, if inflation of the first stage is not checked, there is a danger of its developing into the second stage—an ever-rising level of money wages and of the cost of living. This brings fresh evils in its train. The rise of wages is never even, and generally the workers who are least well organized, and have already the lowest wages, are those who suffer most, so that the 'vicious spiral' increases maldistribution within the working class. Those whose incomes are fixed in terms of money, or whose incomes rise very slowly, suffer more than their share of privation. And these include not only well-to-do *rentiers*, but some of the poorest members of society—the old-age pensioners. Service pay and allowances become more and more inadequate, and the families of soldiers suffer intolerably compared to the families of the better-paid workers.

To a moderate extent, the vicious spiral can be allowed to revolve, and, indeed, we have not been entirely free from it. But if it goes too fast, all these evils become serious. And if it goes beyond a certain point, the phenomena of the third stage of inflation begin to show themselves—a flight from money, leading in the end to complete collapse.

The campaign against inflation, which has been fought with

some success in Great Britain, consists, therefore, in checking inflation in the first stage, to keep its evils within bounds, and to prevent it from developing into the later and more dangerous stages.

The campaign was not worked out systematically, but developed step by step. Many different methods were used, some methods being from a logical point of view inconsistent with others. In this, I think, English pragmatism has been justified by events. The English distrust theory, for a theory may be wrong, and the more logically it is followed out, the worse the confusion that results. But the facts cannot be wrong. So an illogical policy, meeting the facts as they arise, may be more successful than a logical policy based on wrong premises.

According to the old theory of inflation, inflation is due to an excessive creation of the medium of exchange. But this theory is quite misleading, and points to the wrong remedies. Inflation, in the first stage, has nothing to do with the issue of money. It arises from the receipt of incomes in respect of producing goods which are not available for consumption. There is more income to spend, and less goods to spend it on. If incomes increase, more cash is required for circulation, but the increase in incomes cannot be prevented by controlling the issue of money. The increase in incomes, and the reduction of civilian supplies to spend them on, are both inescapable consequences of the war. The only really thorough means of avoiding inflation is not to have the war. Since the war must be fought, and supplies must be cut down, the remedy for inflation must be sought in methods to prevent people from spending.

The first attack upon inflation in Great Britain was the direct control of prices. Under the Prices of Goods Act, introduced at the outbreak of war, all goods had to be sold at pre-war prices, with certain permitted increases to cover increased costs. This was, on the whole, loyally observed. But price-control by itself is no answer to inflation. If demand exceeds supply, and prices are prevented from rising, part of the demand is unsatisfied. People are anxious to buy more goods than are available. If prices do not go up to check demand, some of the would-be buyers get what they want and the rest go without. The result is that the shopkeepers are left with the task of distributing the goods. Queues are formed, and the end of the queue goes home with empty shopping bags. Favourite customers are served, as we say, 'from under the counter'. The shop shuts after a few hours, and late-comers get nothing. The time and trouble to search for what one wants takes the place of high prices as a discouragement to buyers.

I said that the first evil of inflation was the social injustice and hardship which it causes. The state of incipient inflation with shortages in the shops is nearly as great an evil, from this point of view, as the rise of prices itself. High prices distribute goods according to the purchasing power of buyers. Shortages distribute goods according to 'shopping power'. Those who can impress shopkeepers with their wealth and importance, and those who have leisure to crawl from queue to queue get the goods, while the workers who spend their time in contributing to the war have no time to get a share of the goods. Thus the injustice is almost as great as in outright inflation, with waste of time and temper added.

Price-control is relieving a symptom, not curing the disease. A more radical remedy lies in taxation. In discussing taxation we must distinguish clearly between indirect taxes (taxes on commodities) and direct taxes, on income and wealth. British public finance traditionally relies on both types of taxes, and use has been made of both during the war. Before the war, beer, spirits, and tobacco, sugar, and tea were the chief commodities taxed. These taxes were raised in successive budgets, and in 1940 a general purchase tax was added: an entirely new feature in British public finance. Now, a general purchase tax makes some contribution to remedying the subsidiary evils of inflation—it prevents profits from emerging—but it does nothing whatever against the main evil. The tax raises prices, and distributes goods among the population according to their purchasing power. In short, it reproduces the effect of inflation. It would be the ideal method of war finance for a community with equal incomes, but when the whole problem is to get a fairer distribution of goods among consumers than would be brought about by inflation, it is a useless weapon.

The paradox of combating inflation by raising prices was gradually realized by the British authorities, and the need to prevent the Cost-of-Living Index from rising led to the purchase tax being reduced on certain commodities of popular consumption. At the same time, very high taxation of luxuries may be regarded as a method for curtailing demand for necessaries. If people who have money are determined to spend it on something or other, the more that can be taken out of their pockets for a given consumption of materials the better. Thus taxation of unessential goods, although it raises prices, is in a certain sense a remedy against inflation. This system has been evolved in Great Britain, so that we have now a double price level; the prices of necessaries are held at a moderate level, while the few luxuries which are available, for instance, wine and expensive clothes, have very high prices.

Turn now to direct taxation. This is a powerful weapon against inflation, for it takes purchasing power out of the hands of the people. Income tax was increased in each budget up till the last. The standard rate is now 50 per cent, and the limit has been lowered, so that, for the first time in British history, the mass of wage-earners are paying income tax.

Income tax is much superior to commodity taxes, from the point of view of fairness. A tax on a commodity which everyone consumes is regressive. It takes a larger proportion from a smaller income than from a larger income. Income tax is progressive. It takes a larger proportion of a larger income. But, for the very same reason, it takes a larger amount from an increase in the income of an individual than from the average of his income. For this reason it discourages effort. The worker who does over-time may get less for an extra hour of work than for a standard working hour. At the other extreme of the social scale, the super-tax payer can retain only 6d. in the £ of the last increment of his income. People do not work only to make money, but, day in and day out, for five long years, it is impossible to keep at full stretch on patriotism alone. The money motive was to be used to keep up production. This sets a limit to the extent that direct taxation can be used to combat inflation.

This is, indeed, the dilemma of war-time finance. It is necessary that everyone should work as hard as possible, and therefore it is desirable that they should be anxious to earn money. But it is highly undesirable that they should spend money. What use is money if it cannot be spent?

At the beginning of the war Lord Keynes produced an ingenious scheme to solve this problem. His solution was 'deferred pay'.

That is—a high and progressive rate of income tax, a proportion of which should be refunded after the war. Under this scheme the worker has a motive to earn in order to be able to spend later on when goods are plentiful again. Unfortunately, this idea was not very popular. To a minor extent it was embodied in the budget of 1941, and since then we have all received little pieces of paper informing us that we are entitled to such-and-such a sum of 'post-war credit', but no one seems to feel very enthusiastic about these pieces of paper, and they do not provide a strong motive for working overtime.

Nevertheless, the National Savings Campaign, which encourages voluntarily saving, has done a great deal to withhold surplus income from the shops. A part of the work of the Savings Campaign has been directed to what, in my opinion, is a very trivial purpose. It persuades individuals and firms to put money which they have saved in the past, or which they would save in any case, into Government bonds and savings certificates. This is making a very slight contribution to combating inflation. Money which is being held idle in a bank, or in notes under the bed, is not inflationary, and it makes no contribution to war finance to put it into bonds, except in so far as there is a greater moral resistance to cashing savings certificates than there is to drawing on hoarded cash. While savings are held in notes they earn no interest, and if they are put into bonds the Government must pay for them; so that it is more patriotic not to buy bonds than to buy them. But beside this trivial campaign the Savings Movement has also done good work in persuading people to refrain from spending, week by week, and this has made a genuine contribution to the campaign against inflation.

None of these remedies—price control, taxation, and voluntary saving, can be strong enough to prevent inflation. Price control leaves free purchasing power, taxation is limited by the need to maintain incentive, and, however high it is pushed, it leaves inequalities of spendable income. Voluntary saving does not touch the determined spenders. The only remedy which really goes to the root of the trouble is rationing. Rationing at a stroke cuts down demand to equality with available supplies, and distributes available supplies so that everyone gets his share. Price control, combined with rationing, is useful, to prevent the emergence of surplus profits. Saving and taxation are 'mopping-up operations' which deal with surplus income that might be dangerous if left free. But the main battle can be won only by rationing.

This was realized very slowly in Great Britain, and rationing was introduced by stages. At first only a few foodstuffs in particularly scarce supply were rationed. Gradually more were added to the list. Clothes rationing was introduced in 1941. Then came the 'points' scheme covering miscellaneous foodstuffs. Bread has been left free, so have potatoes, vegetables, fish, and fruit. The last three come and go. Sometimes, in one's own town, one can buy some fish or some cabbage, and sometimes one cannot. Bread has always been available, and potatoes usually so. There is thus always something to fall back on to supplement rations.

Restaurant meals are not rationed, and most workers (except miners and agricultural labourers, for whom special provisions are made) have canteens at their works. Municipal restaurants have been set up in most towns, where an unrationed meal can be had at a moderate price. Thus the rationing scheme has been very elastic, and yet at the same time it has been very democratic, and on the whole, I think, most people are satisfied that rough justice has been done.

The history of clothes rationing is interesting as an example of British pragmatism at work. As war demands on labour and material grew, it became necessary to cut down supplies of textiles to the civilian market. The first step was to limit supplies. Each shop was allowed a certain quota of its pre-war turnover. The result was acute shortages and very haphazard distribution according to 'shopping power' of buyers. As a remedy for this rationing was introduced. The ration was specific, so that a wealthy buyer could get much better value for a coupon than a poor buyer. To remedy the consequent injustice a scheme of 'utility goods' was introduced—that is, goods of standard quality at moderate prices. A certain proportion of materials (cotton, wool, etc.) was allocated to 'utility' production, so as to ensure that the buyer of moderate means can get value for his coupons. The rich certainly have an advantage. First of all, the ration takes no account of the wardrobe of the individual, so that those who had plenty of clothes to start with have equal right to buy with those who had no reserves. Second, it is still possible to get better quality by paying more money with each coupon. This advantage has been reduced by exempting 'utility' clothes from purchase tax, while placing 100 per cent purchase tax on other clothes. The resulting system certainly is not an example of perfect justice, but by remedying the worst abuses, each as it appeared, a fairly satisfactory compromise has been arrived at.

The whole picture is certainly lacking in coherent design. Price control, differential commodity taxation, high direct taxes, the savings campaign, rationing made up of a number of separate schemes—all these make up a confused and illogical amalgam; but one which has been pretty successful on the whole in solving the problem of inflation at the first stage.

What of the second stage—the tendency to a vicious spiral? This also has been dealt with in the British way—there has been no definite solution, and yet things have worked out not too badly. The official cost-of-living index number has been held steady. If the price of one article entering into the index rose, a subsidy to some other article was given. The actual cost of living has diverged more and more from the official figure, but it is the official figure on which wage negotiations are based. There has been no law controlling wages, but a sort of 'gentleman's agreement' between the Government and the Trade Unions to keep wage demands within moderate limits.

The whole story is summed up in the following figures: Personal incomes have increased from £4,779 million in 1938 to £7,708 million in 1943, that is, by more than 60 per cent; while real consumption has been reduced by 21 per cent. Prices, to the final consumer (including commodity taxes and subsidies), have risen by about 54 per cent, and prices, excluding taxes and increases by subsidies, have risen 41 per cent. A large part of this rise occurred at the beginning of the war, as a result of the initial exchange depreciation and the rise of shipping costs, raising the price of imported material, which plays a large part in the British economy. Between 1942 and 1943 prices (excluding taxes and subsidies) rose only from 38 per cent above 1938 to 41 per cent above 1938. This is the measure of the success of the war against inflation.

Perhaps it may seem surprising to have spoken so long about inflation without mentioning the quantity of money. The British authorities have learned from experience that if the real cause of inflation—the excess of income over available supplies—is tackled at the root, the quantity of money can be left to look after itself. Actually the note issue has increased from £5 million to £12 million, and bank deposits (which are the main medium of exchange in Great Britain) have almost doubled. This has caused no alarm. It is partly accounted for by the increase in money incomes, and partly by savings. The monetary authorities have learned that if people prefer to hold their savings in cash, no harm is done by giving them the cash to hold—provided there are strong controls to prevent spending. Indeed, much good is done, for the Government can thus finance its necessary borrowing at low interest rates. We are proud of the achievement of a 'war at 3 per cent'. This has been made possible because the authorities were not afraid of increasing the supply of money.

What of the future? The greatest danger of inflation is always after the war is over. But I think that both the people and the Government have had a severe lesson in economics during the war, and if they have the patience and the strength of mind to pursue the same policy after the war is over, to reduce taxation and rationing very slowly, as new supplies become available, that danger also can be averted.

'THE ECONOMICS OF FULL EMPLOYMENT'

(Six Studies in Applied Economics, prepared at the Oxford Institute of Statistics)

THE General Theory of Employment was evolved under the influence of the slump, and, at first, the practical proposals that were drawn from it were concerned mainly with increasing the level of employment. Much argument was expended on the mere question of whether government outlay could increase employment at all. Nowadays the basic principles of the General Theory are so widely accepted that it becomes pertinent to discuss the much more intricate problems of a policy designed, not merely to raise employment out of a slump, but to maintain it continuously at a high level. These problems have been much debated recently, in conferences, articles, and pamphlets (not to mention a White Paper), but a systematic treatment of the subject was lacking. This is now provided by the economists of the Oxford Institute of Statistics, who themselves have taken a leading part in the debate.

Mr. Burchardt summarizes the basic theory. Mr. Kalecki sets out the main lines of the possible alternative policies for maintaining employment in a closed system. Mr. Worswick discusses some problems which the very success of a full-employment policy would raise: how to prevent a vicious spiral of wages and prices; how to ensure flexibility in production without regimentation of labour. Mr. Schumacher discusses the principles of public finance, particularly of government borrowing, appropriate to the modern doctrines. Dr. Balogh deals with international trade. Mr. Mandlebaum illustrates the theoretical essays with an extremely interesting account of the Nazi experiment in full employment. In general, the essays seem somewhat unnecessarily technical and severe in style. This does not apply to Mr. Schumacher's contribution, which provides an interlude in pleasant pastures between the rocky uplands of Mr. Kalecki's austere exposition and the dense forest of Dr. Balogh's close-packed argument.

Each of the essays raises points which it would be interesting to discuss, but, since space forbids a full treatment of all, it seems best to confine this review to those that bear the main burden of the argument.

Mr. Kalecki combs out the tangle of contemporary discussion on employment policy and lays out the alternatives neatly. One or two snarls remain even in his argument. These concern the place of private business investment in a full-employment scheme. Mr. Kalecki draws an important distinction between the rate of investment in industrial equipment required to keep productive capacity expanding appropriately to full-employment output, and the rate of investment which would maintain full employment. There are various impediments which prevent private investment from keeping up with the first standard. The rate of interest may be unnecessarily high. This can be dealt with by monetary policy (more fully discussed in Mr. Schumacher's essay). The tax system may weigh unduly on investment. Here Mr. Kalecki proposes a scheme by which part or the whole of sums devoted to investment are deducted from taxable profits, while amortization allowances are not deducted until they are spent. (This would clearly be a powerful instrument for stimulating investment.) Above all, full-employment demand is not normally experienced, while the fluctuations of the trade cycle further discourage investment, by enhancing risks. When the Government guarantees to maintain the national income continuously at the full-employment level, expanding as productivity increases, and when confidence in the guarantee has been established, these discouragements to investment disappear. When all these policies have been carried out, any investment which is required to expand productive capacity appropriately is also profitable. Therefore, if all business men lived up to the text-book postulates, always aiming to maximize profits and always producing in the most efficient manner available, private investment would regulate itself and productive capacity would automatically expand at the required pace. But, outside the text-books, business men do not behave so. At any moment there are arrears of known technical improvements which have not been digested into the productive system, and new research falls far short of the profitable level. This is certainly admitted by Mr. Kalecki (p. 52), but it does not seem to be woven into his main argument.

In considering the second standard, he discusses the case where the rate of private investment required to expand capacity appropriately falls short of the rate which would give full employment, and exposes the folly of policies based on stimulating private investment beyond the first rate purely for the sake of reaching the second. He does not contemplate the case where the rate of investment required by the first criterion exceeds the full-employment rate. He thus omits to discuss (beyond a passing reference) a problem of both theoretical and practical importance. In this country, with great blocks of antiquated industrial equipment, with under-capitalized agriculture, and a clamorous demand for social investment to raise the level of health and education, the leading problem for many years after the war facing a Government which had accepted the task of framing an employment policy (and which had the powers necessary to carry it through) would not be to find something or other to spend money on, but to adjudicate between urgent rival claims for the available resources of the nation.

Even when arrears have been made up, there is still a problem of the desirable rate of capital accumulation. Mr. Kalecki provides a formula: 'Private investment must be at a level adequate to expand the capacity of equipment *pari passu* with the increase in working population and productivity of labour, i.e. proportionately to full-employment output' (p. 47). But the rate of increase in productivity of labour is not something given by Nature. Both the amount of energy devoted to technical research, and the pace at which old equipment is replaced by improvements, can be varied. To decide the most desirable rate at which to increase the productivity of labour is itself a problem, for, at any moment, a higher rate of increase in productivity requires a higher rate of investment in business capital, and a lower level of consumption or of investment in social amenities. Once the principle of full employment is accepted, the old concept of 'abstinence' comes into its own again, and the allocation of resources between consumption in the present and accumulation for the future becomes one of the central problems of economic policy.

The administrative problem of controlling the rate of investment is not discussed. Mr. Kalecki mentions 'accidental fluctuations in the rate of private investment, for instance as a result of discontinuous technical progress', which would persist after cyclical fluctuations had been eliminated. 'Such accidental fluctuations can best be neutralized by an appropriate timing of public investment.' This entails the existence of some central authority informed in advance of the investment plans of private firms. It also surely requires some powers of regulation? There is no reason why any private investment project should always go to the head of the queue in front of all government projects. But questions such as this open up a field of political controversy which these studies endeavour to avoid.

The relationship of international trade to employment policy is the most intricate part of the whole problem. The task for any one country of maintaining employment is much eased by a high and stable level of employment abroad, but a world-wide employment policy is still a very distant dream. The British proposals for a Currency Union, providing all its members with a large supply of international liquidity, while not in itself a plan for world full employment, aimed to create a setting in which each country would find it easy to carry out an employment policy. In the absence of such a scheme, a country embarking on an employment policy ahead of the rest of the world has to contend, on top of all the difficulties that arise at home, with the problem of keeping out of international debt. When the world falls into a slump, each country finds the demand for its exports decline, while competition of imports rival to home production becomes keener. The government of a country which is determined to maintain employment is then faced with a double task. It must find useful occupation for the workers displaced, and (unless the country is able and willing to borrow from abroad or to sell out capital) it must prevent its foreign balance from becoming negative. The first problem, which presents some difficulties—it is not easy to provide temporary occupation without making it very hard for the export industries to expand again when the market recovers—is hardly discussed in this book. Owing to the way the work has been divided among the various authors, this subject falls between the two stools of internal and external aspects of employment policy. The second problem is discussed by Dr. Balogh.

One line of attack upon it is for the country aiming to maintain employment to compensate for the fall in demand due to the fall in world income by making home goods cheaper relatively to foreign goods. But this may prove impossible. Devaluation of the home currency is not a panacea, for it may happen that there is no exchange rate which will maintain the balance of trade. Selective protection of home industries against 'unemployment dumping' and selective subsidies to those exports for which the foreign demand is most elastic may succeed where general devaluation would fail. In so far as either succeeds temporarily, it does so at the expense of employment abroad, thus giving another turn to the screw of world deflation, and so enhancing the difficulty it is intended to overcome.

A different line of attack is to lay plans against the slump in advance by deflecting trade into channels which will not freeze up. The country resolved on full employment may bargain with its foreign suppliers, guaranteeing to buy from them, wet or fine, in certain quantities, and asking them in return to accept payment in a form which can be spent only in the home country. This arrangement maintains the balance of trade of the home country, and at the same time helps to insulate the supplying countries from the effects of a slump originating elsewhere.

The attractiveness of the bargain to the supplying countries depends largely on the goods which the home country has to offer. There is always a danger that measures to protect home industry against the consequences of a slump will also protect it against the consequences of its own rigidity and inefficiency; and if better and cheaper goods are on offer in third countries, the suppliers may prefer to forgo the bargain, and chance the slump. Dr. Balogh lays emphasis on the bargaining power of the large buyer. This power may be great in a world slump, but, from a long-run point of view, it is the supplying countries whose position is strong. The power of the buyer is only the power of a lover to shoot himself on his mistress' doorstep. The real point is the power of the *steady* buyer to offer an attractive bargain. How attractive it appears to the supplying countries very much depends on the liveliness of their fears of a slump.

If neither line of attack—by devaluation after a slump has set in or by bargains arranged in advance—promises success, or if they are outlawed by international agreement, the alternative is for the country resolved on full employment to cut down imports in a slump by the amount that exports fall, while accommodating a high level of home activity to the slump level of imports. This would be likely to develop into a permanent policy of autarky, for home industries in substitution for imports, once developed, are not easily abandoned.

If a number of countries are resolved on full employment, they can give mutual guarantees of maintaining total demand, and allow a large measure of competition and multilateral trade within the group. This is the policy which Dr. Balogh most favours. He suggests that such a group should trade with the rest of the world on terms which limit the group's imports from outside to the value of its exports, rationing imports among the group where necessary (p. 167). This amounts to something like making the scarce-currency clause of the Bretton Woods proposals permanent. An adequate discussion of this scheme, which raises wide issues of international policy as well as detailed questions of the technique for planning trade in a mainly private-enterprise system, requires a volume to itself.

OBSTACLES TO FULL EMPLOYMENT

VARIOUS definitions of 'full employment' have been used by English writers. Keynes originally used a definition in terms of Marshall's concept of 'disutility of labour'.[1] Beveridge says there is full employment when there are more unfilled vacancies than unemployed workers.[2] Others call full employment the level of employment at which money-wage rates begin to rise.

On all these definitions there may be large numbers of workers unemployed when 'full employment' is said to exist. It is preferable to take a simple-minded definition, and to say that there is 'full employment' when no one is unemployed.

There is a difficulty in giving a precise definition of 'available labour'. Hours of work may vary. The number of married women 'available' for employment may not be clear cut. But if we can take a rough working definition of 'available labour' then we may say that 'full employment' exists when all available labour is employed.

This is a state of affairs that can never be completely attained. In a changing world there are always bound to be, at any moment, some workers who have left one job and have not yet found another.

Technical changes and changes in tastes both at home and in foreign markets bring about shifts in demand between industries. Although seasonal unemployment could be very much reduced by dovetailing operations with different seasonal peaks, there is probably an irreducible minimum of seasonal employment in some districts. Changes in occupation for personal reasons will always be going on. So long as such shifts in employment are taking place, there is always likely to be some unemployment even when the general demand for labour is very high. Thus completely full employment can never be seen.

Nor is completely full employment desirable. The attainment of full employment, in this absolute sense, would require strict

[1] *General Theory of Employment, Interest and Money*, p. 15.
[2] *Full Employment in a Free Society*, p. 18.

Nationalokonomisk Tidsskrift, 1946. This paper is based on a lecture given to the Nationaløkonomisk Forening at Copenhagen on December 6th, 1946.

controls, including direction of labour. To raise the average of employment from 86 per cent (the average for Great Britain, 1921–38) to, say, 95 per cent, would be compatible with a much greater amount of individual liberty than to raise it from 95 per cent to 98 per cent. To raise it from 95 per cent to 98 per cent (not momentarily—but on the average) would involve great sacrifices of liberty, and to raise it from 98 per cent to 100 per cent would involve complete conscription of labour.

No one regards 100 per cent employment as a desirable objective. 'Full employment policy' does not mean aiming at 100 per cent employment, but aiming at a continuous level of employment as near to 100 per cent as is practicable with the methods of control which are acceptable to the public. In what follows I shall use the phrase 'full employment' loosely, to mean 'as near full employment as is reasonable'.

This use of language, though not exact, is sufficiently clear for all practical purposes.

In England, we are now living under a régime where it is generally accepted that it is the duty of government to maintain full employment. This was accepted even before the Labour Government came into power. For us, this is a great revolution in ideas. During the great slump of the '30s it was the orthodox and official view that government action could not increase employment. In 1929, when Lloyd George was running an election campaign on the promise to abolish unemployment by means of government outlay on public works, the Treasury enunciated the doctrine that government outlay could not, in fact, increase the total level of investment.[1]

Looking back now, it seems almost incredible that such views should have been taken seriously. There are still in England many who are sceptical or unsympathetic about the new policy, but they have to use far more subtle and sophisticated arguments than the 'Treasury View' of 1929.

The change in official and orthodox ideas is of the greatest importance. But up to the present we are living in a fool's paradise. We have accepted a full employment policy, and we are in fact enjoying a high level of employment. There is some unemployment in certain areas, where reconversion to peace-time production is held up for want of buildings. Apart from this there

[1] Command Paper, 3331.

is substantially 'full employment' in the sense of as high a level of employment as is reasonable to expect.

But this is largely a coincidence. It has little to do with the new policy, because just now there would be full employment in any case. At the moment we are living in an inflationary situation —that is, there is an excess of demand over supply for labour as a whole. The acute shortage of houses, due to bombing and to the cessation of building during the war; the drive for exports, which is being conducted not in order to maintain employment, but in order to balance our trade; the great reduction in private stocks of clothes, furniture, and so forth combined with war-time savings ready to be spent on goods as soon as they become available; and the requirements of industry for reconversion to peace-time production—all these add up to an effective demand for labour in excess of supply.

The consequent tendency to inflation is kept in check by the methods evolved during the war. Heavy taxation, rationing, control of prices, a vague and unformulated, but nevertheless fairly successful wages policy, control of imports, licensing of private investment, propaganda for saving, in short, all war-time methods of checking inflation are still in force. These methods are fairly well understood by the Government, and accepted with more or less good-natured grumbling by the public.

If it were possible to keep up permanently a condition of near-inflation and run the machine on the brakes—that is, with controls to curb excessive demand—employment policy would be straightforward and comparatively easy to manage.

The real test of the new policy will come when there is a fall in demand. How will it be met? The danger may come from within or from without. Let us first consider the internal danger. There may be a fall in the rate of private investment when the reconstruction boom comes to an end, but this is unlikely to be serious. Industrial investment, in equipping factories and so forth, has never been a very large part of all home investment. The main bulk of home investment is in building and civil engineering. If the Government can control the rate of building, the investment plans of nationalized industries, and the timing of large schemes, such as the electrification of rural districts, then it should be possible to plan for a steady level in the great bulk of investment. This in itself would help to steady private investment because it would go a long way towards stabilizing incomes, and therefore the general level of profits. Further, by consultation and persuasion, without overt control, the large firms can probably be induced to fit their investment plans into a national scheme. And a small uncontrolled fringe would probably not be very unstable.

The White Paper on Employment Policy[1] issued by the late Coalition Government was not based upon this point of view. It was based rather on the conception of 'counter-cyclical' government investment, that is, the idea that the Government should step in and increase its own investment when private investment falls off, and slow down its own investment when private investment increases. In my view, this policy is fundamentally wrong. It means giving private enterprise the first choice. When private firms choose to make investment they can. When they no longer want labour, the Government will use the labour for something or other. When private investment recovers, the Government must release labour again, so that it can be used for profitable investment. This whole point of view is subject to the gravest objection. Once we have accepted the idea that it is the business of the Government to see that labour is always employed, we must go on to admit that it is the business of the Government to see that labour is employed in the most useful possible way: that is to say, that schemes of investment should be directed to meet the needs of the community, and not to suit the whims and fancies of profit-seeking firms.

Indeed, it is impossible for the State to divest itself of responsibility for the direction of employment once it has accepted responsibility for the total amount of employment. There are many in England at present who advocate the use of 'global methods' designed to affect the total employment without exercising any discrimination over the allocation of labour between uses. But this is in fact impossible. Any policy, even if it is purely global in conception, will produce concrete results and have an influence upon the direction of employment. The decision not to interfere with private investment is itself a positive decision.

Thus the responsibility for deciding how the influence of the State upon the direction of employment is to be used cannot be escaped.

The problem of deciding what are the 'needs of society' and of

[1] Command Paper 6527.

adjudicating between conflicting needs is by no means simple. There is no one Platonic ideal of the 'best use of the nation's resources'. Conflicts of interest and conflicts of ideology are bound to persist. But somehow or other a democracy does decide what it wants. In England at present there is no doubt that the people want more than, in fact, can be done at all quickly. Housing—first in the sense of some kind of a roof over everyone's head, later in the sense of improving the disgraceful condition of our great cities and our backward rural districts. Re-equipment of industry —not for the sake of profit, but for the sake of meeting our desperate foreign trade position and for raising the general standard of production and therefore of consumption. Improvement of our education and our health services, which involves large investment in building and equipment as well as in training of personnel. Improvements in the efficiency and amenity of our transport system. Improvements in the amenity of the countryside (there are many cottages in England which are without gas or electricity and even without piped water) which are desirable both for their own sake and to check the drift away from agriculture, which is one of our serious economic problems. These and many other 'social needs' are agreed by the nation, in the vague and yet definite sense in which democracies do agree upon their needs.

The task of deciding between these needs, and reducing them to a scheme of priorities, must be the duty of the Government. The methods to be used are still in course of evolution, and no doubt they will work clumsily, and be the subject of much dispute and criticism. But a merely passive policy of compensating the vagaries of private enterprise would be the least hopeful of all possible methods of solving the problems involved.

The 'counter-cyclical' policy is subject to another objection. It is very unpractical. It is not at all easy to switch on and off schemes of investment at a moment's notice, or even at six months' notice. Besides, private and public investment are often closely bound up together. You cannot have factories built during the boom and wait for the next slump to make roads up to their gates. It is essential for a sane employment policy that investment should be planned as a whole and not merely stabilized by 'counter-cyclical' public works.

The second branch of the White Paper policy is to maintain

consumption when investment falls off. When investment falls, incomes decline and there is 'secondary unemployment' due to the fact that consumers have less money to spend. The suggestion is that, at such a moment, the purchasing power of consumers should be increased, and the general level of demand for consumption goods kept up, so as to fend off the 'tertiary unemployment' which follows when consumer goods industries become less profitable, and investment in them in turn falls off.

The prejudice which still exists in the British Treasury (or which, at any rate, still existed when the White Paper was written) made it impossible to advocate remission of taxation and the deliberate creation of a budget deficit as a means of maintaining purchasing power. They did, however, suggest the creation of a deficit in the social insurance funds by reducing weekly contributions when demand threatens to fall. This would make rather a feeble contribution to solving the problem. Many more or less fanciful schemes for regulating purchasing power have been suggested by English economists. These seem often to be rather perverse. There is something repugnant to common sense in the idea of giving money to people to spend just in order to keep up the market for goods and make industry profitable. Ordinary people consider that they should be given money either because they deserve it, or because they need it, not just in order to make a market. It is necessary to provide at least the appearance of equity in releasing purchasing power even if the motive is to stabilize employment. The least arbitrary of these schemes is the device of 'deferred pay' invented by Lord Keynes as a measure of war-time finance. Part of the income tax paid is credited to the individual to be refunded at the decision of the Government. This provides a fund of purchasing power which people regard as their own money, which can be released when demand for consumer goods is threatening to fall.

This scheme was used, to a small extent, during the war, and the arrears of tax credited to the public are held up at present, to be released when the supply of consumer goods becomes adequate —that is to say, when normal demand no longer exceeds supply. The release of the credits would provide a stimulus to demand which could be regulated, in time and in amount, so as to give a salutary shock to the economy when a failure of demand is threatening. There is no reason why this system should not be permanent, so that there are always arrears of potential purchasing power in hand, to be released when required to maintain demand.

These methods can be used to prevent an internal failure of demand. But for Great Britain, and equally in Denmark, the main danger does not lie inside the country, but outside—that is, in a fall in demand for exports, whether due to a slump in the outside world or to a long-period change.

This would present a difficult situation even for a fully planned economy. It creates two problems—how to maintain employment and how to deal with the balance of payments.

If demand falls in export industries, work must be found for the labour released. If exports are highly specialized, this is by no means an easy matter. It is of little use just to increase purchasing power in general. Plans should be drawn up specifically for (a) buying up and using or storing products formerly exported, (b) turning labour to alternative products, or (c) arranging an alternative foreign outlet to replace the lost market. Such plans are not easy to work out satisfactorily, and although there is much talk in England now about employment policy, it may be doubted that plans on these lines are actually being prepared. If the world slump were to come soon there would be little difficulty, for the home market is starved of goods, and would eagerly absorb what is at present being exported. So far as miscellaneous consumer goods are concerned, actually the same goods could be sold at home. And where the same goods are not appropriate, alternative uses for labour could easily be found. For a country whose exports are primarily agricultural the difficulty would probably be greater, and alternative employment might be harder to arrange.

If the immediate problem of maintaining employment is solved by switching labour from the foreign to the home market, the further problem will arise of switching it back again when the foreign market recovers. This must require a fairly high degree of control over industry. For if we are to do without the brutal methods of a market economy—unemployment and bankruptcy —we must have other means for directing production.

The problem of maintaining employment when export demand falls off is complicated and difficult enough, but if it is solved a worse difficulty remains—the problem of the balance of payments.

The 'natural' remedy for a fall in exports, under *laissez-faire* conditions, is a fall in employment and in income, which reduces demand for imports also (though not necessarily to the same extent). But if employment is successfully maintained, then the demand for imports does not fall, and the balance of trade runs into a deficit. For a country with ample monetary reserves this would not matter. But for Great Britain it would present a very serious problem. Discussions are going on now as to means to help countries which do their duty to the world by maintaining their demand for imports in face of a slump elsewhere. Let us hope that some world agreement will be arrived at on these lines, for the provisions of the Bretton Woods fund only scratch the surface of the problem.

The main remedy for a trade deficit envisaged under Bretton Woods is exchange depreciation. But this is not a remedy appropriate to the disease. If the trouble is caused by a decline in total world demand, there is first of all very little reason to expect that depreciation would bring about a recovery of exports for a particular country. Depreciation works by reducing the *relative* price of the country's exports, and, in a general slump, there are probably very few commodities for which price-elasticity of demand is high. Moreover, even if it does do good from the point of view of the country in question, it can do so only at the expense of other countries, for it works by improving the competitive position of the depreciating country, and securing for it a larger share of the shrunken world trade, by reducing the share of its rival producers. No remedy is beneficial to the world as a whole that does not increase the total of world demand.

Behind this balance of trade problem again lies a further difficulty—the difficulty of distinguishing cyclical from long-period changes in foreign demand. The remedies required are quite different in the two cases. If demand for exports has fallen temporarily, the capacity of the export industries should be preserved with the utmost care, and any transfer of labour from them made with an eye to restoring it to them as soon as possible. Imports should be kept up as far as reserves permit. But if the change is permanent it is necessary as quickly as possible to reduce the productive capacity of the trade which has lost its market—to foster, if possible, alternative exports, and if that cannot be done, to set about cutting down imports. Thus a misdiagnosis of the situation would lead to a totally wrong policy being pursued; the medicine for one disease is poison in another, and diagnosis will never be easy, since long-run and cyclical changes are often mixed up together.

At the present time, framing of policy is particularly difficult, for one great unanswerable question hangs over everything—what will the U.S.A. do in the coming slump? We can be pretty sure that history will not repeat itself, and economists planning now for the return of the 1930s would be like the generals who are accused in peace-time of planning to win the last war.

The most that one can say is, that we must prepare for a flexible policy and for an intelligent and quick response to events.

Flexibility requires control. It is a popular error that bureaucracy is less flexible than private enterprise. It may be so in detail, but when large-scale adaptations have to be made, central control is far more flexible. It may take two months to get an answer to a letter from a government department, but it takes twenty years for an industry under private enterprise to readjust itself to a fall in demand.

For this reason, full-employment policy requires a high degree of central control over the economic system. Just how much control remains to be seen. The problem of combining the necessary degree of control with the traditional methods of democracy is the dominating political problem of the present time.

If all these problems are successfully solved, certain difficulties arise from the very success of the full-employment policy.

For people who have a secure income in any case, full employment is a great nuisance. There are no domestic servants, the theatres are always full and the holiday resorts overcrowded. Goods are in short supply, not because less are produced, but because other people are consuming more. Shopkeepers become over-bearing instead of obsequious.

For managers in industry discipline is hard to preserve because workers are no longer frightened of losing their jobs.

Unpleasant tasks such as coal-mining cannot recruit labour on the old terms.

All these 'drawbacks' are, of course, the reverse side of the advantages of full employment for the mass of the people.

Finally, there is the problem of preserving the value of money.

If the demand for labour is strong, money-wage rates tend to rise, and since the demand for commodities is also high, prices rise with costs. A successful employment policy, just because it is successful, entails a chronic danger of inflation.

Up till now, in England, the 'vicious spiral' has been kept within bounds, but we have no definite wages policy, nor are we likely to have one, for individual Trade Unions are jealous of their independence.

The danger of an all-round rise in wages could probably be dealt with by an over-all understanding with the Trade Unions, but the problem of relative wage changes is not easy to solve. There are many trades, of which mining is the chief example, where wages are obviously too low, whether we consider it from the human point of view of the disagreeableness and danger of the work, or from the economic point of view of the need to attract labour away from less onerous occupations. So long as unemployment was general, a completely irrational wage system could persist, but once there is full employment, wages must conform broadly to the text-book rule of equalizing the 'net advantages' of different occupations. The process of raising wages which are too low, involves raising the general level of wages (no one advocates lowering wage rates which are relatively high) and therefore is likely to involve a rise in the cost of living. Thus even right and necessary wage changes contain the threat of the 'vicious spiral'.

All this sounds pessimistic, but only because dangers and difficulties can be clearly foreseen. Whatever may happen, we are better off if our eyes are open, and nothing that can happen now can be so bad as the blind misery of the great slump.

PART III

ECONOMIC CONSEQUENCES OF A DECLINE IN THE POPULATION OF GREAT BRITAIN

EMPLOYMENT

THE relationship between growth of population and growth of employment is not easy to disentangle, for all the elements in economic development interact upon each other and no one can be isolated. It seems fairly clear that the great development of production in the nineteenth century was a necessary condition for the great increase in population which took place in the western world, for if there had not been that increase in productivity the Malthusian checks would have come into operation. Equally it is clear that the increase in population was a necessary condition for the development of industry which took place. How far the industrial revolution can be said to have caused the increase in population is a question of great historical interest which does not now concern us. Whatever may have been true in the past, the development of industry clearly does not cause an increase of population in the conditions which now prevail in the western world. What we have to discuss is whether an increase in population causes an increase in employment.

In primitive conditions an increase in productive employment is limited by known techniques and the amount of land available. When that limit is reached, and population continues to increase, an absolute over-population occurs in the sense that more hands add nothing to the wherewithal to fill more mouths. This is a problem of the utmost urgency, for instance, in India, but it has no bearing on our immediate problem.

In an advanced industrial country, does an increase in numbers lead to a corresponding increase in employment? An increase in numbers certainly increases needs, but needs are not the same thing as market demand. With every pair of hands God sends a mouth, but a mouth without a shilling to buy bread does not

---

This paper was written during the war. Then a decline in the population of Great Britain was expected in the near future. It has not been published previously.

constitute a market. It is doubtful whether an increase in population without the other concomitants of nineteenth-century expansion—the development of new continents and rapid technical progress—could be relied upon to keep industrial expansion going.

At the same time, in a society such as our own, where no one is allowed to starve outright, and a certain minimum standard of housing and other services is maintained, an increase in needs sets up a pressure towards increase in outlay, for in so far as the minimum standard cannot be maintained by private outlay, it will be supplemented by social services.

For most industrial countries, and for this country in particular, all questions concerning employment are much complicated by international trade. Let us rule them out, at the first stage of the argument, by assuming that exports are continuously adjusted to imports. An increase in imports, then, gives employment (in the export trades) just as much as an increase in consumption of home produced goods. The question of the balance of trade will be discussed below.

To illustrate the immediate effect of an increase in numbers on employment, it is useful to construct a simple picture, omitting many complications which occur in reality. Let us suppose (1) that an increase in unemployment relief is financed by borrowing, (2) that unemployment relief on the average is equal to half the earnings of an employed man, (3) that wages costs are equal to half the net value of the product of an employed man, (4) that an addition to wage incomes is fully spent on consumption, (5) that half of an addition to non-wage incomes is spent on consumption and half saved (whether privately or through undistributed profits). On these assumptions the multiplier is equal to 2; that is to say, when one additional man is employed, the consequent repercussions of additional spending lead to the employment of another man. Now suppose that four men come into the labour market as a result of population increase (their places as juveniles being filled up by the rising generation). Assuming that there is general unemployment and no unfilled vacancies, the first effect is to add four to the number of the unemployed. On our assumption, four doles make up the value of the product of one employed man. One man is therefore employed to provide for the consumption of the new entry, and one more man is employed by the operation of the multiplier. Now employment is increased by two men and unemployment by two men. Both the number and the proportion of unemployment is increased. The additional borrowing of the unemployment funds is equal to the additional saving out of non-wage incomes.

If the unemployed are supported by their friends and relations, or if the social security funds maintain a continuously balanced budget, the four new mouths would add very little, if anything, to total consumption and little or no increase in employment would take place. The addition to the population would remain unemployed.

So far it seems as though an increase in population, when general unemployment already prevails, tends to increase unemployment. But this is by no means the whole story. The number of people requiring house room, public services such as drainage and transport facilities and medical attention, is increased. In so far as this merely increases overcrowding in houses, trams, and hospitals, it has no further effect on employment. But if an increased pressure of overcrowding leads to investment in housing and ancillary services, employment is increased, both in the constructional trades and (owing to the multiplier effect) in consumption industries also. The additional total consumption helps to maintain investment in private industry. The repercussions of an increase in population may therefore go very far in increasing employment.

The pressure of overcrowding is likely to increase investment partly because individuals will forgo outlay in less capital-consuming lines in order to provide house room for themselves, and partly because public authorities will feel obliged to maintain a certain standard of ancillary services, and possibly also to subsidize house-building. So long as a constant standard of housing and services is maintained, it requires a continuously increasing population to maintain investment of this type at a given level. This is a point of the utmost importance, for investment of this type in recent years has represented something like three-quarters of all home investment. If the coming cessation of population growth were to lead to a rapid decline of this type of investment to replacement level, there can be little doubt that the problem of unemployment, far from being relieved, would be much exacerbated; *a fortiori* if a decline in numbers reduces it below replacement level.

The effect of changing numbers on industrial investment can best be considered in terms of its influence at various phases of the trade cycle. First consider the top of a boom. The boom comes to an end when the rate of investment falls off, and investment falls off when the emergence of surplus capacity reduces the prospective profit to be obtained from creating more capacity. Now, surplus capacity may emerge for two quite different reasons. It may emerge because the accumulation of new equipment by investment made during the boom overtakes the up-swing of income and consumption due to the boom. As soon as the rate of investment ceases to increase, income (and the demand for commodities) also ceases to increase, and remains for a time poised at its maximum level. But, meanwhile, new equipment is being completed and coming into use. Equipment therefore increases relatively to output, and surplus capacity emerges. So far as this is concerned, changing numbers of population (except for the influence on relief payments and on social investment discussed above) has no effect. But surplus capacity may also emerge because it is impossible to find labour to man the new equipment. A boom may knock its head against the limit of full employment before profitable investment opportunities have been exhausted. As soon as the rate of investment falls off, for whatever reason, income and consumption decline, and the cumulative down-swing of the slump sets in. In such a case an increase in numbers taking place over the years of prosperity may permit a boom to go on longer than it could if numbers had not increased. It may well be that the influence of increasing numbers in permitting booms to develop unchecked was of importance in the past, but during the whole of the inter-war period there was such a large untapped reserve of unemployed labour that it appears extremely unlikely that scarcity of labour played any part in limiting employment. It is true that scarcities of particular craftsmen occurred in 1937, but this was due to the drying up of recruitment and training during the depression, and it is obvious that a more rapid increase in overall numbers would have done nothing to relieve these scarcities.

Now consider the trough of a slump. The bottom stop, below which total income cannot fall, is higher the larger the population, particularly if the social insurance funds meet their increased outlay by borrowing or drawing on reserves. A decline in numbers during the slump, both by reducing relief payments and by relaxing the pressure for social investment in the manner described above, is likely to prolong and deepen the slump, both directly and through its influence on the profit expectations which govern private investment.

There may also be a general and vague effect of declining numbers on private investment. In the past, the knowledge that total numbers were increasing may have been at the back of the minds of entrepreneurs laying out plans to increase their productive capacity, and this may have helped to keep up the rate of investment. Correspondingly, public discussion of the coming decline in numbers may have a depressing effect. Prosperity, in a private enterprise economy, is largely a matter of 'thinking makes it so'. If entrepreneurs in general expect a decline in the market for their products, their investment plans will be curtailed and consequently the market will, in fact, decline.

The changing age composition of our population is likely to make labour less mobile (this is discussed below). Immobility of labour can only be said to be a cause of unemployment when unfilled vacancies appear. Apart from the case of special crafts, unfilled vacancies only appear in a boom stronger than any experienced in this country in the inter-war period. Immobility, like an overall scarcity of labour, may theoretically check the development of a boom, but the booms that we have experienced recently have checked themselves long before this factor came into play. It cannot therefore be regarded as an important cause of unemployment in the conditions then prevailing.

We must also consider the reaction of a decline in numbers upon the possibility of a secular exhaustion of investment opportunities in private industry. Unless the average of unemployment (over good and bad years) increases very much, the total national income may be expected to increase, as a result of technical progress and the accumulation of capital, even if population is constant or declines moderately. The question then is: does a given increase in national income representing only an increase in the standard of life generate as large a demand for new capital as an equal increase accompanied by a rise in population? At the upper levels of income it is fairly clear that it does not. For the mass of the people better (as opposed to more) housing comes very high on the list of demands which are at present over the horizon. So do travel, holidays from home, and entertainments of all kinds which involve new construction. Moreover, the development of mass demand for manufactures which were formerly regarded as luxuries creates large outlets for industrial investment. But it seems unlikely that such demands can be an adequate substitute for the enormous absorption of capital represented by the growth of towns. If new demands take a less capital-using form as population ceases to grow, the problem of the secular decline in investment opportunities will be exacerbated by the decline in population.

In any case, we have argued above that a decline in numbers is likely to have the effect of deepening and prolonging slumps, while in some circumstances it may curtail booms, and this would increase the riskiness of industry and so reduce the inducement to invest. There is a further reason why instability may be expected to increase with a rising standard of life. Durable consumers' goods (e.g. cars and refrigerators) are an important ingredient in rising standards. Now, when such a durable commodity first comes within the horizon of effective demand for large numbers of families, the industry producing it has a large market, which continues to expand as long as the incomes of families which have not yet bought it for the first time continue to rise. But sooner or later saturation will be reached, and the industry must bump down to the level of replacement demand. This may be fended off by creating artificial obsolescence through keeping up a stream of heavily advertised new models, but this, as well as being socially wasteful, is a precarious basis for demand. This type of demand sets up a tendency to industrial fluctuations similar in nature to the cycle of investment. Moreover, with a high standard of life the pattern of demand has great scope to change in ways which are not at all easy to foresee (the demand for men's shoes in the U.S.A. fell off with the increase in use of motor cars) while the changing age composition accompanying a decline in population brings about changes in demand which may not be correctly foreseen. Such influences tend to make investment more risky, so that the allowance for obsolescence which capital is expected to earn, before investment will be undertaken, is kept high, and the inducement to invest represented by any given level of current profits is correspondingly reduced.

The long-run reaction of declining numbers on the propensity to save is very problematical. Saving may be divided into three broad types: small savings of the mass of the public, savings of the wealthy, and company reserves. Small savings are mainly of the insurance type, and represent a redistribution of consumption over the lifetime of an individual rather than net accumulation. This class of saving produces net saving only so long as the numbers are increasing or the habit of saving is spreading. So far as the first element is concerned, a reduction in the rate of population increase is likely to reduce accumulation some time before an overall decline in numbers sets in, because of the rise in the proportion of elderly people, drawing on past savings, to the earning and saving population. So far as the second element is concerned, it is hard to make predictions. It seems likely that the saving habit will continue to spread rapidly. Social insurance, which is now extremely popular, is a kind of compulsory saving, and the extension of social insurance is probably likely to increase rather than to reduce private saving, since it raises many families above the threshold of hopelessness and fecklessness below which saving does not seem worth while. But this is independent of population trends. The specific influence of population on small saving turns on the question: Does a family with few or no children tend to save more or less from a given income than a family with many children? *A priori* one is inclined to answer more. The margin of disposable income after meeting bare needs is higher in the small family, and probably the very same desire for security and improvement which leads to family limitation also promotes saving, so that the spread of the new pattern of living down the income scale is likely to be accompanied by an increase in the habit of saving. The conclusion that saving varies inversely with the number of children is borne out by Mr. Madge's survey,[1] but the evidence is sketchy, and more investigation is required into this question.

At the other end of the income scale it seems in general probable that the effect of family limitation is adverse to saving. Saving to leave a fortune, or to offset death duties, probably springs

---

[1] *Wartime Patterns of Saving and Spending*, N.I.E.S.R., Cambridge Press, 1943.

largely from consideration for one's heirs, and the fewer the heirs
the weaker the motive for saving.

In any case, personal savings in this country are generally
reckoned to represent less than half of all savings. The main bulk
of saving comes from undistributed profits. The most important
influences upon the thriftiness of the community as a whole are
the share of total income going to profits and the policy pursued
by corporations. In the past the share of profits in total income
has been remarkably stable over the long run. Unfortunately,
economists have no simple and agreed explanation of this phenomenon to offer. Probably the most plausible explanation is that
any tendency for the share of profits to fall is offset by a growth
of monopolistic practices designed to defend profits. Fiscal policy,
interest policy, and policies connected with the prevention of
unemployment and the control of monopoly may influence the
share of profits in the future, but except in so far as population
trends react on these policies, it is difficult to trace any strong
influence of population movements on the share of profits. Nor
does there seem to be any obvious connection between population
movements and the policy of corporations.

The above discussion is not very conclusive. Any influence that
there may be of population movements upon thriftiness is likely
to be swamped by other influences which would be operating in
any case. At least we may say, however, that there is no reason
to expect a decline of population, in itself, to bring about a
decline in thriftiness sufficient to offset the generally depressing
effect upon investment which it seems likely to produce in an
uncontrolled system.

We have so far been discussing the reaction of a decline in
numbers on unemployment in an uncontrolled system. We find
that, to say the least, a decline in numbers is not likely to reduce
the need for a national policy to prevent unemployment, and it
is now very widely accepted that in future there must be such a
policy. It is not to our purpose to enter into a discussion of the
nature of an employment policy, or of the relative merits of
various types of policy, but it is necessary to discuss in general
terms the problems presented for employment policy by a decline
in numbers.

First of all there is the question of deciding what is the best use
to make of the resources which without a national policy would

be unemployed. With a stationary or declining population, continued full employment would lead to a more rapidly rising standard of life than with increasing numbers, and there is always more room for dispute about what form a rise in the standard of life should take than about the necessity of maintaining more people at an already accepted standard. But, in present circumstances, this difficulty is remote. The need for improved nutrition, housing, health services, and education, as well as for a very considerable re-equipment of industry and mechanization of agriculture is widely accepted, and provides a target for employment policy which will stand for at least a generation. There is no need to tease ourselves about a possible *embarras de richesses* which may conceivably set in in the future. Moreover, in so far as a rising standard is taken in the form of more leisure, the problem will solve itself.

The most immediate relevance of present population trends to employment policy is connected with the age composition of the population rather than its total numbers. Adequate mobility of labour is a necessary condition for the success of an employment policy that aims at all high. The adjustment of the supply of labour to the demand for it is easier to secure when shifts can be brought about by the painless process of inducing new workers to go into expanding trades, and allowing contracting trades to lose workers by retirement and death, rather than by the more difficult process of inducing older workers to change their jobs. There is a certain critical rate of shrinkage for any industry which can take place in a painless manner, and this critical rate is higher the larger the proportion of its workers who are near retiring age; up to a certain point, therefore, the ageing of the labour force actually helps mobility. But if the required shrinkage exceeds the critical rate, mobility is harder and more painful because the workers who have to change jobs are older. This problem, however, can be much exaggerated. The versatility of modern industry has been demonstrated by the war. A man may change from producing locomotives to producing tanks without altering his craft or even changing his shop. The general run of semi-skilled occupations are much the same, whatever the final product. And a high degree of flexibility can be given to industry by varying hours of work without requiring any mobility of labour at all. In framing an employment policy it is extremely important to combine it with a location policy, so that the dependence of any particular district upon a single trade is kept as low as is practicable. If the need for geographical shifts of labour is small, industrial shifts on any scale likely to be required in normal times can probably be brought about without much difficulty, even with an ageing population. The post-war situation, however, will be far from normal.

The overall problem of abnormal age composition is overshadowed by the problem of the still more abnormal age composition of the labour force of particular industries. The industries of districts which took the main brunt of the depression lost their younger workers and drew in new recruits at a rate below replacement level even for the scale to which the industries had shrunk. The industries most depressed before the war are, therefore, likely to be faced with an acute scarcity of labour when normal conditions return. Policy will have to be evolved to deal with these problems in any case, and the general abnormal age composition of the population at worst adds some difficulties to a situation which would in any case be formidable.

THE STANDARD OF LIFE

We will now assume that at least a moderately successful full-employment policy is in operation, so that any influence upon unemployment coming from the side of population is offset, and consider the influence of population trends on real income per head.

The first point to be considered is the age-composition of the labour force. This is by no means uniquely determined by the age-composition of the population. At one end the promised rise in the school-leaving age will have a considerable effect upon it. At the other end, the rage for early retirement, which was setting in before the war, was largely the product of the depression. Under the influence of a full-employment policy, inducements to elderly workers to carry on might take the place of inducements to remove themselves from the labour market. Thus the age-composition of the labour force is likely to change, even apart from changes in the age-composition of the population as a whole. The reduction in the proportion of juveniles is likely to raise average efficiency. There can be few occupations in which a lad is absolutely more efficient than a man, and where juvenile labour is preferred it is usually because the difference in wage rates more than offsets the difference in efficiency. The disappearance of one type of cheap labour is likely to promote more efficient organization of industry. At the other end of the scale, a greater proportion of elderly workers may lower average productivity, but this loss also can probably be kept low, or even turned to positive advantage, by stimulating managers to take trouble in adapting conditions of work to the capacity of workers. There is little reason, if management is responsive, and does not confine itself to lamentations over rising wage costs, why the further change in age-composition of the labour force due to the change in the age-composition of the population at large should reduce average productivity.

A change in the age-composition of the labour force is accompanied by a change in the ratio of dependents to workers. Here again the effect of social policy may swamp the effect of changing age-composition of the population, but assuming any given social policy, the population trend will have its effect through altering the proportion of those within the socially-determined period of working life to those outside it. This proportion is expected to remain fairly constant during the next thirty years, but there will be a marked change in the composition of the dependent population, pensioners taking the place of children. However dependents are supported, whether by their families, by their own past savings and social insurance contributions, or by the Exchequer, their current consumption is provided by the current production of the active part of the population. Assuming a given level of employment, the real consumption of the active population plus the rate of capital accumulation is therefore greater the smaller the consumption of dependents. It is therefore of some interest to inquire into the relative average cost of the consumption of a child (including costs of education) and of a pensioner. If these are roughly equal, the effect of changes in the age-composition of the population upon average income will be slight.

A full-employment policy has two main branches—a redistribution of income calculated to increase consumption, and an increase in the average rate of investment. A stabilization of numbers (and *a fortiori* a decrease in numbers) reduces the amount of investment necessary to maintain a given standard of capital per head, as compared to the situation where numbers are increasing. It therefore enlarges the scope for increased consumption as a means of maintaining employment. Thus, if the first branch is followed alone, a greater rise in the standard of life would come about with a stable or slowly falling population than with a rising population.

The influence of numbers would also be important if an increase in the average rate of investment is the main ingredient in employment policy. There are many reasons why investment policy is likely to play an important part in any employment policy. First of all, the need for social investment in housing, public utilities, schools and hospitals, and in building up a stock of trained personnel of all kinds (teachers, doctors, nurses, and social workers) is much in the forefront of the public mind; while the need for building up equipment to improve the competitive position of British industry and agriculture is urgent. Secondly, a rapid reduction in the proportion of investment to consumption at a boom level would require large structural changes in industry and large switches in the labour force, so that a pure consumption policy would meet with much greater difficulties than a policy in which investment played a large part. Thirdly, a pure consumption policy would have a strong tendency to increase imports, and so add to the difficulties of the balance of trade, while investment policy can be directed towards activities which require a low proportion of imported materials. Fourthly, prejudices in favour of financial orthodoxy tell strongly on the side of investment. We may therefore assume that full employment policy will largely take the form of attempting to stabilize the rate of investment at something higher than the average level experienced in the past, at least for some years to come.

If such a policy is adopted, and is even moderately successful, the importance of population for the standard of life becomes very great. Lord Keynes has estimated[1] that over the period 1860 to 1913 something like half of all the capital accumulation that occurred was required merely to maintain capital per head. Such estimates are admittedly very rough, but they serve to give an impression of the orders of magnitude involved. The estimate suggests that, with stable numbers, we may look forward to a rise in capital per head at twice the pace which took place during

[1] 'Some Economic Consequences of a Declining Population', *Eugenics Review*, XXIX, I, 1937.

a fairly prosperous period in the past. In the same context, Lord
Keynes estimated that the national capital is not more than four
years' purchase of the national income. Thus, with stable numbers, a rate of net investment of 16 per cent of the national income
would raise capital per head at the rate of 4 per cent per annum.
This, again, is of course very rough guesswork. Such a rate of
increase, if wisely directed, holds out very great promise of a
rapidly improving standard of life. Its most obvious relevance is
in the sphere of housing. With enormous arrears of normal building,
slum clearance, and reparation of war damage on our hands, it is
clear that the scope for improvement in the standard of housing
is much greater if we do not have to provide for increasing numbers as well. Once the arrears are overcome, and the bulk of
building activity can be directed to replacing bad old houses with
good new ones, an absolute rise in the standard will become
practicable. The same argument applies to public utilities (e.g.
light and water for the countryside), and to schools, hospitals, and
clinics. A cessation in the growth of towns would relieve many
threatening economic and social problems (but this depends even
more upon control over the location of industry than upon total
numbers of the population), and if we can look forward to some
shrinkage, so that it becomes possible to roll up the ribbons, the
benefits would be still greater.

In the long run, when a satisfactory standard has been reached,
there will be a problem of tapering building activity to replacement level. This is a particular aspect of the general conclusion
that a far-sighted employment policy is made all the more
necessary by a cessation of population growth.

As far as industrial investment is concerned the prospect is also
favourable. It is sometimes maintained that the rate at which
industry can digest an increase in capital per head depends (as
soon as the influence of falling interest rates is exhausted) upon
the uncontrollable vagaries of technical progress. But this is by
no means the case. There is a very great spread in most British
industries between the equipment of the most modern and the
oldest plants; in many industries America has already pioneered
the way to high productivity based upon high capital per head;
five war years of unusually rapid technical progress have accumulated a fund of new knowledge ready to be adapted to civilian
use; and the adjustment of capital structure to lower interest rates

has still to be made. There is thus great scope for industrial investment, even with existing knowledge.

Moreover, technical progress, especially with modern methods of systematic research, is not a rigid self-determining process, but is strongly influenced by its economic environment. The combination of a foreseen cessation in population growth with full employment would create conditions of continuous scarcity of labour combined with continuous strong demand for commodities —a state of affairs highly propitious to technical progress. Thus, even when arrears have been made up, it is not likely that the scope for investment, under a full employment policy, will be rapidly narrowed. In a very long—and very peaceful—run, no doubt, capital accumulation will approach the point at which the scope for new investment vanishes. This is the state of 'Bliss' in which capital ceases to be scarce. As this point is approached, the rate of investment must be tapered off, and employment policy must be directed towards increasing consumption and increasing leisure. In so far as future technical progress takes a 'capital-saving' form, the approach to 'Bliss' will be so much the more rapid. Such speculations, however pleasing, have little relevance to the immediate future, but they point once more to the increased need for long-sighted planning occasioned by the cessation of population growth.

A cessation in the growth of numbers increases land per head relatively to what it would be if numbers continued to grow, while a decline in numbers increases it absolutely. For this country, food-producing land per head (the classic ground of Malthusianism) is relevant to the problem of the balance of trade rather than directly to the standard of life, but from the point of view of amenities, land per head or rather per family is of great importance. To-day we have roughly one acre per head of population. This means that the present middle-class standard of life, based upon a house and garden, a summer holiday in the country, and a motor-car, is quite out of the question for the mass of the people, and the more people rise to that standard the greater the inconvenience to those who already enjoy it. Even if numbers decline, a less land-consuming pattern must be found for our rising standards, but a considerable consumption of land in open spaces, green belts, and national parks is certainly required for a rising standard. This will be easier to provide the smaller are total numbers.

We have come to the conclusion that, provided employment policy is even moderately successful, falling numbers mean rising standards of life. Is there any limit to this process? Can population fall to a sub-optimum level, from a strictly economic point of view?

This is not the same problem as the question of whether the rate of decline may be excessive; that question turns upon the effects of a changing age of composition of the population. What we have now to discuss is whether a moderate rate of decline will continue to raise average real income however long it goes on.

It is obvious enough that a population starting from scratch in a given space may be too small to allow industry to develop. But a small population which inherits the capital designed for larger numbers is in a very different position from a population which has been small all along. There is a general presumption that, in an old country, any population, at a given moment of time, is super-optimum in the sense that a decline in numbers would increase capital per head and raise the average productivity of labour. This is all the more likely to be true if capital equipment varies much in quality, so that a decline in numbers makes it possible to concentrate on the most efficient plant, the most productive mines and the most convenient sites. As time goes by, disinvestment will take place in part of the inherited capital. But a great deal of investment is irreversible—once the equipment has been created it is there for good (the original layout of a road and railway system is an important example). A still larger part of equipment can be kept in permanent repair by a very small rate of outlay. Thus a great part of the increase in capital per head due to a decline in numbers will persist over any length of time. The stock of inherited capital is likely to grow progressively less appropriate to existing requirements with the fall in numbers and the passage of time, and some of it (owing to the cost of demolition) may become a positive nuisance, but there is always likely to be some net gain. A large reduction in numbers in a heavily capitalized country would involve losses to capitalists and landlords, which might raise serious social and political problems and would be inimical to investment in an uncontrolled system, but with a successful employment policy it is always likely to raise real national income per head. The above argument applies with full force to foreign capital owned by home nationals. Its yield provides purchasing power over imports without any current expenditure of labour, and the capital provides an invaluable war chest. The relevance of this argument to our own situation is all the greater because of the loss in total foreign capital which has taken place during the war.

We must next consider the possibility of a loss of economies of large-scale production as a result of decline in numbers. There are circumstances in which this might have some importance, but we must observe, first, that a large element in the economies of scale is purely financial—the spreading of given overheads over a larger output. If physical capital is kept intact and its financial value deflated with its earning power there is no loss to society, but merely the loss to capitalists already referred to. Second, a great part of the technical economies of large scale can be achieved by concentration of output. So long as there is more than one plant of the most efficient size in each line there need be no loss of economies due to a reduction in total output. It is true that growing concentration increases the danger of monopoly, but the growth of monopoly is one of those extremely serious problems of the future with which we shall be faced, and with which we shall have to deal, whatever happens to population. Thirdly, many of the most important economies of scale apply to the total development of industry rather than the scale of any particular line of production, and depend upon the total of income rather than its composition. If average income increases as numbers decline, total income falls off much more slowly than numbers, and may even increase while numbers are falling. Finally, in a peaceful world with international trade there need be no loss of economies at all in any transportable goods, but merely an increase in national specialization.

Taking all these considerations into account, there seems little reason to fear a sub-optimum population. Such arguments cannot be pressed too far, for any large decline in numbers would take place over a long time and be accompanied by all sorts of influences, so that any prediction of its consequences is necessarily highly speculative. If we allow our minds to dwell on Dr. Charles' estimate of a population of four million in the year 2035, we may either draw an agreeable picture of England's green and pleasant land, exporting the product of a highly mechanized agriculture, running two trains a day over an electrified railway system, and obtaining coal entirely by surface mining, or we may indulge a taste for horrors by depicting handfuls of decrepit Methuselahs sharing the grass-paved ruins of their cities with owls and foxes. But such predictions are too fanciful to be of serious value.

THE BALANCE OF TRADE

The structure of British foreign trade is closely connected with population movements. Broadly speaking, the reason that Great Britain did not succumb (as Ireland did) to the Malthusian devil during the period of great population growth was that she developed a highly advantageous trade in manufactures against food and raw materials. Now that British industry shares world markets with powerful rivals, while a special and acute problem is presented by the abrupt fall in net invisible exports due to the war, her large population is a source of weakness to this country. Any decline in numbers which may now set in will relieve the situation, but is unlikely to be large enough to make a substantial contribution to solving it.

Pre-war imports were roughly £800 million per annum, of which half were foodstuffs. Food imports were thus about £9 per head, taking population as 46 million. It is generally reckoned that one-third of food consumption was home produced. The disappearance of one mouth from the population would thus reduce food imports by £9 per annum and release £$4\frac{1}{2}$ of home-produced food for other mouths to consume. Home food is not strictly substitutable with imported food, nor is it physically distinct (milk is partly imported as cow-cake and eggs as maize). Moreover, the rise in the standard of life which would accompany a better average of employment with declining numbers is likely to bring about a rise of average food consumption. £$13\frac{1}{2}$ per mouth (at pre-war prices) must thus be taken as an upper limit to the reduction of food imports which would result directly from a decline in numbers.

So far as raw materials are concerned, and 'manufactured' imports (which consist largely of oil products and other partially processed materials) there is very little substitution between home and imported goods. And if the contemplated rise in the standard of life is not strongly deflected towards home products it will raise imports per head. It would therefore be an exaggeration to credit a reduction in numbers with a relief to import requirements at the average rate of £9. Even if we take the upper limit in each case, we get a reduction in import requirements of only £22½ per head at pre-war prices. Thus there is little hope of an appreciable contribution to the balance of payments problem from any decline in numbers which can be expected in the immediate future. At the same time it is obvious that every increase in numbers must add to the difficulties with which this country will in any case be faced.

From a long-run point of view the outlook is extremely speculative. In the '30s rapid technical progress in agriculture, combined with a world-wide collapse of effective demand, created a glut of foodstuffs. Even a moderate improvement in the average of world prosperity, combined with the immense population growth which is going on outside the western world, would create a huge demand for food, and it would be optimistic to rely upon technical progress keeping pace with it. We must therefore reckon with the possibility of a strong unfavourable trend in the terms of trade between manufactures and foodstuffs. On the other hand, it may happen that gloomy forecasts will be belied by the spread of improvements in agricultural technique and the release of acreage for foodstuffs by the development of synthetic substitutes for agricultural raw materials. Whichever turn development takes, the international position of Great Britain would be less precarious the smaller (within reason) the population requiring to be fed. A considerable decline in numbers would relieve her from acute difficulties or put her in a strong position to take advantage of favourable developments, as the case may be.

MARX AND KEYNES

THE relationship between Marxist and academic economists has changed in recent years. During the time of Marshall an impassable gulf still divided them. The one party was engaged in exposing the evils of the capitalist system, the other in painting it in an agreeable light. One regarded the system as a passing historical phase, containing within itself the germs of its own dissolution; the other regarded the system as a permanent, almost a logical, necessity. This fundamental difference of outlook was supported by a difference of language, each party using terms strongly coloured by its own point of view. Thus, the academics described the interest obtained by owning capital as the *reward of abstinence*, or *waiting*, and profit as the *reward of enterprise*, while Marx treats interest and profit (and rent) as *unpaid labour*, or *surplus value* (the surplus of the value produced by labour over the value paid to labour). This complete difference of attitude made inter-communication between the two schools impossible.

Latter-day academics have, for the most part, undergone a striking change. The circumstances of the times have forced them to concentrate on two problems, monopoly and unemployment, which naturally raise doubts as to whether all is for the best in the best of all possible economic systems, and they are more inclined to analyse the defects of capitalism than to dwell upon its merits. The attempt to represent merely owning capital (waiting) as a productive activity has been abandoned, and the view is gaining ground that it is misleading to treat capital itself as a factor of production, on the same footing as labour. 'It is preferable to regard labour . . . as the sole factor of production, operating in a given environment of technique, natural resources, capital equipment, and effective demand'.[1] What is more important, capitalism is no longer regarded as an eternal necessity. Thus, Keynes writes: 'I see the *rentier* aspect of capitalism as a transi-

---

[1] Keynes, *General Theory of Employment, Interest and Money*, p. 213.

This paper appeared in Italian in *Critica Economica*, November, 1948. The first two paragraphs are taken from an article which appeared in the *Economic Journal*, June-September, 1941.

tional phase which will disappear when it has done its work'.[1] And Professor Hicks: 'I do not think one could count upon the long survival of anything like a capitalist system [in the absence of a trend of innovations sufficiently strong to maintain investment] . . . one cannot repress the thought that perhaps the whole Industrial Revolution of the last two hundred years has been nothing else but a vast secular boom'.[2] These *dicta* are much closer to Marx than anything that can be found in Marshall, while Mr. Kalecki's epigram: 'The tragedy of investment is that it causes crisis because it is useful',[3] has a close affinity with Marx: 'The real barrier of capitalist production is capital itself'.[4]

This change, however, had no direct relation to Marxism. It was rather the result of an explosion of academic economics from within.

The system of thought which dominated academic economic teaching (and greatly influenced policy) even after the onset of the great slump in 1930, allowed no place for unemployment as more than a mere accident or friction. 'Natural economic forces' tended to establish full employment. Crises were treated as a special problem, and kept, as it were, in quarantine, so that theory of crisis did not infect the main body of economic doctrine. Confronted with massive and persistent unemployment in the first post-war period, the orthodox theory was baffled and ran into a tangle of unconvincing sophistries. Out of this situation arose Keynes' General Theory, by which I do not mean simply the book called *The General Theory of Employment, Interest, and Money*, but the whole stream of ideas, or rather the analytical system, to which that book made the main contribution, but which is still in process of developing and perfecting itself, finding new applications and modifying its methods to treat new problems.

Keynes' main achievement was in a sense negative (though it has many positive consequences both for theory and for policy). It was to show that there is no automatic self-righting mechanism tending to establish full employment in an unplanned private-enterprise economy.

The basis of the orthodox doctrine was Say's Law of Markets— the theory that supply creates its own demand—production and

---

[1] Ibid., p. 376.   [2] *Value and Capital*, p. 302.
[3] *Essays in the Theory of Economic Fluctuations*, p. 149.   [4] *Capital*, Vol. III, chap. 15, §2.

sale of one lot of commodities provides the purchasing power to buy other commodities. Thus general over-production cannot occur. This doctrine was accepted generally without much criticism. Marshall called it an axiom—that is, something self-evident.[1] But it was also elaborated and defended by a sophisticated argument.

The orthodox conception of a natural self-equilibrating mechanism in the *laisser-faire* system had two branches.

According to the first, the rate of money-wages provides the mechanism. If men are unemployed they will be prepared to accept lower wages. The fall in wages will increase demand for labour, and so unemployment will quickly disappear. If it does not disappear, that is due to the stupid obstinacy of trade unions in refusing to accept a cut in wages. Keynes showed that this theory was based on a very simple fallacy—the fallacy of composition. It is true for any one employer, or for any one industry —to a lesser extent for any one country in international trade— that a cut in wages, by lowering the price of the commodity produced, will increase its sales, and so lead to an increase of employment in making it. But if all wages are cut, all prices fall, all money incomes fall, and demand is reduced as much as costs. No one employer then has any motive to take on more men. In a crowd, anyone can get a better view of the procession if he stands on a chair. But if they all get up on chairs no one has a better view.

The second line of orthodox argument concerned the rate of interest. If the demand for consumer goods falls, this causes unemployment in making consumer goods. But, according to the orthodox argument, reduced demand for consumer goods means increased saving. An increase in saving means that there is more money to be lent to industry, so that the rate of interest falls. As a consequence, industry will want more capital (as it can now borrow on cheaper terms) and so there will be an increase of employment in making capital goods. This will exactly compensate the fall of employment in making consumer goods.

Here again Keynes pointed out a very simple error; this time the error of assuming what it is required to prove. If employment, and incomes, are unchanged, then a fall in consumption entails an increase in saving. But the first effect of a fall in consumption

[1] *Pure Theory of Domestic Values*, p. 36.

is to reduce incomes and cause losses, and with lower incomes there is less saving. If the rate of investment in new capital does not increase, incomes will fall to the point at which saving is no greater than before, and there is no tendency for the rate of interest to fall. (This led to discarding the theory that the rate of interest is determined by the supply and demand of saving, and putting in its place a totally different theory of the rate of interest based on demand for the stock of money.)

In so far as it is possible to summarize a complex system of thought in a few words, we may say that the essence of Keynes' theory is as follows: an unequal distribution of income sets up a chronic tendency for the demand for goods to fall short of the productive capacity of industry. Those who desire to consume have not the money to buy, and so do not constitute a profitable market. Those who have the money to buy do not wish to consume as much as they could, but to accumulate wealth, that is, to save. So long as there is a sufficient demand for new capital investment (in houses, industrial equipment, means of transport, growing stocks of goods, etc.), savings are utilized, and the system functions adequately. But saving in itself provides no guarantee that capital accumulation will take place; on the contrary, saving limits the demand for consumption goods, and so limits the demand for capital to produce them. Booms occur when there are profitable outlets for investment. Long periods of prosperity could occur in the nineteenth century when there were large opportunities for profitable investment in exploiting new inventions and developing new continents. Pseudo-prosperity occurs in war-time because war creates unlimited demand. But prosperity is not the normal state for a highly-developed capitalist system, and the very accumulation of capital, on the one hand by increasing wealth and promoting saving, and on the other by saturating the demand for new capital, makes prosperity harder to attain.

Thus crises appear, not as a superficial blemish in the system of private enterprise, but as symptoms of a deep-seated and progressive disease. Though Keynes' theory arose out of the problem of unemployment, it has many other applications. It has proved invaluable in the analysis of post-war inflation. It has revolutionized the theory of international trade. And it has implications, not yet fully worked out, which undermine the

traditional academic theory of the long-run supply of capital and
of the distribution of the product of industry between labour and
capital.

Academic theory, by a path of its own, has thus arrived at a
position which bears considerable resemblance to Marx's system.
In both, unemployment plays an essential part. In both, capitalism
is seen as carrying within itself the seeds of its own decay. On the
negative side, as opposed to the orthodox equilibrium theory, the
systems of Keynes and Marx stand together, and there is now,
for the first time, enough common ground between Marxist and
academic economists to make discussion possible. In spite of this
there has still been very little serious study of Marx by English
academic economists.

Apart from political prejudice, the neglect of Marx is largely
due to the extreme obscurity of his method of exposition. There
are two serious defects in the Marxian apparatus, which are quite
superficial in themselves, and can easily be remedied, but which
have led to endless misunderstandings.

In Marx's terminology C, constant capital, represents productive equipment (factories, machinery, etc.), and raw material and
power; V, variable capital, represents the wages bill; and S,
surplus, rent interest, and profits. Now, if we write (as Marx
habitually does) $C + V + S$ to represent the flow of production,
say per year, then C is not the stock of capital invested, but the
annual wear-and-tear and amortization of capital. $\dfrac{S}{C + V}$ is the
share of profits in turnover, and not the rate of profit on capital
invested. The rate of profit which (for Marx as in orthodox
systems) tends to equality in different lines of production, and the
rate of profit which tends to fall as capital accumulates is not
$\dfrac{S}{C + V}$, but the rate of profit on capital invested.

Marx himself was well aware of this point, but his habitual use
of the expression $\dfrac{S}{C + V}$ for the rate of profit on capital is excessively confusing. Moreover, lumping raw material and power
along with equipment in the single concept of constant capital
makes it impossible to distinguish between prime and overhead

costs, since prime costs consist of V and part of C (raw materials and power), while another part of C is overhead. Thus Marx's apparatus is useless for many of the problems in which academic economists have interested themselves, especially in connection with short-period supply price and the influence of monopoly on the share of wages in output.

The second main difficulty arises from Marx's method of reckoning in terms of *value* or labour time. With technical progress and capital accumulation, output per man-hour tends to rise, so that the *value* of commodities is constantly falling. Academic economists are much concerned with output, and with concepts such as the 'real national income', the 'level of real wages', and so forth. To measure these in terms of *value* is to measure with a piece of elastic. Thus academic economists, if they get as far as considering Marx at all, are apt to form the impression that his methods of thought are quite useless, and to dismiss the whole of his analysis as an inextricable mass of confusion, which it is not worth the trouble of understanding.

This impatience has been further encouraged by the perennial controversy over the labour theory of value. In my opinion, this has been much ado about nothing, and the pother that there has been over it has disguised both from the academics and from the Marxists the real nature of the question at issue. To the academic economist, the 'theory of value' means the theory of *relative* prices —the prices of commodities in terms of each other. Now Marx's theory of relative prices, as set out in Volume III of *Capital*, is quite simple. The rate of profit on capital tends to equality in all lines of production. Wages of labour also tend to equality in all occupations (allowing for differences in skill). The amount of capital per unit of labour employed is governed by the state of technical development. The normal price (apart from errors and perturbations of the market) for, say, a year's output of any commodity, is equal to the wages of the labour employed in producing it *plus* cost of raw materials, power, and wear and tear of plant *plus* profit, at the ruling rate, upon the capital invested. Prices would be proportional to *values* if capital per unit of labour (the organic composition of capital) were the same everywhere, but, in fact, for technical reasons, proportionately more capital is employed in some industries than in others, and since the rate of profit on capital invested tends to equality, profits, relatively to wages, tend to be high where the ratio of capital to labour is high. Thus normal prices are equal to long-run costs of production, and the ruling average rate of profit on capital is the supply price of capital to any particular line of production. Conditions of demand determine the amount of each commodity produced.

There is nothing in this that contradicts orthodox theory. It leaves out such refinements and complications as price rising or falling with the scale of output (much emphasized by Marshall), and it does not touch upon questions of oligopoly and imperfect competition (which have been elaborated in recent years), but it is the obvious first starting-point for any theory of relative prices. The academic economist may consider it too simple and primitive to be of much interest to him at this time of day, but he has no reason to regard it as either mysterious or fundamentally erroneous. Equally, the Marxist has no reason to regard the labour theory of value, *as a theory of relative prices*, either as particularly important or as fundamentally opposed to orthodoxy.

What divides Marx's theory from others is not at all the question of relative prices of commodities but the question of the *total* supply of capital and the rate of profit on capital *as a whole*. On this question there is a sharp difference between Marx and the pre-Keynesian academics.

In the Austrian theory of value, the supply of capital is somehow given. For Marshall, capital accumulation represents a 'real cost' to capitalists—the 'sacrifice of waiting'—and accumulation goes on so long as profit exceeds this cost. In equilibrium, the rate of profit is just sufficient to cover the real cost of waiting. Thus there is a supply price for capital as a whole, and the amount of capital tends to be such that the rate of profit is equal to this supply price.

In Marx's system an urge to accumulate is inherent in the capitalist economy, the amount of capital, at any moment, is the result of the process of accumulation which has been going on in the past, the total of profits is the difference between total net receipts and the amount which it is necessary to give to the workers to ensure their reproduction, and the rate of profit is simply this total of profits averaged over the total of capital in existence. Thus the real differences between Marx and the orthodox schools concern the question of what governs the accumulation of capital and the distribution of the total product of industry between workers and capitalists. Compared to these problems, the determination of relative prices of commodities appears as a secondary question which has been too much flattered by all the attention that has been paid to it. It is precisely upon these large questions that the old orthodox system has been profoundly shaken. Thus, as between Marxists and Keynesians, the labour theory of value is a totally irrelevant issue.

What remains to divide them? Primarily, of course, a difference in philosophical and political outlook, but here I wish to discuss the question as far as possible on the plane of ideas rather than of ideologies, and to confine the argument to problems of economic analysis, for I believe, with Professor Schumpeter,[1] that Marx was a great economist, in just the same sense as Ricardo, Marshall and Keynes were great economists, and that his merits simply as a theorist have been concealed by the prophetic robes in which he has been dressed up.

The central issue is the theory of crises. I have argued elsewhere[2] that the theory adumbrated in Volume II of *Capital* has close affinities with Keynes. But it is possible that I have overemphasized the resemblance. The last two volumes of *Capital*, which Marx did not complete, are excessively obscure and have been subjected to many interpretations. The waters are dark and it may be that whoever peers into them sees his own face.

Here I wish to concentrate on the differences rather than the resemblances between the two systems. In Keynes' system the clue to crises is found in variations of the *inducement to invest*, which depends primarily upon the prospect of future profit from new investment. As capital accumulates, the profitability of further investment declines. This accounts both for the sharp onset of a slump after a period of high investment, and for the secular tendency for unemployment to develop with growing wealth and productive capacity. Of this there are only scattered hints in Marx, and it is incompatible with his main argument. For in Marx's system the amount of investment is governed by the amount of surplus which the capitalists succeed in extracting from the system, that is to say, it is the rate of saving out of profits which governs the rate of investment. Competition and technical progress set up an urge to accumulation, for each capitalist fears to fall behind in the race if he does not continuously invest in new

---

[1] See below p. 152.   [2] *An Essay on Marxian Economics*, Chapter VI.

capital equipment embodying the latest developments. Thus the problem of effective demand does not arise, and though Marx explicitly repudiated Say's law as childish nonsense, yet he no more than Mill or Marshall admits the divorce between decisions to save and decisions to invest, which, in Keynes' system, appears as the root cause of crises and unemployment.

This does not mean, however, that Marx neglects the problem of unemployment. On the contrary, 'the reserve army of labour' is an essential feature of his system. In his view, the amount of employment offered by capitalists depends upon the amount of capital in existence, and there is unemployment because there is insufficient capital to employ all the potentially available labour. When accumulation catches up upon population growth (and the growth of the supply of 'free' labour as peasants and artisans are sucked into the labour market by the spread of the capitalist system), a temporary relative shortage of labour stimulates labour-saving inventions and so replenishes the reserve army once more. Now, unemployment of this type, in the world at large, is a phenomenon of the greatest importance. It exists in the backward, over-populated countries of the east, and, indeed, everywhere except amongst the most developed industrial nations. And something analogous has reappeared in war-shattered economies where unemployment results from the mere lack of equipment and material to work with. Unemployment of this kind is radically different from unemployment due to a deficiency of demand. It seems, then, that Marx and Keynes are discussing two different problems, and that each theory is required to supplement the other. Marx, however, regarded his system as all-inclusive, and he purported to derive from it an explanation of the crises which develop in advanced capitalist economies. It is here that, in the light of Keynes' argument, Marx's analysis appears inadequate and unconvincing.

There are two distinct strands of thought to be detected in *Capital*. According to the first, which is fully developed in Volume I, real wages (broadly speaking, with exceptions and reservations) tend to remain constant at subsistence level (though the subsistence level contains a 'moral and historical element' due to the customary standard of life). As productivity increases with capital accumulation and technical progress, the rate of exploitation (the ratio of profits to wages) therefore tends to rise. Capital at the same time tends to be concentrated in ever fewer hands as large units prevail in the competitive struggle over smaller units. Thus there is an ever-growing difference between the wealth of the few and the poverty of the many which in the end will lead to an explosion—the overthrow of capitalism and the 'expropriation of the expropriators'.

Now, the course of history since Marx's day has disproved this prediction. In the foremost capitalist countries the level of real wages has indubitably risen, and the gap in the standard of life of the workers and the capitalists has narrowed, most markedly in England and the Scandinavian countries, but to some extent in all capitalist nations. Marx did not foresee to what an extent capitalism would be able to buy off the workers with refrigerators and Ford cars.

Marxists often seek to explain away the rise in the standard of life of the industrial workers in the advanced countries by attributing it mainly to the exploitation of colonial peoples. The white workers are fatted 'palace slaves', and the capitalists can afford to pamper them so long as they extract profit from the exploitation of the coloured peoples. But this theory is unconvincing. If the profit obtainable abroad is high, there is no reason why any individual capitalist should be willing to accept a lower rate at home. Investment in colonial regions will be kept up and investment at home retarded, so that the bargaining position of home labour is weakened, not strengthened, by the existence of cheap labour abroad.

Colonial exploitation clearly does raise the level of real wages of home labour, but it does so by a different mechanism from that postulated by the theory of 'palace slaves'. The low wages of the colonial workers influence the standard of life of the home workers through low prices of raw materials and foodstuffs relatively to manufactures. (At the present moment, when the terms of trade are relatively favourable to primary producers, the industrial workers are feeling the difference.) This advantage is not confined to workers in the imperial nations. The innocent Swedes gain as much from favourable terms of trade for tropical raw materials as the British or the Dutch.

The importance of cheap colonial labour to the standard of life of the industrial workers has never, so far as I know, been systematically evaluated. But though it has been of obvious importance, particularly in England, it would be absurd to attribute to it a predominant share in the rise of the standard of life in the United States in the last fifty years, even if we extend the conception of colonies to include the Southern States, for raw materials 'imported' from regions of colonial exploitation play too small a part in the total of American consumption to account for more than a fraction of the spectacular rise in American wealth.

Thus it appears that Marx's prediction of 'increasing misery' of the workers has failed to be fulfilled. At this point Keynes once more supplements Marx, for he shows how increasing wealth brings its nemesis in a different way. Growing susceptibility to unemployment appears instead of growing poverty of the masses as the weakness at the heart of developing capitalism.

There is a second strand of thought in *Capital* which is quite different from the first, and which, indeed, is hard to reconcile with it. This is the Law of Falling Rate of Profit, elaborated in the third volume. In this argument (once more with exceptions and qualifications) it is the rate of exploitation, not the rate of real wages, which tends to remain constant. If the rate of exploitation is constant, real wages rise with productivity, the workers receiving a constant share in a growing total of real output. Now, according to Marx, there is a broad tendency for the organic composition of capital to rise as time goes by; that is to say, capital-using inventions are the predominant form of technical progress, so that capital per unit of labour employed is continuously rising. If capital per unit of labour is rising, but profit per unit of labour is constant (or rises more slowly) then the rate of profit on capital is falling. Thus capitalists undermine the basis of their own prosperity by their rage for accumulation. The connection between this theory and the theory of crises is made in the most tangled and confusing passages of Volume III, and has been the subject of many conflicting interpretations. Instead of plunging into that jungle, it is better to concentrate upon the first stage of the argument—the rising organic composition of capital.

Marx (or rather Engels for him) clearly admits that it is not the case that all technical progress increases capital per unit of labour. Historically, the key to development has been transport, and inventions which save time, save capital. It is therefore by no means obvious that organic composition has really been rapidly rising with the development of capitalism. Huge investments in machinery are obvious to the naked eye, but it is impossible to assess how far the saving in stocks and work in progress due to speeding up communications and speeding up processes has in the past offset growing investment in equipment. And it is impossible to tell what the predominant type of invention will be in the future. Certainly many great capital-saving inventions (such as wireless in place of cables) have been made in recent times. This is a question to be investigated. Meanwhile, it is at least possible to imagine, for the sake of argument, that from now on capital-saving inventions will balance capital-using inventions, so that organic composition ceases to rise (capital per unit of labour employed will tend to remain constant), while technical progress continues to raise productivity just as rapidly as before. A world in which organic composition is constant (or, for that matter, falling) is perfectly conceivable. To such a world, Marx's analysis would have no application, and the whole of that part of his theory of crises which depends upon the declining tendency of profits would fall to the ground. His case for a tendency to ever-deepening crises as a necessary and inevitable feature of capitalism therefore cannot be sustained. If there is a fundamental defect in capitalism it must have deeper roots than in a mere accident of technique.[1]

Keynes' theory does not depend upon any particular tendency in organic composition. Capital-saving inventions are likely to offer less outlet for investment than capital-using ones, and so tend to make a smaller contribution to maintaining effective demand. At the same time they may reduce the share of a given output going to capital (for in Keynes' system there is no reason why the rate of exploitation should be constant) and so tend to reduce the excessive propensity to save. But, either way, the question, in Keynes' system, is of secondary importance, and his theory is equally cogent whichever form technical progress in the future may happen to take.

Thus it appears that whichever branch of Marx's theory of crises we follow, it is necessary to call in Keynes' analysis to complete it, and neither part of Marx's argument can stand up by itself.

At the same time, Keynes' system of thought operates within

---

[1] In my *Essay on Marxian Economics* I have tried to show that even granted the assumption of rising organic composition, the theory still fails to be convincing.

a restricted field. He does not touch at all upon the major questions with which Marx was concerned, and he has undermined the orthodox theory of long-period equilibrium without putting anything very definite in its place. Thus Marx's theory, or at any rate some theory on the questions which Marx discussed, is as much required to supplement Keynes as Keynes' theory is to supplement Marx.

THE LABOUR THEORY OF VALUE

WHAT was all the fuss about? In Volume I of *Capital* Marx set out his theory of *value*. The *value* of, say, a week's output of a commodity is the labour-time expended in making it, including the labour-time expended in the past to make raw materials and capital equipment now used up in the process of production. The net output (total output minus the *value* of raw materials and wear and tear of plant) is divided between wages and surplus—that is, profit interest and rent. The ratio of surplus to wages is the rate of exploitation.

In Volume III of *Capital* Marx gives his theory of prices. The exposition is confused by his habit of using one expression for two meanings—*variable capital* means both the annual wages bill of a concern and the capital locked up, at any moment, in the wages-cost of work in progress. He does distinguish between *constant capital* in the sense of the annual wear and tear of physical capital, and in the sense of the amount of capital represented by equipment and the raw material in work in progress, but he often loses his grip on the distinction. These, though tiresome, are minor difficulties, and the essence of his theory of prices is quite simple. Wage rates per man-hour are assumed equal in all industries (Marx deals with the complications when they are not), and, when prices are normal, the rate of profit on capital invested is equal in all industries. Thus the price of a week's output of a commodity is equal to the costs of replacing the raw materials and wear and tear involved in its production, *plus* the week's wages, *plus* profits at the general rate on the capital involved in plant and in work progress.

This is broadly the same as Marshall's theory of long-period normal prices (without the complications of increasing and diminishing returns) or, as Sombart puts it, 'a "quite ordinary" theory of cost of production' (quoted, p. 31).

It is obvious that the prices of various commodities and their

A review of: *Karl Marx and the Close of his System*, by Eugen von Böhm-Bawerk. *Böhm-Bawerk's Criticism of Marx*, by Rudolf Hilferding. *On the correction of Marx's Fundamental Theoretical Construction in the Third Volume of Capital*, by Ladislaus von Bortkiewicz. Edited by Paul Sweezy. *Economic Journal*, June, 1950.

values can be in the same ratio to each other only in a very special case. When prices are proportionate to *values* the net product of equal quantities of labour-time must be sold for equal amounts of money. If wage-rates are everywhere the same, this is compatible with the condition that profits per unit of capital must be uniform only if capital per unit of labour is the same in all industries. (Marx describes the ratio of capital to labour in an industry as the 'organic composition' of its capital, but, owing to the double meanings referred to above, it is hard work to make sense of his definition of organic composition.)

Why, then, does Marx state (in Volume I) that normally prices equal values? From the modern point of view, the best line of defence is to argue that in Volume I he is assuming, just for convenience, that all industries are alike. Relative prices of commodities, after all, are of little interest in 'macro-dynamic' analysis, and it is quite legitimate to use a 'model' in which the ratio of capital to labour is uniform, for the purpose of disentangling the large questions with which Marx was concerned —movements in the total supplies of capital and labour, the development of productivity in the economy as a whole, and the distribution of the product of industry between labour and capital.

Mr. Sweezy hints that this is how he would like us to take it (p. xxiii). But it was not the way Marx looked at the matter. For him *value* and prices were important, and were connected with each other in a fundamental way. He did not think of exchange-value as a relationship between commodities which has no significance when the total of output is considered, but as a quality inherent in each of them—a quality analogous to weight or colour.

Let us take two commodities, e.g. corn and iron. The proportions in which they are exchangeable, whatever these proportions may be, can always be represented by an equation . . . e.g. 1 quarter corn = x cwts. iron. What does this equation tell us? It tells us that in two different things— in 1 quarter of corn and x cwts. of iron there exists in equal quantities something common to both. . . . This common 'something' cannot be either a geometrical, chemical, or any other natural property of commodities. . . . If, then, we leave out of consideration the use-value of commodities, they have only one common property left, that of being products of labour. (Quoted, p. 10.)

This, no doubt, is mere assertion, disguised as argument. But having committed himself to the assertion, Marx had to reconcile it with his theory of prices.

The reconciliation (published long after his death, in Volume III of *Capital*, but conceived much earlier, p. 155) is purely formalistic and consists in juggling to and fro with averages and totals. Marx's contention is that the quantity of surplus in terms of *value* generated by a unit of labour is the same in each industry, whereas actual profit per unit of labour varies with capital per unit of labour. The *value* generated in each industry is conceived to be pooled and shared out again, through the competitive process, so as to bring this about. Once more pure assertion is masquerading as argument, for we have nothing but Marx's bare word for it that the *value* generated per unit of labour is the same in each industry—all we can know in concrete reality is the actual profit per unit of labour, which admittedly varies from industry to industry.

The real meaning of all this lies on a quite different plane. What Marx was trying to convey was a view of the operation of the capitalist system which, right or wrong, is highly significant; but what he actually wrote, taken literally, is a rigmarole entirely devoid of content.

Böhm-Bawerk seized upon the rigmarole as soon as Volume III was published, and made sport of it. His manner is urbane, his argument elegant, and the essay is still worth reading for its entertainment value. But it is totally superficial. The theory of *value*, in the narrow sense of a theory of relative prices, is not the heart of Marx's system (though both he and Böhm-Bawerk believed that it was), and nothing that is important in it would be lost if *value* were expunged from it altogether. Böhm-Bawerk makes out his case, but nothing follows.

In his counter-attack (first published in 1904), Hilferding argues that the theory of *value* is not intended to deal with relative prices, but with the law of motion of society (p. 147). All the same, he cannot discard any part of Marx's system, and he has to find some sense in which it is also true that *value* governs price. To do so he falls back on the historical argument. Before capitalism developed, each worker owned his own tools and the prices of commodities were proportional to the labour-time required to produce them. *Value* then ruled in the market, and, as capitalism developed, *values* were gradually transformed into prices.

The argument about how prices were determined in the pre-capitalist world is conducted in much the same style as the 'bourgeois' economists' argument about how Robinson Crusoe equalized his marginal utilities, and is no more convincing. But, even if it were true, it would not serve to rescue Marx from Böhm-Bawerk's attack, for his so-called equation, '1 quarter of corn $= x$ cwts. of iron', was supposed to apply, not in an idyllic past, but in the contemporary capitalist market.

For the rest, though Hilferding scores one or two telling points against Böhm-Bawerk's own theory, he throws no light whatever (indeed, he throws darkness) on the meaning of the theory that *value* determines price.

Why is it that Marxists, even to this day, have to carry on all this mystification? Why could not Marx's system have been freed, by constructive criticism, from irrelevance and contradictions and clearly shown to be the original and penetrating system of analysis that, with all its blemishes, it certainly was? The reason is, no doubt, that the Labour Theory of Value has long ceased to be a theory and become a creed. Perhaps, from one point of view, the Marxists are right to defend it. Religions which take a firm stand upon dogma have shown, in the course of history, great cohesion and toughness, which reason might have weakened. 'The spirit killeth, the letter keepeth alive'. But the theological style of argument has a corrupting effect upon the intellect.

The last item in this collection is one of the very rare examples of a constructive criticism on a point in Marx's system. Not being a pious Marxist, Bortkiewicz was able to notice an error in Marx's text, and at the same time he was sufficiently interested and sympathetic to put it right. The point at issue is purely formal and of no importance, but it has the same kind of cross-word-puzzle fascination as the 'adding-up problem' in 'bourgeois' economics.

As we have seen, Marx in Volume III discarded the assumption that prices are proportional to values, but in calculating the output of industries, in some numerical examples, he carelessly reckons raw materials and wear and tear (constant capital) at

prices corresponding to *values*. Since the raw materials for one
lot of industries are the output of another lot, his examples fail
to hang together.

Bortkiewicz makes an elaborate job of exposing and correcting
Marx's slip. Mr. Sweezy refers approvingly to other contributions
which have been made to the problem and looks forward to new
work being done upon it (p. xxx). He evidently fails to realize
that it is just a toy and that the whole argument is condemned
to circularity from birth, because the *values* which have to be
'transformed into prices' are arrived at in the first instance by
transforming prices into *values*.

Marx conceives of exploitation in terms of the division of
working time into the part necessary to produce the subsistence
of the workers, and the rest, which produces surplus. This has
no meaning as applied to individual industries. Obviously, in a
specialized industrial economy, it would take any group of workers
more time than there is to produce for themselves the goods
which they consume. The division must be conceived as applying
to the output of the economy as a whole. We must take the sum
of all profits received, find its ratio to the sum of all wages paid,
and divide the total working time in the corresponding proportion. Suppose that, of total net output, 40 per cent goes to wages
and 60 per cent to profits, then the *value* of the wages paid for
100 man-hours of work is 40 man-hours, and the surplus generated
by them is 60 man-hours. Now, each group of workers is conceived to generate surplus at this rate, irrespective of the actual
share of profits in the industry concerned. In an industry with
more than average capital per unit of labour, where the ratio of
profit to wages is, say, 70 to 30, the surplus per 100 man-hours
being reckoned as only 60, the extra 10 man-hours' worth of
profits actually received is attributed to the fact that the price of
the commodity produced 'exceeds its *value*'. But this *value* is
purely notional, and corresponds to no actual feature of the
industry in question. The *values* of commodities are imputed by
crediting each group of workers with the average rate of exploitation of labour as a whole, and the 'transformation of values into
prices' consists of breaking the average up again into the separate
items from which it was derived. It is possible to make a logical
slip (as Marx, in fact, did) in either half of the process, but if the

imputation and the transformation are both done according to the rules, the answer is bound to come out right.

The above type of methodological criticism appears to a Marxist to be tiresome and beside the point, because the whole rigmarole has a symbolic meaning for him. *Value* precedes price, because the fact of exploitation lies behind the phenomena of the market. May be so—but this is not the kind of proposition that can be established by a tautological argument. Why not state the point of substance openly and leave the tautologies to look after themselves?

POSTSCRIPT

The problem of the falling rate of profit is connected with the problem of *value* in this way: when the rate of profit and the ratio of capital to labour (organic composition) are uniform throughout the economy, the prices of commodities are proportional to their *values* at a given moment of time. As time goes by, technical progress increases output per man hour, so that the *value* of commodities falls through time. If the rate of profit and organic composition remain constant, prices in wage units (that is, taking the money wage per hour of standard labour as the unit of account) fall, through time, with *values*. With a uniform rate of profit, price for a particular commodity exceeds *value* where organic composition is above average. Similarly, if organic composition rises through time, a constant rate of profit entails that prices fall less fast than *values*. Marx granted the point in respect to individual commodities, but for the system as a whole he assumes that prices move with *values*, so that rising organic composition entails a falling rate of profit.

'CAPITALISM, SOCIALISM AND DEMOCRACY'

By JOSEPH SCHUMPETER

PROFESSOR SCHUMPETER takes his stand on a highly original and personal point of view. Most of those who advocate or expect the supersession of capitalism by socialism have a strong sympathy with the idea of socialism and, indeed, call themselves socialists. Professor Schumpeter, as many tart phrases reveal, has little love for socialism, and none at all for socialists. His natural sympathy is all with the heroic age of expanding capitalism. But yet he regards capitalism as doomed and socialism as inevitable. His reasons are set out in Part II of the book, *Can Capitalism Survive?* This forms the central core of his argument. Before considering it, we may glance at the outlying portions of the work.

First comes an essay on Marxism. Professor Schumpeter treats Marx primarily as a great economist: 'It is easy to see why both friends and foes should have misunderstood the nature of his performance in the purely economic field. For the friends, he was so much more than a mere professional theorist that it would have seemed almost blasphemy to them to give too much prominence to this aspect of his work. The foes, who resented his attitudes and the setting of his theoretic argument, found it almost impossible to admit that in some parts of his work he did precisely the kind of thing which they valued so highly when presented by other hands'. He distinguishes between Marx's vision and his analysis. He holds that Marx's analysis is often faulty, but that, in particular in connection with the theory of value and the theory of crises, his vision of the general development of capitalist society is substantially correct, or at least far superior to that of most of his critics. On one major point, however, both analysis and vision fail—the theory that there is an inherent tendency in capitalism to lower the standard of life of the masses. With this, Marx's theory of the cataclysmic end of capitalism falls to the ground.

Next, turn forward to the sections on Socialism and on Democracy. Can socialism work? Is socialism compatible with democracy? In each case the answer is affirmative. The section on Socialism is somewhat perfunctory, though illuminated with many telling points, such as that one of the important economies of socialism would be the release of numerous first-class brains, now occupied in the business of legal tax evasion, for more productive uses. The section on Democracy is, perhaps, the weakest part of the whole. The reader is left with a baffled feeling that Professor Schumpeter is not really as cynical about democracy as he pretends, and that the main issues have not been discussed. Professor Schumpeter freely succumbs to the temptation to tease and provoke; perhaps this section is aimed mainly at pricking some specifically American bubbles.

Now return to the main argument. Section II is arranged on the plan of a detective story. It opens: 'Can capitalism survive? No. I do not think it can'. But none of the obvious suspects are guilty. We have already seen that Professor Schumpeter does not accept Marx's diagnosis. Nor does he agree with the usual run of contemporary analysis. Monopoly is not a blemish in capitalism, but an essential factor in its development. A competitive system of the textbook type is simply impracticable in a dynamic world. What appears in any given situation as restriction is necessary to maintain the profitability which makes expansion in the long run possible. (In this chapter Professor Schumpeter is at his most brilliant, and his argument blows like a gale through the dreary pedantry of static analysis.) Nor is unemployment the villain of the piece. With the continuous advance of productivity which capitalism brings about, society can easily afford to keep the unemployed in sufficient comfort to prevent unrest (it must be remembered that Professor Schumpeter is writing on the other side of the Atlantic; in a European setting, perhaps he would not take so airy a view). The spectre of declining investment opportunity is an illegitimate projection of the great slump into long-run prospects. None of these is responsible for the decay of capitalism. The real secret is that capitalism destroys itself, not by its vices, but by its virtues. Its rationalism undermines the authority of the governing class, which capitalism inherited from the feudal age, and without which it cannot control the masses. The rising standard of life and the spread of education create a class of discontented intellectuals who canalize and make articulate the resentment of the masses at the inequality without which capitalism cannot function. Above all, technical development leads to the obsolescence of the entrepreneurial function. With the growth of big business and of experimental science innovation itself is reduced to routine, and the entrepreneur sinks into a bureaucrat. Subsidiary reasons, of which the decay of the family is the most important, undermine his will to survive, and when, in the fullness of time, the system becomes ripe for transformation, his resistance will be negligible, and socialism will come into being without any break in the process of evolution.

The reader is swept along by the freshness, the dash, the impetuosity of Professor Schumpeter's stream of argument. But pause on the brink a moment and look around the contemporary scene. On reflection some rather large elements seem to be missing from the analysis. First, what about U.S.S.R.? 'It must be remembered that the bolshevik conquest of rule over the most backward of all the great nations was nothing but a fluke'. Perhaps. But in that case the exception seems rather more important than the rule. Who knows what flukes may accompany the end of the present war? And, even if the bolshevik fluke remains unique, there cannot be much doubt that the existence of a socialist Great Power will play at least as important a part in the future development in other countries (even without any deliberate intervention in their affairs) as the more subtle processes of evolution according to the imminent characteristics of capitalism. And then, what about Fascism? Does present-day experience really lead us to expect that capitalism is destined to a quiet and pious death? But, no matter whether it convinces or not, this book is worth the whole parrot-house of contemporary orthodoxies, right, left, or centre.

MR. HARROD'S DYNAMICS

No one will disagree with Mr. Harrod that modern economic theory lacks, and badly needs, a system of analysis dealing with a dynamic society. Keynes' *General Theory of Employment* broke through the husk of static analysis, but, apart from some *obiter dicta*, scarcely developed any theory of long-run development. Mr. Kalecki's pioneering work has been very little followed up (Mr. Harrod makes no reference to him); many others have shot at a venture into the mists, but we have no systematic body of long-run dynamic theory to supplement the short-period analysis of the General Theory and to swallow up, as a special case, the long-run static theory in which the present generation of academic economists was educated. Mr. Harrod has boldly set out to sail these uncharted seas, and there is no doubt that he has undertaken a voyage of the greatest interest. Unfortunately his exposition is so idiosyncratic, and the matter is so closely packed in the small compass of five lectures, that his book is extremely hard to follow (the original audience of the lectures must have had a strenuous time of it). In this article I shall attempt to give an outline of what I understand him to be saying, omitting his algebra, and somewhat re-arranging his order of presentation.

As is natural in a discussion of this kind, the level of abstraction is high. What sort of world does Mr. Harrod contemplate? First of all we must notice that he takes a high line with the index-number problem. He operates throughout with a 'constant goods-value of money' and deals with quantities of output, real income and capital without any reference to changes in their composition in terms of concrete commodities. He is dealing with a world in which output and consumption per head are rising through time, and productive technique is improving. Thus it is natural to suppose that new commodities are constantly coming into existence, and new types of machinery must certainly be coming into use. He does not discuss what, in such a case, a constant value of money means, and for purposes of the present

---

A review of: *Towards a Dynamic Economics*, by R. F. Harrod. *Economic Journal*, March, 1949.

discussion we must follow him in leaving this skeleton locked up in the cupboard.

Next, his world is dynamic in the sense that continuous change is going on through time, but it is a world without history. Every change that took place in the past was digested, so to speak, as it occurred. Time rolls on in a homogeneous stream, and it makes no difference at what point we dip into it. Also it is a world without politics. There are no conflicts of interest within society, and almost no influence of the social environment upon individual behaviour. At the same time it is a capitalist world, with entrepreneurs, *rentiers* and workers, and with a monetary and fiscal system. The greater part of the argument is confined to the problems of a closed economy.

The first question which Mr. Harrod examines is whether there is any natural tendency for the propensity of the community to save to adapt itself to the rate of capital accumulation required to sustain a steady expansion in production.

What is this 'required' rate of accumulation? There are no arrears of investment needed to adapt the stock of capital to changes which have occurred in the past (no war-damage to make good, no revolutionary new discoveries not yet fully digested into productive technique). Change, however, is going on currently. The population may be growing, and technical progress is taking place. Mr. Harrod simplifies the problem by postulating that any change which is going on takes place at a steady rate. He puts diminishing returns from land on one side as a problem which would complicate the argument out of proportion to its importance. For the purposes of the first stage in the analysis he assumes a constant rate of interest. Now, in these conditions there is a certain rate of increase in total output which is possible, with continuous full employment (full employment being interpreted in a loose sense, admitting of adequate flexibility in production). This rate of expansion depends, with a constant rate of interest, upon the increase in working population and the increase in output per head due to technical progress. Mr. Harrod calls this the 'natural rate of growth' (Gn). It is important to be clear that it is not natural in the sense of being the rate of growth which will tend to come about under the free play of economic forces. It is rather to be understood as the maximum rate of growth which the underlying conditions make possible.

This rate of growth requires a certain rate of capital accumulation. Let us look at the two components of the rate of growth separately. If technique is unchanged while population is growing, output per head is constant (diminishing returns from land having been ruled out). Investment is required to equip growing numbers with the already prevailing amount of capital per head. If population growth takes the simple form of a constant proportional rate, *x* per cent per annum (age-composition and the proportion of workers being constant), then capital accumulation at the rate of *x* per cent of the amount of capital will give the required expansion. Each year the increment of numbers is larger than the year before, the required value of net investment is larger than the year before, and the value of replacements of capital is larger than the year before. (In Mr. Harrod's world, with time but no history, there cannot be any indestructible equipment. With constant technique and a given rate of interest, there is a given length of life of capital goods, which determines the annual amount of replacements required.) If investment at the right rate is carried on (thriftiness being such that consumption per head is constant), national income, gross and net investment and total consumption all expand at the same rate, and the proportion of workers engaged on new investment, on replacements and on production of consumption goods are each constant.

Now consider technical progress with a constant population. Changes in technique may alter the ratio of capital to output (at normal-capacity working). Mr. Harrod divides inventions and improvements into neutral, capital-using and capital-saving, according as they cause the ratio of capital to output, at a constant rate of interest, to remain unchanged, to increase or to diminish.[1] In Marxian language, with neutral technical progress the organic composition of capital does not alter. With capital-using progress (which Marx assumed to be the rule) the organic composition of capital is rising through time.

Mr. Harrod makes great use of the conception of neutral technical progress, and we must pause to examine what it means. It does not entail that every invention is neutral, but that inventions are neutral on balance. Neutral progress in Mr. Harrod's conception results from an equal rate of increase in output per head at all stages of production. To reduce the conception to its

---

[1] Cf. 'A Classification of Inventions,' *Review of Economic Studies*, February, 1938.

simplest possible form, and to keep the index-number problem safely immured, let us imagine that production can be divided into two departments—making machines and making final output with the aid of machines, only one type of machine and one type of commodity being produced. Proportions of factors employed are not necessarily rigidly fixed by technique, but the most profitable amount of machinery per unit of output is governed by the ratio of the price of commodities to the price of machines, and by the rate of interest. Now some device is introduced which increases output per man-hour equally in both departments. Since both are affected in the same way, the relative prices of machines and final commodities are unchanged, and, the rate of interest being constant, the ratio of machines to output will be unchanged. The relative shares of labour and capital in real national income are constant. Labour is released from producing the old rate of output and from maintaining the old stock of machines in the same proportion. This labour is available for producing additional output, and this additional output requires an increase in the stock of machines which bears the same ratio to the old stock as the new rate of total output bears to the old. Thus the rate of capital accumulation required for the expansion of output made possible by the progress which is going on (with continuous full employment) is proportionate to the rate of increase in output, just as it is when population increases with constant technique. As soon as we depart from some such simplified case the index-number problem becomes formidable. Technical progress is largely bound up with alterations in equipment. Amortization funds attached to old machinery are being continually reinvested in improved machinery, and the conception of a constant stock of capital, or a given rate of increase in the stock of capital, becomes extremely vague, not to mention the difficulty of defining the rate of increase of output when new commodities are coming into existence. But Mr. Harrod does not stop to discuss these questions.

With neutral technical progress and a constant rate of interest, the ratio of capital to output is constant and the required rate of accumulation is proportionate to the rate of increase of output. If progress is on balance capital-using, the ratio of capital to output is increasing (at a given rate of interest). New investment is then required to provide additional capital for the old rate of output. (Now our simple example does not apply, and the skeleton rattles disturbingly in the cupboard.) The required rate of accumulation no longer bears a simple relation to the rate of increase of output, but has two terms, one depending upon the rate of increase of output, and the other upon the level of output. Mr. Harrod puts this on one side for separate discussion, and assumes throughout the main part of his argument that progress is neutral on balance. Even then, Mr. Harrod recognizes that to reduce capital requirement to a function of income is an over-simplification. His 'relation' (which used to be known as the 'acceleration principle') cannot bear all this weight. He admits that some investment may be of a long-range character not closely related to the requirements of current output (armaments and war must come into this category). He provides us with a symbol for it (k) and says we may make it as large as we like, but he does not discuss it in detail, and it is easier to follow his analysis in its purest form, without regard to k.

Neglecting k, and combining population growth with neutral technical progress, we arrive at the rate of accumulation required if the maximum possible rate of expansion in total income, corresponding to continuous full employment, is to be enjoyed, the required rate of accumulation being proportionate to the rate of growth of income.

Now the question to be considered is whether there is any natural tendency for thriftiness to adjust itself to capital require-ments. Here we notice the shift of emphasis when the General Theory is transposed from short-period to long-period terms. In most of the discussions arising out of the General Theory, thrifti-ness is taken as given. There is a certain rate of saving corre-sponding to full employment, and the main question is whether investment tends to reach that level, and, if it fails to do so, what should be done to make it. This is apt to lead to the state of mind of regarding investment as an end in itself, and to the justification of digging holes in the ground and filling them up again. In its original context this was perfectly correct, but long-term policy cannot be based on hand-to-mouth expedients for curing a slump, and Mr. Harrod's analysis is certainly salutory in directing attention to long-term problems.

To make the next step in the argument it is necessary for him to consider the influences which determine thriftiness, and to inquire whether there are any cross-connections between capital requirement and thriftiness which tend to keep them in harmony. He distinguishes between net saving and the amortization of existing capital. He assumes that the rate of technical progress is allowed for by entrepreneurs, who adjust amortization funds to the rate of obsolescence of capital equipment, so that the stock of capital in existence at any moment is being continuously adapted in form without change of value (any exceptions are dumped into that convenient hold-all, k). Thus a more rapid rate of invention is offset by a higher rate of amortization, and no net saving is required to adapt past accumulated capital to new forms.

Here Mr. Harrod makes a curious point. Suppose that instead of assuming prices constant we assume money wages constant; then prices of commodities (including capital goods) are falling continuously as progress takes place. If individual concerns aim at keeping the money value of their capital intact, amortization funds as they are reinvested provide continuously increasing amounts of physical equipment and of stocks. In the simple case where population is constant, the rate of interest given, and progress neutral, amortization funds provide for the whole of the required accumulation of physical capital, and no net saving at all is required. However, in the rest of the argument Mr. Harrod continues to assume constant money prices, so that all adaptation of existing capital is looked after by amortization, and all additions to the stock of capital require net saving.

Mr. Harrod discusses the influences determining the supply of net saving mainly in terms of the thriftiness of individuals. He distinguishes between time-preference and the effects of falling marginal utility of income, and shows how they were confused in the traditional concept of 'discounting the future'. He regards the elasticity of the income-utility curve of a representative individual as something which exists in nature, and proposes a new method of discovering it experimentally. Let income be paid in the form of a lump-sum bonus plus a piece-rate per unit of work. At the starting rate the individual freely chooses how much work he is willing to do. Now raise the bonus, and see what change in the piece-rate is necessary to keep the amount of work he does unaltered. By this means the marginal utility of income could be measured in terms of the marginal disutility of a given amount of work. (Mr. Harrod playfully suggests that managers and shop stewards should organize the experiment, but the ideal field for it is the ancient universities. Increase our fellowship dividends, and then see at what rate per hour we will take a given number of pupils.) Unfortunately this method contains the same basic fallacy as earlier attempts, such as Dr. Frisch's method of measuring the marginal utility of income in terms of the marginal utility of a given quantity of sugar. The unit of measurement is not independent of the magnitude to be measured, because the utility of leisure to an individual is strongly influenced by the funds available to him for having a good time, so that the disutility of work rises with income. If we cannot measure marginal utility of income it is impossible to say what it means. The foundation of much of this part of Mr. Harrod's argument is thus exceedingly shaky. But even though the answer he gives may be somewhat mystical, the question he is asking is real and important.

He divides saving into three categories: savings designed to be spent in old age or emergencies of private life—the amassing of a 'hump'; saving for heirs; and corporate net saving carried out by a firm for the sake of the business, over and above the saving which individual shareholders might wish to make, through its agency, for their private purposes.

Mr. Harrod considers that population growth favours 'hump' saving, as each successive generation contains more individuals than the last at saving ages relative to the number of retired persons living on their humps. This is disputable. The more rapid the rate of growth of population the larger is likely to be the average size of a family, and the smaller the margin above subsistence from a given individual income. A good deal more investigation is required before we can say on which side the balance is likely to be, and it seems doubtful whether an element of harmony is here to be found between saving and capital requirements.

After an argument of some subtlety Mr. Harrod concludes that 'hump' saving is likely to grow at a greater rate than income per head, so that here there is a potential element of disharmony. He has little to say about the effect of the total stock of wealth on the rate of saving.

About saving for heirs he has no very definite conclusions to offer, but again finds no presumption in favour of harmony. In general, private saving is likely to rise with real income, but it is related to the level of income, not to its rate of growth.

Only in the case of corporate saving is there likely to be some harmony between thriftiness and capital requirements, because favourable prospects for investment in the future are likely to promote the building up of company reserves, but even here the connection is weak and uncertain.

Although Mr. Harrod devotes a good deal of space to these questions the analysis does not go very deep. To mention only one point, a discussion in terms of individual psychology leaves out of account the major influence on the thriftiness of a community—the distribution of income between its members. But, however that may be, there is no reason to doubt Mr. Harrod's conclusion that there is no presumption that thriftiness (with a constant rate of interest) tends to adapt itself to the rate of capital accumulation required to sustain a steady expansion of production.

The next question is whether the rate of interest will tend to move in such a way as to secure harmony between thriftiness and capital requirements. This question has two parts. First, how a movement in the rate of interest would affect thriftiness and capital requirement if it took place; and, second, whether it is likely to take place.

On the first question Mr. Harrod, applying his formula for time-preference and income utility, concludes that a fall in the rate of interest will tend to reduce 'hump' saving, and that the traditional view that some individuals will save more (from a given income) at a lower rate of interest is fallacious, but the argument is not set out fully enough to make it clear from what assumptions this follows. He hazards no guess as to the effect of a fall in the rate of interest on saving for heirs. A fall in the rate of interest will increase capital per unit of output capacity, in a given state of knowledge, in so far as technical conditions permit of variation. Mr. Harrod is highly sceptical of the influence of the rate of interest on methods of production, and gives little weight to this factor. In any case it would be partially or wholly offset by the stimulus to corporate saving which would be given by an increased demand for capital within firms. It is to be observed that the increase in capital per unit of capacity (in so far as it occurs) due to a given once-and-for-all fall in the rate of interest requires a once-and-for-all bout of capital accumulation (which may, however, be imagined to be spread over many years). When the appropriate 'deepening of capital' has taken place there is no further need for accumulation. Thus to maintain a given rate of accumulation, under this influence, a continually falling rate of interest is necessary.

To sum up—if thriftiness can be represented as a constant proportion of saving to income at a given rate of interest, and if this proportion falls with the rate of interest, then in any given state of population growth and technical progress, there exists a certain value of the rate of interest which would equalize the full-employment rate of saving with capital requirements, and fulfil the conditions for steady progress at the maximum possible rate. If the proportion of income saved increases with income, while the required rate of accumulation is constant, a continually falling rate of interest is required for steady progress, in this case the influence of thriftiness being possibly helped out by a continuous increase in capital per unit of output. If the required rate of accumulation is rising relatively to thriftiness (owing to capital-using technical progress) a continuously rising rate of interest is required.

Is there any reason to expect the rate of interest to behave in the appropriate way? Mr. Harrod makes an attack upon the traditional view that the rate of interest tends to establish equilibrium between saving and capital requirements which is more drastic than Keynes'. Keynes showed that the traditional view was fallacious. Mr. Harrod maintains that it was non-existent. He gives it two possible interpretations. One is that the capital market foresees the long-term movements in the rate of interest which underlying conditions require, and brings those movements into existence. This leads to violent paradoxes. For instance, if the situation requires a continuous fall in the rate of interest, and this fall is foreseen, the present value of irredeemable stock becomes fantastically great. Alternatively, the traditional view may be interpreted to mean that the market takes no view of the long-run course of prices of assets but writes them up and down from day to day in response to the current state of demand and supply of new capital. This would involve revaluing the whole outstanding stock of assets in response to every chance discrepancy between current investment plans and full-employment saving, and it leads to results no less absurd than those arising under the first interpretation. Neither interpretation provides an account of market behaviour remotely resembling what actually happens, and Mr. Harrod falls back (rather in the spirit: if you know a better 'ole, go to it) upon Keynes' theory of the rate of interest in terms of demand and supply of money. He concludes that there are no grounds for expecting the rate of interest to behave in such a way as to secure steady progress, though it may have a vague and feeble influence in the right direction.

Is there an influence promoting harmony to be found in the movement of wages? When thriftiness is excessive in relation to capital requirements there is unemployment, and money-wage rates may be expected to fall. Following Mr. Kalecki's version of the General Theory on this point, Mr. Harrod shows that falling wages and prices are more likely to increase the disharmony than to cure it.

He does not touch upon the sophisticated argument that falling wages will drag down the rate of interest (by reducing the demand for money) and so bring it to the required level. Presumably he would dismiss this contention on the ground that the effect of prospective falling prices in reducing the inducement to invest and increasing the burden of debt would swamp any possible stimulus which a falling rate of interest might give.

We have thus come to the conclusion that there is no presumption that harmony between thriftiness and capital requirements will be maintained. This is the projection into the long period of the central thesis of the General Theory. We must now introduce a fresh layer of complications into the analysis.

It might happen by chance that the relationship between thriftiness and capital requirements was just right, so that the rate of saving corresponding to full employment was continuously equal to the required rate of capital accumulation (in Mr. Harrod's terminology G_n is then equal to G_w, of which more anon). There is then a definite rate of capital accumulation which could be maintained continuously, and which would ensure constant full employment (in the loose sense) and the growth of national income at the maximum rate made possible by changes in population and technical progress. But even when such a rate of accumulation exists, there is no guarantee that it will be realized. If all entrepreneurs got together and found out what the rate was they might agree to put it into effect, but so long as investment is determined by innumerable private decisions there is no reason to expect that the right rate will be arrived at. And once the rate of accumulation is off the steady course it can never get on to it, but reels along drunkenly below it.

Mr. Harrod provides a rough sketch for a theory of the trade cycle to be superimposed upon the long-period analysis. If, at any moment, the rate of investment falls below the level corresponding to steady growth, the consequent slackening of effective demand causes the expansion of output to fall below the steady rate. Capital requirements are thereby reduced. The rate of investment falls further, and production declines in the familiar self-propelling downward movement into a slump. In a revival, which starts from a position with unemployed man-power available, the self-propelling up-swing may increase output at a much more rapid rate than that which is possible once full employment has been reached. If the actual rate of growth of income (G) exceeds the long-run rate (G_n), then according to Mr. Harrod's system of ideas, the increment of capital required to provide for the expansion of output which takes place over a short period is greater than the rate of accumulation which can be continuously maintained. As an analysis of the trade cycle this seems rather unsatisfactory, for a system of ideas in which investment is governed purely by the 'relation' cannot easily deal with the fact that in the slump there is unused capacity, as well as unemployed labour. The investment required to provide equipment to produce an increment of income is by no means a simple function of the increment of income when there is surplus capacity, and perhaps redundant stocks, left behind by the last boom. Working capital, however, lends itself to this kind of analysis, and if all equipment were very short-lived Mr. Harrod's method would not be far wrong.

His analysis applies most easily to the breakdown of a boom. Once investment has reached a level exceeding the long-period rate (the rate of accumulation corresponding to G_n) it is clear that it cannot be maintained for long. There are two quite distinct ways in which the inevitable breakdown may come. The boom may knock its head against the limit set by available labour while it is still in full swing. Investment projects may be great enough (combined with the propensity to consume) to generate a demand for more labour than there is. Then a wage inflation may set in, or, if wages are held down, there will be a sharp rise of prices relatively to wages causing an increase in the share of profits in national income and so reducing the propensity to consume; or mere physical difficulties in getting hold of the right kind of labour may check the expansion of investment. In one way or another the expansion of output will be brought to a halt. And as soon as output ceases to expand, the rate of investment begins to fall. Alternatively, the boom may come to an end before full employment has been reached because the rate of growth of income is smaller than the rate of growth of the stock of capital, so that capital grows relatively to output during the course of the boom, surplus capacity begins to emerge, and the inducement to invest falls off. In either case, as soon as the actual rate of investment falls, the self-propelling down-swing into a slump sets in.

Mr. Harrod does not seem to distinguish quite clearly between the case where the boom is cut off in its prime (or explodes in hyper-inflation) because it reaches the physical limit of employment, and the case where it comes to an end because the rate of expansion is too great to be profitably maintained. But, in any case, he is not concerned to codify the theory of the trade cycle (he freely admits that his long-period G's are not a handy instrument for short-period analysis) but simply to show that, even when underlying conditions make steady progress possible, there is no reason to expect that it will occur.

Still worse, as we have seen, there is no reason to expect that conditions will be such that steady progress is possible (under *laissez-faire*). To reduce the argument to its simplest form, suppose that thriftiness can be represented as a constant proportion of income saved, and that the rate of capital accumulation required for steady progress with full employment is also a constant proportion of income (as would be the case with neutral technical progress and a constant rate of interest). Now, the first proportion may be smaller or greater than the second (thriftiness less or greater than required accumulation). Mr. Harrod suggests that this can also be expressed by saying that the ruling rate of interest is below or above the rate required for steady progress, but this way of putting the matter is somewhat artificial, for it may be that the influence of the rate of interest is so weak that no conceivable rate of interest would do the trick, so that the 'required rate of interest' has no meaning; and even when there is a definite value for the required rate it may be one which could not conceivably obtain (for instance, it might be negative).

If the required rate of accumulation exceeds thriftiness then it is likely that, underlying the ups-and-downs of the trade cycle, there will be a constant buoyancy of the inducement to invest, periods of near-full employment will be frequent, inflation a danger that has to be guarded against, the rate of progress actually realized will be held below the maximum possible rate by scarcity of saving, and thriftiness will be a social virtue, in the sense that any increase in thriftiness would make a more rapid growth of income possible. In short, conditions will be those to which the maxims (though not the analysis) of nineteenth-century economics apply.

Mr. Harrod suggests that the *General Theory* fulfilled only half its task because it neglected the possibility of deficient thriftiness (or a market rate of interest below the required rate). This appears to be rather misleading. It is true that Keynes, being interested in the problems of the 1930s, did not elaborate the analysis of conditions of excessive effective demand, but he provided a sketch for that analysis, and the methods of thought of the *General Theory* have proved indispensable in discussing the present-day inflationary situation.

Turn now to the opposite case, where the proportion of income saved exceeds the rate of accumulation required for steady progress with full employment. Then the level of investment which would ensure full employment results in a rate of increase in the stock of capital in excess of that corresponding to the rate of increase in output. The new capital which would come into existence if this rate of investment were continuously maintained would be partly redundant to requirements. Therefore that rate of investment cannot be maintained. This is something quite apart from the trade cycle and corresponds to what is sometimes called secular stagnation, or chronic unemployment. The analysis seems to bear a close resemblance to Hobson's thesis that saving causes crisis because there is no outlet in consumer demand for the goods which new capital equipment produces. Mr. Harrod's analysis provides the missing link between Keynes and Hobson.

So far we have had fairly plain sailing. We must now introduce Mr. Harrod's third G, G_w, 'the warranted rate of growth', which is the element in his exposition which makes it baffling and

mysterious. The 'warranted rate of growth' is such that, if it is
maintained, producers will be content with what they are doing
and will continue to maintain it. Mr. Harrod does not enlarge on
the subject of what makes producers content. The meaning for
contentment which best seems to fit his scheme of ideas is that
capital is always kept working at normal capacity. Entrepreneurs
are satisfied with investment decisions taken in the recent past if
the new capital (as well as all pre-existing capital) is being profitably utilized (though the question of what rate of profit will keep
them happy is nowhere discussed). To put the matter in terms
of how entrepreneurs feel is rather confusing, because we are all
the time dealing with averages, and particular industries are all
the time moving faster or slower than the pace of the economy
as a whole. One entrepreneur, whose new investment has over-
shot the mark and whose new plant is working under capacity,
will not be consoled by the fact that another is straining his plant
beyond normal capacity to keep up with a super-average share of
demand. However, if I have understood Mr. Harrod aright, the
'warranted' rate of growth is that rate of growth of output which
ensures the continuous full-capacity working of the stock of
capital considered as a whole (full capacity, like full employment,
being taken in a loose sense, allowing for some play in the rate of
production).

What does this imply? The full utilization of the stock of
capital in existence at any moment yields a certain rate of output
and income. Corresponding to that rate of income is a rate of
saving, depending upon the thriftiness of the community. For
that rate of income to be realized, investment must be equal to
that rate of saving. This rate of investment yields a certain rate
of increase in the stock of capital. Thus the 'warranted' rate of
growth is that rate of growth of output which would result from
the continuous operation at full capacity of the stock of capital,
when the stock of capital is continuously growing at a rate
dictated by the investment which just absorbs the rate of saving
corresponding to full-capacity income.

What is the relationship between full capacity and full employment? On this question Mr. Harrod's line of thought is particularly elusive, but the following seems to be what is implied in his
argument. When thriftiness is deficient, the 'warranted' rate of
capital accumulation is less than the rate required by steady

progress with full employment. The actual rate of accumulation will pursue a cyclical course, but taking good times with bad, the rate of accumulation is held in check by the fact that the full-capacity rate of saving yields a rate of increase in the stock of capital less than the required rate. Now, if population is increasing, the stock of capital will be growing more slowly than available labour, while the amount of employment associated with a given stock of capital is continually falling as technical progress takes place, so that there will be a progressive increase in unemployment. (Here we cannot avoid history, for the amount of unemployment at any moment will depend upon how long this process has been going on.) This unemployment is not susceptible to Keynesian remedies, for, if the level of effective demand were boosted up, for instance, by putting some of the redundant labour to work on public investment schemes, the demand for consumption goods would be raised above the capacity output of existing capital equipment, and an inflationary rise of prices would set in. (To solve the problem, measures to increase investment would have to be combined with measures to check the propensity to consume, by taxation and rationing.) This is a kind of unemployment which is not contemplated in the *General Theory*. It may be appropriately called Marxian unemployment (as opposed to Keynesian unemployment, which is due to deficiency of effective demand). For though nothing is farther from his thoughts, Mr. Harrod has led us to Marx's theory of the reserve army of labour, which expands and contracts as the growth of population runs faster or slower than the rate of capital accumulation.

This analysis applies to the situation of over-populated, backward countries. Mr. Harrod is more interested in advanced economies suffering from the reverse problem of excessive thriftiness. When thriftiness is excessive relatively to the rate of accumulation required by steady growth with full employment, the rate of investment which would maintain effective demand at the full-capacity level would result, if it were realized, in a rate of growth of the stock of capital in excess of the required rate. Such a rate of accumulation cannot be maintained, for, if investment ruled at this level for a time, surplus capacity would presently emerge. Either this will be foreseen, and there will be a continual drag on the rate of accumulation, or an occasional burst of high investment will create surplus capacity, and will consequently be followed by a prolonged slump.

There are two quite distinct ways in which surplus capacity may emerge if investment is maintained for a time above the rate required for steady progress with full employment. The first is the Hobsonesque situation in which effective demand is not expanding fast enough to keep the stock of capital in profitable use as capacity grows. The second is that there may not be sufficient labour available to man up new equipment as it comes into being. Technical progress is continually reducing the number of men required to produce the current rate of output, and the working population may be growing. But it might happen that the rate at which labour was thus becoming available for increased output was less than in proportion to the rate at which the stock of capital was expanding. Then equipment would presently be standing idle because workers could not be found to operate it. In Marxian language there would be over-production of capital. This would deter further investment, and a slump would set in. Now, indeed, there is unemployed labour available, but the fall in the rate of investment has started the self-propelling down swing of income, and there is not enough effective demand to keep even the old stock of equipment in use.

It may be that this is a mare's nest. It is hard to imagine investment being deterred by a prospective scarcity of labour. Rather, necessity being the mother of invention, it would be natural to suppose (as Marx does) that technical progress in such a case would be given a capital-using twist, so that labour required per unit of capital would be reduced at a faster rate. But then, we fall out of the frying-pan into the fire, for, with capital-using inventions and a constant rate of interest and rate of profit on capital, the relative share of labour in national income is falling, and the share of profits rising, through time, so that thriftiness is increasing (all the more because corporate savings will be deliberately stepped up to finance the new investment) and the Hobsonesque limit upon accumulation will come into play.

In Marx's system, also, capital-using progress (rising organic composition of capital) leads to crisis, but not because the relative share of labour falls, reducing effective demand: on the contrary, the trouble arises because the relative share does not fall (the rate of exploitation tends to be constant) so that the rate of profit on capital falls as capital accumulates.

This excursion has carried us some way from Mr. Harrod's text, but it serves to show the vistas which his analysis opens up. Mr. Harrod himself makes an excursion into the analysis of international investment which is full of pregnant suggestions, but limitations of space prevent us from following it here.

Mr. Harrod's main purpose is to lead up to some prescriptions for policy (though he derives most of them straight from the analysis of the *General Theory* without much dependence on his own new contributions). He regards the problem of secular stagnation, for the United States if not for us, as waiting around the corner of post-war inflation, and he proposes remedies, elaborated with a wealth of fancy, which may be baldly summarized as follows: get the rate of interest gradually down to vanishing point (by appropriate increases in the quantity of money). Set up stores of staple commodities, with instructions to buy and sell at fixed prices (on the analogy of a gold reserve). In conjunction with a wages policy which keeps the average rate of money wages rising at the same pace as average output per head (rather a tall order, this) the operation of the commodity reserve would keep the price level stationary. When effective demand was tending to flag and prices tending to fall, the stores would find themselves buying, thus supplementing other kinds of investment and checking the fall in prices; when demand was in excess of current output the stores would be selling, and disinvesting from their stocks. This provides an anti-cyclical stabilizer. Meanwhile, correct the deficient or excessive effective demand by budget deficits or surpluses, financed by the issue or retirement of interest-free paper. By these means a sort of automatic pilot would be introduced into an otherwise *laissez-faire* system, to keep output smoothly on its course.

It is a common vice of present-day economic argument to jump from a highly abstract piece of analysis straight to prescriptions for policy, without going through the intermediate stage of examining how far the assumptions in the analysis fit the facts of the actual situation. There is a big gap between Mr. Harrod's ingenious and instructive manipulation of his three *G*'s and the conditions of any actual economy.

First of all, the effect of distribution of income and of wealth upon thriftiness has been omitted from the argument (Mr. Harrod dismisses the whole question of distribution with some dark hints about the political instability of an egalitarian society). It can be plausibly argued that the phenomenon of excessive thriftiness is a product of excessive inequality, and that measures to correct inequality, which may be advocated on their own political or humanitarian merits, would, as a by-product, permanently reverse the position, and make deficient thriftiness the normal rule. There seems very little point in discussing artificial measures for absorbing excessive savings until this great question has been argued out.

Next, we must recall that Mr. Harrod's world is one in which there are no arrears of investment requirements to be made up. There is no war-damage to repair; no slum clearance and re-design of towns to clean up the mess which the past has left upon our hands; no rehabilitation of dust-bowls and deserts created by individualistic exploitation of the soil; no backward sections of the community to be brought up to the level of the rest; no massive 'Marxian unemployment' to be overcome by industrial-ization of over-populated regions; no adaptation of antiquated equipment in the light of already existing technical knowledge; no recent large-scale scientific discoveries to be embodied in industrial equipment. In short, Mr. Harrod's world must not be confused with Europe, Asia, or America. (It is true that arrears of investment, along with other complications, can be looked after by Mr. Harrod's k. But the issue here is not the formal correctness of the analysis, but the relative importance of the various elements in it.) Before we have examined what arrears of beneficial invest-ment remain to be made good, there is little point in discussing schemes to throw away potential savings by budget deficits caused by tax-remissions to the wealthy, or schemes of investment in piling up stocks of commodities which (beyond the point at which they are useful in themselves) would be scarcely more productive than digging holes in the ground.

Again, Mr. Harrod's interest policy consists in purely monetary manipulations. Even when the gilt-edged rate of interest has been reduced to vanishing point there would still be great scope for agencies to cheapen the supply of finance to worthy enterprises. There is no knowing how much potential investment, which would provide a genuinely useful outlet for saving, is now held up by the imperfections of the capital market.

Finally (though by no means exhaustively) in Mr. Harrod's world, technical progress drops like the gentle rain from heaven and is not susceptible to any economic influence (we departed from his scheme of ideas, above, in suggesting that a scarcity of labour would promote capital-using inventions). Now, the technical progress which is relevant to the argument is not merely scientific discovery, but the embodiment of new ideas in actual production. The rate of utilization of new techniques is not in practice maintained at the optimum level. Even in the most progressive nations and industries there are a great number of relatively backward producers. There is no knowing how much the rate of growth of output per head, at any stage of scientific knowledge, might be raised by appropriate policies. Moreover, scientific discovery itself is not just like the weather, but is susceptible to being directed and speeded up. In short, Mr. Harrod's G_n is not a natural datum, but an object for policy and organization.

All this goes very much against Mr. Harrod's grain, because to discuss either the distribution of income or measures to increase useful investment brings politics into the economic argument. But his is no way to keep politics out. His resolution to avoid these questions is itself a political decision.

Without a thorough examination of the relationship of his assumptions to reality we cannot take Mr. Harrod's proposals as more than a *jeu d'esprit*, but that does not detract from the interest and importance of his analysis upon its own plane.

POSTSCRIPT

The above argument does not bring out sufficiently clearly that the 'warranted rate of growth' is simply an expression of the long-run average propensity to save. If the community saves 10 per cent of net income, and the stock of capital is always five years' purchase of net income, then accumulation at the rate of 2 per cent per annum could be continuously maintained. But there is no reason to expect this rate to be realized.

Mr. Harrod's diagnosis of stagnation is that the 'natural rate' of growth falls short of the 'warranted rate', that is, that there are not enough profitable outlets for investment at the rate corresponding to thriftiness. But his own argument shows that it may easily happen that a rate of accumulation that would turn out profitable if entrepreneurs had faith enough to embark on it, is not realized simply because they never begin.

THE THEORY OF PLANNING

THERE has been a good deal of discussion among English economists of the theory of planning, the principles of pricing in a socialist economy and so forth, but for the most part the discussion is carried on entirely in the air, without any reference to what happens in the only known example of a fully socialist economy. Mr. Dobb breaks out of the closed circle of academic argument and sets out both to illuminate the history of Soviet development by economic analysis and to illuminate economic theory by Soviet experience. For this task he has the unique advantage of being at the same time a Marxist and an academic economist.

The historical part of his book (an enlarged and revised version of his earlier work) is of great interest, but it inevitably leaves the reader vaguely dissatisfied. The story is told mainly in terms of the published evidence of the controversies over matters of policy in the Soviet Union, and the reader cannot help feeling that he is seeing through a glass, darkly. What picture of English life could even the acutest foreign student derive from even the closest study of *Hansard* and the *Economist*? But, whatever its limitations (for which the world situation rather than Mr. Dobb must bear the blame), he has made an invaluable contribution to the understanding of a passage of history of which it is impossible to exaggerate the importance.

The book is also valuable as a contribution to economic theory. The first chapter in particular, which discusses the general principles of planning, puts the rather niggling and arid debate into a fresh setting and should be the starting-point of a new discussion far more fruitful than any we have had hitherto.

Looking to traditional economic teaching for some light on planning problems, Mr. Dobb finds little to help him. Economic theory may be roughly divided into two parts—a static analysis, designed to show how delicate and beautiful is the mechanism by which the pricing system adjusts supply to demand and assures that maximum satisfaction is obtained from available resources, and a dynamic analysis, dealing with innovations, investment,

---

A review of: *Soviet Economic Development Since* 1917, by Maurice Dobb. *Soviet Studies*, October, 1949.

and the trade cycle, which shows how a private enterprise system is inherently unstable and condemned to waste resources in mis-investment and periodic slumps. Neither is of much application to the questions at issue.

Mr. Dobb shows that the static theory fails to apply, first of all, because it starts too late in the story. The analysis begins: given that there are n commodities. But for planners organizing the development of a potentially wealthy but actually poor and backward community the first problem is to decide what com-modities to produce. The orthodox theory of 'consumers' sovereignty' is based (though not very explicitly) on the notion of a great number of independent entrepreneurs continually trying out new commodities or varieties, of which some succeed and others fail, while consumers' tastes act like the forces of natural selection in biology. This has always been a weak point in the theory of consumers' sovereignty, for, even apart from advertisement and all the arts by which salesmanship moulds demand to supply, there is bound to be a strong influence of producers upon tastes, for the consumer has no way of knowing what he wants until he sees it. The function of initiating produc-tion has to be taken on by the planners, and there is no way by which they can hand the responsibility over to consumers' choice.

Mr. Dobb emphasizes the difference between the problem of deciding what to produce in a planned economy and the evolution of products under capitalism. Hitherto new industries have generally started with fairly small-scale production by a number of independent entrepreneurs (so that the above theory of con-sumers' choice as a process of natural selection has some plausi-bility). Economies of large scale gradually reduced the number of independent producers, and mass production by a few supervenes. In Russia there is no need to reproduce the stages of this long and costly historical process. Industries jump into being at the mass-production stage, both because the most advanced capitalist techniques are available for imitation and because, in a relatively egalitarian society, it is preferable not to put a new article on the market at all until the demand of the bulk of the population can be satisfied. But it is not possible all at once to create the equip-ment for mass production of a large number of commodities. A choice has to be made, and in the very nature of the case the trial and error method of picking commodities is not feasible. Mr.

Dobb points out that in this situation the possible loss of welfare due to errors of judgment on the part of the planners is far greater than the costs of trial and error under private enterprise. But, at the same time, the difficulties of arriving at a choice are not so formidable as orthodox theory would suggest. If we think in terms of n different commodities (n being the number of separate commodities it is possible to visualize) imagination boggles at the task of picking between them (and the text-book maxim that, for a commodity to be chosen, its total utility must exceed its total cost, is not very helpful) but in reality the choice is fairly narrow; first of all, because commodities are not independent from the consumers' point of view, but must be supplied in complexes (a point which our own quasi-planners overlooked when they encouraged the production of electrical household gadgets but failed to provide enough power to work them) so that the choice has to be made in terms of a few coherent patterns of consumption rather than an indefinitely large number of different permutations and combinations. Secondly, the choice is narrowed by the very same fact which makes a correct choice desperately important— the poverty of the country, which gives a fairly obvious answer to the question of what is most needed. Mr. Dobb therefore suggests that instead of the economic calculus developed in the text-books we should think in terms of military strategy, and finds the conception of a list of priorities, based on obvious needs, more relevant than the nice calculation of marginal utilities and marginal costs, which, even on its own showing, can deal only with the proportions in which already existing commodities should be produced, and not with the selection of commodities to be produced at all.

Here it seems that he is in danger of being at once too vague and too sweeping. Too vague, because while 'economic strategy' and 'patterns of consumption' are useful metaphors, they do not tell us concretely how the decisions are taken. When the standard of life has risen to the stage where, say, hot-water bottles and fountain pens come over the horizon of the possible, how do the planners actually decide which to go for in next year's investment plan? Too sweeping, because in his impatience with the brittle fabric of economic theory he throws aside the lumps of common sense which are embedded in it. If commodities are arranged in a priority list and worked through in order, the last units of one

are likely to be of lower utility than the first units of the next.
Rather than make an all-or-none choice between two commodities
it would obviously be better to produce some of each and allocate
them (whether by price or rationing) to the consumers to whom
their utility is greatest (say, hot-water bottles to the aged and
fountain pens to authors). There is some evidence that the Soviet
authorities themselves were worried about such problems, and
that they were making a drive, just before the war threw the
economy back on to the basis of bare necessities, to allow the
principle of consumers' sovereignty greater scope (p. 374 *et seq.*).

A related question which has been much discussed by academic
economists is the desirable degree of variegation of a given
commodity. Mr. Dobb points out that, in the absence of marketing risks and of product-differentiation as a means of competition,
Soviet plants can be far more closely specialized on a narrow
range of products than private-enterprise firms (for instance, mills
each weave no more than two types of cloth, p. 17). Indeed, they
can achieve the degree of specialization (unknown hitherto)
which would occur in an ideal text-book world of absolutely
perfect competition. This gives great technical advantages, but
generally the economies of specialization are exhausted when a
single plant of the technically optimum size is fully specialized.
Should standardization be pushed beyond this point, so that
many plants produce identical goods? In some cases standardization is desirable from the consumers' point of view, for example,
where the object produced is a component of something else
(screws are a topical example in the western world) but in others
(clothes and furniture) variety is an end in itself. Do the Soviet
planners deliberately arrange for variety, in such cases, by making
the number of designs at least as great as the number of plants?
Or do they sometimes go further and sacrifice relatively slight
economies of specialization to make variety greater? Some might
object that this is a very 'bourgeois' question and that the desire
for variety is inherently mixed up with snobbery, but there is no
evidence for such a view, and the Soviet authorities seem to have
been anxious (perhaps as part of their concern with the incentive
to work) to indulge the fancies of the consumer within the limits
set by their productive possibilities.

There is another point which Mr. Dobb raises, but does not
discuss, and that is the scale of production of a newly introduced

commodity which has a long useful life. He points out that at first, demand (at a price within the means of the mass of households) extends to, roughly speaking, one per head (or per family) for the whole population, but when every first purchase has been made, demand sinks to replacement level. For what scale of production should investment be made? One extreme would be to lay down plant just sufficient for production at the expected replacement rate, and to work off demand for first purchases slowly; the other extreme would be to aim at the most rapid saturation of demand possible, at the cost of redundancy of plant in the future. Where between these extremes does the best solution lie? *Laissez-faire* theory here cannot pretend that free market forces establish the right answer; it can only show how economic fluctuations are set up, in such a case, in a private enterprise economy. Nor does it seem possible to devise any method of discovering what premium above long-period cost represents the advantage to consumers of having the commodity sooner rather than later, so as to weigh the loss due to postponement of satisfaction under the first policy against the cost of redundant plant under the second. Trial and error would upset the conditions in the process of exploring them. Yet the question is a practical one, and requires a practical answer. Presumably the planners take a rough and ready view, and adopt an intermediate policy on some kind of commonsense basis. Questions such as this, which are started on almost every page, expose the hollowness of theoretical economics, and challenge the academic economists to reduce their analysis to a form which can be brought to bear upon the actual problems of planning.

What part does pricing policy play in the planning system? Mr. Dobb does not make it quite clear how relative prices are used. The over-all problem is clear enough. It is necessary that the total purchase price of consumer goods as a whole should exceed the incomes distributed as their costs of production, to provide a fund for investment, defence and free services (private saving being trivial). In principle this could be arranged by means of an income tax, but income tax plays a very small part in the Soviet fiscal system, and, indeed, it is not easy to see why it is used at all, for paying out income with the right hand and taking it away with the left is one of those Gilbertian absurdities into which historical evolution has led capitalist nations, which there seems no reason to reproduce in a rational socialist system. Another method would be to allow the Soviet enterprises to collect a profit equal to the difference between prices and costs. But profits are used as a check upon efficiency, and for this purpose they would be much less effective if swollen by the whole margin representing collective saving. Therefore the required gap is established by a turnover tax. In order to dispense with rationing it is necessary to fix the level of prices (including tax) so that total consumer demand just absorbs the total available output of consumer goods. If the tax is pitched too low (relatively to money incomes) there is inflation: if too high, an accumulation of stocks. This is the socialist equivalent of the full employment policy towards which capitalist nations are now feeling their way.

The solution of the over-all problem is simple in principle, though no doubt complicated to administer. But what of relative prices? Mr. Dobb implies (p. 373 *et seq.*) that the rate of turnover tax varies between different commodities in such a way as to reflect their scarcity relatively to demand, and that rates of tax so determined are used as an indicator to show what outputs should be expanded in the next period's plan (though the indication may be disregarded where social considerations require particular kinds of consumption to be pushed or discouraged). This suggests a system much more like the economic text-books than his first account of 'strategic' planning. But it is not clear how far this is a gloss which Mr. Dobb has put upon the matter, rather than a conscious principle of Soviet planning. Nor does he tell us at what intervals tax rates are altered, how the estimates of 'what the traffic will bear' are arrived at, or whether the system ever falls into the trap known to economists as the 'cobweb effect' (a high price due to scarcity in one period leading to over-supply and sales below cost, or rather with less than average turnover tax, in the next).

There is another point which is not quite clear. Mr. Dobb states categorically (p. 13) that the basic costs to which turnover tax is added include amortization of capital but no interest charge (more accurately these costs are 'targets'; any enterprise which can produce at less than target cost is allowed to keep part of the gain to use for amenities or investment undertaken on its own initiative, p. 354). But he implies (p. 374) that account is taken of the varying amounts of capital equipment involved in the production of different commodities, those which are less expensive in capital being given preference. If turnover tax is then related to scarcity the effect is the same as though an interest charge were included in price. These points are of some scholastic interest. If turnover tax is everywhere proportional to cost, prices reflect Marxian 'values'; if they are dictated by scarcity relative to demand they conform to Marshall's 'short-period prices'; while in so far as they include a concealed charge for capital they conform to Marshall's 'long-period costs' or Marx's 'prices of production'.

Mr. Dobb shows some impatience with such nice questions as those discussed above, which indeed appear trivial against the broad sweep of Soviet development. The grand moral of this thirty years of history is not so much for the western industrial countries, where the standard of life is already high, as for the undeveloped nations. That communism is destined to supersede capitalism is in the nature of a dogma, but it is a proven fact that the Soviet system shows how the technical achievements of capitalism can be imitated (in some spheres surpassed) by those whom the first industrial revolution left as hewers of wood and drawers of water.

In his references to the prospective industrialization of backward peoples there is one great question which Mr. Dobb refrains from raising. Because Malthus was a sanctimonious reactionary, and because Russia had huge reserves of untapped natural resources, Marxists have always brushed over-population aside as a capitalist bogey. Now that, it seems, communism is about to be established in a Malthusian nation, the future course of history will be strongly influenced by the philosophy of population which Marxism evolves.

PART IV

THE PURE THEORY OF INTERNATIONAL TRADE

THE classical theory of international trade is very remote from the problems which perplex us at the present day. Nevertheless the traditional teaching has a vague but penetrating effect on current thought. In particular there is always lurking at the back of our minds the conception of a natural position of equilibrium in international trade which would establish itself if the economic forces of the market were allowed full play. It therefore seems worth while to re-examine the classical theory and to try to see what basis it offers for the belief in a natural tendency towards equilibrium.

I

The classical model for the discussion of international trade, as we find it, for instance, in Marshall's *Pure Theory*, is based on the following assumptions[1]:

1. Given productive resources within each country, all fully employed, and no mobility of factors of production between countries.
2. Given tastes and technical knowledge.
3. Perfect mobility of factors between industries within each country.
4. Perfectly competitive conditions within each industry.
5. Annual value of imports and exports equal for each country.

The assumption of full static equilibrium is made merely for convenience, and the classical model can be adapted to deal with a world in which capital accumulation is going on. But the assumption that trade balances for each country is central. This entails that there are no international capital movements. So long as owners of wealth are free to lend their money where they please, a world without capital movements can be conceived only if the rate of interest and the prospect of profit are the same in

[1] Marshall's *Pure Theory of Foreign Trade*, pp. 1-2.

Review of Economic Studies, Vol. XIV, No. 36, 1946-7.

each country, so that there is no motive for international lending. Since this requires that capital accumulation has reached the same stage all over the world, we are pushed by the initial assumptions into contemplating a position so remote as to be entirely without interest.

The alternative is to postulate that international lending is non-existent simply because it is unknown—the owners of wealth in each country never contemplate acquiring foreign capital. The rate of interest and the level of profit on capital can then be different in different countries. Within each country the rate of interest is such that there is zero saving with full employment, and the stock of capital equipment is such that the rate of profit is adjusted to that rate of interest. Rich and thrifty countries attain equilibrium with a low rate of interest and a high ratio of capital to labour and land. Poor and unthrifty countries have a high rate of interest and a low ratio of capital. This interpretation seems more congenial than the first to the spirit of the classical analysis, which draws a sharp distinction between the principles of international and domestic trade, and it is on this basis that the argument of the first three sections of this paper is conducted.

The classical model can be adapted to the case where capital accumulation is taking place in the various countries, so long as we retain the assumption that there is full employment in each country when trade is balanced. On this assumption, the rate of interest in any one country is such as to assure whatever rate of home investment, in prevailing conditions of thriftiness, will maintain full employment there. The actual stock of capital at any moment is then the result of past history, and the stock of capital is changing through time.

The assumption that trade is balanced for each country entails that relative levels of prices in different countries are such that traders, each acting individualistically in the pursuit of profit, selling in the dearest market and buying in the cheapest, between them produce the result that imports for every country are equal to its exports. What mechanism ensures that equilibrium price levels are established? There are two main factors governing the relationship of prices in any one country to prices in the world outside—the exchange rate of its currency, and the relative level of its money wage rates. To simplify the argument, let us postulate that exchange rates are rigidly fixed, and that a universal and smoothly working gold standard is in operation. Then the establishment of equilibrium price levels must come about through movements in relative money-wage levels.

When, by chance, prices in one country are below the equilibrium level, its exports exceed its imports, and gold flows in. Or, when prices are above the equilibrium level, gold flows out. In its simplest form the traditional analysis, relying on a crude quantity theory of money, states that the movement of gold of itself brings about a movement of relative prices, gold continuing to flow until relative prices reach the level at which exports and imports are brought into equality.[1] In a more sophisticated form, the traditional analysis states that when gold is flowing out of a country its interest rate has to be raised. This checks investment, causes unemployment, thus reduces demand for consumption goods as well as for investment goods, and consequently lowers prices. Conversely, when gold flows in, the rate of interest is lowered, employment increases, and prices rise.

This argument, as we find it, for instance, in the Cunliffe Report,[2] blurs over an essential point. The reduction in investment, caused by the rise in interest rates, and the consequent unemployment and fall in consumption, reduce the demand for imports, quite apart from any fall in home prices. Indeed, it is conceivable for the short-period elasticity of supply to be so great that the fall in home prices accompanying a fall in output is negligible. It is the fall in real income, in the first instance, which reduces imports and staunches the outflow of gold. But this equilibrium in the balance of payments is maintained only on condition that incomes remain at their reduced level. Recovery to full employment would start the outflow of gold again. Meanwhile, however, it may be assumed that unemployment is leading to a fall in home money-wage rates. The consequent fall in home costs relatively to the world level (which at the same time may be rising because of the contrary effects produced in countries gaining gold) will increase the volume of exports and reduce the volume of imports corresponding to a given level of home income. If activity remains at its reduced level, an inflow of gold then

---

[1] Marshall, op. cit., p. 3.
[2] *First Interim Report of the Committee on Currency and Foreign Exchanges after the War*, 1918, paragraphs 4–7 and 16–17.

develops, relaxing the restriction of credit. A sufficient fall in home money-wage rates will allow the rate of interest to be restored to its former level and full employment to be re-established. This is all implied in the Cunliffe doctrine, but the vital distinction between restoration of the balance of payments due to reduced home activity and restoration due to the competitive advantage given to home production by a relative fall in home costs, is not clearly brought out in the analysis.

The traditional account of the operation of the gold standard is not very convincing. The rise in interest rates on which it relies is primarily a rise in bank rate. A rise in bank rate, in a stable world, could be relied upon to check an outflow of gold by attracting short-term loans from abroad, but it is highly disputable that it could fulfil the more fundamental task of reducing employment. The direct effect of a rise in bank rate on investment is very uncertain. It may be doubted whether the sympathetic rise in long-term rates due to a rise in bank rate was ever very great,[1] and it may be doubted whether even an appreciable rise in long-term rates is a very powerful influence in checking long-term investment, when other circumstances are favourable to it. This is a complicated subject, which has given rise to much controversy. It is, fortunately, not necessary to settle the point before proceeding with our argument.

Once it is admitted that a fall in money-wage rates plays an essential part in the supposed mechanism, we can short-circuit the whole argument about interest rates, and assume simply that money-wages fall when there is unemployment. To postulate absolutely full employment raises unnecessary complications. Let us suppose that in equilibrium conditions, with balanced trade, there is a small margin of unemployment, sufficient to give some flexibility to production, but not sufficient to allow any large change in total output to take place. We must further assume that with this normal level of unemployment wages are stable; with more unemployment, wages fall continuously, and with less, wages rise continuously.

Now, since there is a normal level of unemployment when trade is balanced, an excess of imports (if investment remains the same) causes more than normal unemployment, and a fall in wages. An

[1] Kalecki, *Essays in the Theory of Economic Fluctuations*, p. 107 *et seq.*

excess of exports reduces unemployment below the normal level, and raises wages.

On the assumption of perfect mobility of labour, any change in money wages must be uniform throughout the country, and on the assumption of perfect competition, prices are governed by marginal costs, and therefore by wage rates. A relative change in home and foreign wage rates will produce a relative change in the prices of home-produced goods embodying imported materials. Apart from this, the prices at a given level of output of home-produced goods will move proportionately with money-wage rates.

On these assumptions, when there is disequilibrium in trade, home money wages and prices will continue to move, relatively to the world level, until trade balances, and the normal level of unemployment, which may be called 'full employment' for short, is restored. This interpretation seems to be congenial to the spirit of the classical model, and the intention of the argument is no more than to bring its implications into a clear light.

If this interpretation is accepted, the next question to be met is: Can equilibrium in the balance of trade necessarily be established by the mechanism of changing relative money-wage rates? It may be objected that in some concatenations of elasticities of demand and supply a rise in wages (or an appreciation in exchange rate) may increase a surplus of exports, or a fall increase a surplus of imports, instead of wiping it out,[1] but it can be shown that, from a formal point of view, this objection is not fatal to the classical analysis.

Let us first consider the case where departure from equilibrium consists in a surplus in the balance of trade of a certain country, Alpha. Money-wage rates rise relatively to the world level.[2] This raises the costs of goods produced in Alpha, and raises the purchasing power of a day's earnings over goods produced abroad

---

[1] Cf. Lerner, *Economics of Control*, p. 377; and Joan Robinson, *Essays in the Theory of Employment*, 1947 edition, p. 142.

[2] For simplicity of exposition we may assume that money-wage rates in all other countries remain unchanged. But our whole argument is conducted in terms of relative wage rates, and the absolute level of world prices does not come into it. It is possible, however, to use as a standard of value the wage unit of any one country—that is, the money value of a day's earnings of a representative worker in that country. Wages in Alpha and in the rest of the world can then be calculated in terms of this standard unit. The relationship between Alpha wages and world wages which gives equilibrium is the same in whatever unit they are calculated.

(the terms of trade have turned in Alpha's favour). Consider first the effect upon the value of Alpha's imports. Foreign goods have become cheaper relatively to home goods (because home costs have risen relatively to the world level). This increases the demand for imports. Real home incomes have increased (because home money incomes, which are partly spent upon foreign goods, have risen relatively to world prices) and for this reason also there will normally be an increase in demand for imports. Furthermore, the increase in demand will cause an increase in the prices of the goods concerned (neglecting cases of falling supply price) to an extent depending on their elasticity of supply. The total value of imports is therefore increased, and this tends to reduce the trade surplus with which the story began.

A perverse case can be conceived in which the main imports into Alpha are 'inferior goods', the demand for which falls off as real income increases. There may then be a decline in the value of imports when home money-wage rates rise, so that the disequilibrium would be enhanced instead of mitigated, as far as the import side of the balance is concerned.

Now look at the export side of the balance. Costs in Alpha have risen, and the price in world markets of Alpha's export goods tends to rise. The change in the value of Alpha's exports therefore depends on the elasticity of the rest of the world's demand for Alpha goods. If Alpha is a small part of the world, selling in competition with rival sources of supply, the demand for her exports will be elastic and their value will fall off as their prices rise. If Alpha is the sole source of supply of some specialities, world demand may be inelastic; there will then be a perverse reaction, the value of exports increasing with home money-wage rates. But this can be true only over a certain range. So long as the export surplus persists, wages (on our assumptions) continue to rise, and at some point the specialities in question become so expensive, relative to world money incomes, that the demand for them turns elastic. Moreover, real income in the rest of the world is reduced when money-wage rates in Alpha rise, and the goods which she supplies go up in price. (This is the converse of the rise in real income in Alpha referred to above). If Alpha is a small country this effect on the rest of the world is insignificant, but if Alpha represents an important fraction of world production, then the impoverishment of the rest of the world will cause a decline in Alpha's exports. Thus, though there may be a perverse reaction over a certain range, at some point, as Alpha money-wage rates rise, the value of Alpha's exports must fall off, and there is some level of Alpha wages at which exports fall to zero. Therefore, even if there is a perverse reaction in imports, the fall in value of exports must sooner or later counterbalance it. The mechanism of rising wages can be relied upon to wipe out an export surplus, at some level or other.

Now consider the converse case, where disequilibrium consists in a surplus of imports. There is a deficit in the balance of trade of a country, say Beta. Wage rates in Beta fall. The reduction in the price of her exports may lead to a rise in their total value, and so contribute to wiping out the deficit. But there may be a perverse reaction, the value of exports falling with price. In this direction, the perverse reaction does not tend to be reversed as the fall in wages continues, for demands tend to become less elastic as prices fall and the saturation point is approached. On the import side, however, equilibrium is bound to be restored, later if not sooner. Both the substitution of home for imported goods, and the decline in real income due to the fall in home money income relatively to world prices, reduce the demand for imports, and consequently also reduce their prices (to an extent depending upon elasticity of supply from the rest of the world). There is a limit to the possible fall in price of imported goods, but no limit to the possible reduction in their quantity. At some level of relative money wages Beta becomes too impoverished to import anything at all. The value of exports can never sink to zero, as wages in Beta fall, but the value of imports can. Thus, even if there is a perverse reaction upon exports, sooner or later the fall in Beta wages must wipe out the surplus of imports.

From a formal point of view, the classical analysis (on its own assumptions) can thus be vindicated. It is to be observed, how-ever, that there is nothing in the argument to show that balance can necessarily be established for a deficit country with its existing population. If it is densely populated (relatively to the fertility rather than the extent of its soil) and depends upon imports of food, the process just described, by which a fall in home money incomes relatively to world prices reduces the physical volume of imports, will involve extreme distress. There will be strong pressure to emigrate, and if emigration is impossible, Malthusian misery will reduce the population. The hidden hand will always do its work, but it may work by strangulation.

While the traditional theory was being developed by Marshall, the assumption of 'given factors of production in each country' was belied by large-scale migration (as well as by international investment), and it was not necessary to take the assumption seriously. Nowadays the safety-valve of migration is choked up, and many countries are faced with the problem of excessive population relatively to their opportunities to export. The classical argument requires whatever reduction in the price of their exports relatively to imports (that is, whatever cut in their terms of trade) will establish balance, and the required cut may entail a steep fall in their standard of life, unless the number of mouths to be fed on imports can be reduced. We need not go to the Malthusian east to find examples, or to the defeated nations of Europe. It may well be that our own country has been left by the war in some such situation.

A good deal of present-day discussion of international trade seems to be based on the notion that there always is a position of equilibrium to be found by relying upon the operation of the pricing system, and it is necessary to recognize that the classical doctrine does not exclude starvation from the mechanism by which equilibrium tends to be established.

Our argument is conducted in terms of varying money-wage rates with rigid exchanges, but it applies equally to varying exchange rates. The effect upon relative prices at home and abroad of a change in exchange rate is the same as the effect (on our assumptions) of an equal proportionate change in wage rates. A fall in money-wage rates entails certain evils for the home economy—a rise in the value of money gives an unearned increment of real income and wealth to creditors which may be socially undesirable, and the corresponding increased real burden of debt is deleterious to industry; expectations of future falls in prices check demand for all durable goods, and may make the maintenance of full employment impossible. These secondary evils do not occur if adjustment is made by way of exchange rates. But this does not affect the main issue. The deterioration in the terms of trade of a deficit country necessary to wipe out the deficit is the same whether it is brought about by exchange depreciation or through reductions in money-wage rates. The loss involved in the passage to equilibrium cannot be evaded by choosing one route rather than the other.

In what follows we shall continue to assume fixed exchange rates, and argue in terms of changing relative wage rates, in order to simplify exposition, but at every point the argument can readily be transposed into terms of changing exchange rates.

II

We are now able to set out the classical doctrine of 'comparative costs' without tying ourselves up uncomfortably in the classical 'bales of goods'.

The first point to be established is what determines the relative money-wage levels in the various countries. The stock of capital equipment in each country is given, at any moment, and it is assumed to be always adapted in the most appropriate manner to whatever type of production is being carried on. The rate of investment in each country is such that there is full employment when trade balances and the rate of interest must be such as to fulfil this condition. We can therefore determine the net productivity of labour in each country.

The gross productivity of labour (value of output divided by labour employed) is determined, in each country, by the capital stock in that country, by natural conditions, the level of skill and of education, and so forth, and by the conditions of world demand for the commodities which it produces. The net productivity of labour is the gross productivity *minus* the cost of capital and land. Thus in poor or unthrifty countries, where the stock of capital equipment is relatively small, and the rate of interest which ensures equilibrium relatively high, the net productivity of labour will be lower than in countries plentifully supplied with capital, unless this disadvantage is offset by natural endowments, such as a high ratio of fertile land to population, or natural facilities for producing some rarity which commands a high price in world markets. The productivity of labour falls as employment in any one line is extended, partly because of diminishing physical returns (which, allowing for transport, will be the normal rule) and partly because of the fall in price of any one commodity when more of it is sold.

Since perfect mobility within each country is assumed, there is a uniform level of real-wage rates throughout all industries in any one country, and net productivity at the margin of production in each industry is the same throughout the country. The level of money wages, in equilibrium, reflects the national level of productivity. Thus there is a definite pattern of relative national money-wage rates (corresponding to national productivities) which will give equilibrium. The competitive advantage of high productivity is offset by high money costs of labour, so as to ensure that trade balances. High-productivity, high-wage countries then trade on even terms with low-wage, low-productivity countries, each country being a high-cost producer for some commodities and a low-cost producer for others. This is the basis of the familiar doctrine that 'no country can undersell the rest all round'.

Suppose that one country, Alpha, has a money-wage level, in equilibrium twice that prevailing in the rest of the world (treating the rest of the world as a unit for the sake of simplicity). Then Alpha will export those commodities for which the net productivity of labour, at quantities sufficient to supply the home market only, is more than twice the world level. Exports will be pushed up to the point at which the value of net product at the margin is equal to no more than twice the world level, that is, to the point at which net productivity is equal to wages in Alpha. She will import those commodities for which the net productivity of labour, if the whole home market were supplied, would be less than twice the world level. For some commodities (grapes in Scotland) there is no output at which productivity in Alpha would be twice the world level, and the whole of Alpha's consumption will be imported. For other commodities productivity is twice the world level for small quantities, but falls below that level before the whole of home demand is satisfied. Of these, part will be produced at home and part imported.

Another country, Beta, has a money-wage level in equilibrium half that in the rest of the world. She will export commodities in which productivity is more than half the world level, and import commodities in which it is less than half the world level.

For a high-wage country like Alpha the purchasing power of an average day's earnings over world produce is relatively high, and her citizens benefit in so far as imports enter into their standard of life. It is high productivity in tradeable goods which necessitates high money wages. If Alpha's advantage lies in some freak of nature, such as valuable mineral deposits, and her general productive efficiency is not great, the purchasing power of a day's earnings over home goods will be relatively low, and the benefit from her high productivity is confined to high purchasing power over imports. If her advantages spring from a plentiful supply of capital equipment, superior technique, efficiency of management and skill of labour, productivity will be high in many lines which do not enter into international trade, as well as in those that do, so that over a wide range of home goods, as well as over imports, the purchasing power of a day's earnings is high, and for a further reason her standard of life tends to be high. But it so happens that there are a number of lines in which general industrial efficiency has little scope to show itself and in which importation is impossible. This is true especially of direct personal services. The wages of a valet in America are higher than those of an Indian bearer, not because the American is more efficient at valeting (the reverse may well be the case), but because superior productivity of industrial and agricultural labour in America has set wages there at a higher level than in India. This is of particular importance for those who are trying to support a middle-class standard of life on a moderate income. Middle-class pensioners often prefer to retire to industrially backward countries where 'money goes further' than it does at home. The same principle applies, to some extent, to services such as retailing, which enters into the final price even of imported goods. And house-building is generally a relatively backward industry where importation is impossible (though 'pre-fabrication' may perhaps change this situation). For these reasons, the cost of living tends to be higher in high-wage than in low-wage countries. Differences between countries in their standard of life therefore generally tend to be less than differences in their average money incomes.

In the foregoing paragraphs we have strayed here and there from the strict conditions of the classical model and appealed for examples to the real world. This is permissible because in a very broad sense the classical model does reflect reality. It is certainly not the case that balanced trade and full employment generally prevail, but surpluses and deficits are generally small relatively to a country's total trade, and (taking good times with bad), unemployment is small relatively to the total of employment.

Great differences between productivity in different countries must therefore be broadly offset by differences in money-wage rates.

The offset, however, is never exact, and the classical doctrine that no country can undersell the rest all round is not fully applicable to the real world.

Starting from a position of balanced trade, suppose that one country, Alpha, improves in efficiency in producing tradeable goods. She now develops a surplus of exports. If there were already nearly full employment in Alpha at the beginning of the story, money-wage rates would start to rise, and the surplus would be wiped out in the manner described above. But if there was sufficient unemployment (in open or disguised form) to permit the increase in output to take place (along with any further consequential increase due to increased home investment) and still to leave a reserve of labour, there is no reason why money wages should rise. Alpha is now a country of cheap labour, in the sense that her productivity, relatively to the rest of the world, exceeds her wage level relatively to the rest of the world, and she is under-selling the rest of the world all round, in the sense that she is a low-cost producer.[1] Her terms of trade are less favourable than they would be if wages rose to the equilibrium level, and the rest of the world benefits to the extent that her goods are sold to it so much the cheaper. But the rest of the world experiences the disadvantage of having lost markets to Alpha and is consequently suffering from unemployment or from greater difficulty in maintaining employment. It also experiences monetary difficulties owing to the drain of gold to Alpha, but this matter can be better discussed later, when we have removed the assumption that international lending is unknown.

Complaints by producers in other countries who are suffering from competition from cheap labour are often raised in connection with a low standard of life in the cheap labour country. 'The native can live on a handful of rice', and this gives his employer an unfair advantage. The foregoing argument has no necessary connection with the 'handful of rice'. The United States is just as likely to be a cheap labour country, in the sense that money-wage rates lag behind productivity, as Japan or China.

At the same time it is true that cheap labour, in this sense, will often be found where there is a low standard of life. When

[1] I am indebted to Mr. John Knapp for this method of setting out the argument.

industry begins to develop in a backward, over-populated country, the rates of money wages which it is necessary for employers to offer are held down by an elastic supply of labour, accustomed to very low earnings, from the over-populated countryside. At first, productivity in the new industries may be so low that, even with very low wage rates, it is a struggle to compete with industrially advanced, high-wage countries; but, as time goes by, efficiency in industry is likely to improve. If the total population is constant, average real income in agriculture rises as surplus population is drawn away, and consequently the level of wages which will attract workers to industry also rises. The rise in wages, however, may lag behind the increase in industrial productivity, and if population in the countryside is increasing, there may be no rise of wages at all. Thus labour in industry grows progressively cheaper as efficiency increases.

Whether the standard of life is high or low, a surplus tends to develop wherever productivity increases faster, relatively to money-wage rates, than in the rest of the world. Since technical progress and capital accumulation proceed very unevenly over the world, while the response of wage rates to increased employment is very sluggish, the tendency to establish the equilibrium wage rates never works fast enough to catch up with changing circumstances.

The classical model, therefore, shows us that in reality disequilibrium is the normal rule.

III

The chief purpose to which the analysis of comparative costs has been put is to demonstrate the merits of free trade. But actually, as we shall see, the classical model cannot be used to show that protection is harmful to the interests of any one country,[1] though it can for the world as a whole.

Starting from a position of equilibrium, the effect of introducing a tariff in Alpha is to reduce her imports (unless the demand for imported goods is perfectly inelastic) and to increase home production for the home market. Home production will increase even if there is no direct substitution of home for imported supplies. Alpha may import nothing but copper and caviare,

---

[1] Quite apart from the 'infant industry' case, which is not here discussed.

neither of which can be produced at home under any circumstances. When the price of these commodities is raised to final consumers in Alpha, less will be consumed, and the sums paid for them to foreigners will be reduced (though total outlay upon them by Alpha consumers may have been increased). The proceeds of the import duties may be disbursed to Alpha citizens, for instance, by remission of other taxes in such a way as to compensate consumers for the import taxes which they pay. The sums formerly paid to foreigners for those quantities of copper and caviare which are no longer imported will then be spent on home goods. If the proceeds of the import duties are used for government outlay, which would not otherwise have been undertaken, again home production is stimulated.[1] In one way or the other, home expenditure on home production in Alpha is increased. Employment is therefore increased above the normal level and money-wage rates in Alpha rise. Her exports therefore fall in physical volume, and the labour released from producing them is absorbed into the expanding home industries.

If Alpha is a sufficiently important part of the world, unemployment in the rest of the world due to loss of Alpha markets[2] will cause money wages there to fall, until labour released from exporting to Alpha is absorbed into home production substituted for imports from Alpha.

When adjustment to the situation created by Alpha's tariff has been completed, and full employment once more everywhere prevails, labour has been transferred from export to home production, both in Alpha and in the rest of the world.

The same equilibrium position, as has often been pointed out,

---

[1] If the proceeds are used as a sinking fund for the national debt our assumptions require that the rate of interest shall be lowered to the point at which other forms of saving are correspondingly reduced, or home investment correspondingly increased. This applies also if thriftiness is increased because some Alpha citizens, when they find caviare unduly expensive, prefer to increase their saving instead of their expenditure on other things. Thus even in this case, home production is increased. If investment is increased, the stock of capital accumulates faster than it would have done otherwise. This may lead to a change in the position of Alpha industries in the scale of comparative advantages which would not have taken place if the tariff had never been introduced. But this belongs to another part of the story.

[2] During the transitional phase, unemployment in the rest of the world will reduce demand for Alpha exports. If the marginal propensity to import from Alpha is large, the initial fall in employment in Alpha's export industries may be sufficient to offset the increase in employment in her home industries, so that money wages in Alpha do not rise. In this case equilibrium is restored entirely by the fall in money-wage rates in the rest of the world.

could be established by a tax on Alpha's exports, calculated so as to bring about the same change in their total value in world markets. In this case the initial effect is a rise in the price of Alpha exports, a fall in their physical volume, unemployment in Alpha, and a fall in money-wage rates until the labour released from exporting industries is absorbed into home production displacing imports, which have now become more expensive relatively to Alpha money incomes and home costs. Although the final position is the same in real terms, the transition takes the form of a slump in Alpha, instead of a boom, which introduces an important difference. The following discussion is confined to the case of import taxes.

Now, Alpha's tariff causes a loss to the rest of the world, in so far as its opportunities to sell to Alpha, and therefore to buy from her, are curtailed. In Alpha, the tariff reduces productivity in real terms. After the transition has been completed, net productivity of labour in money terms is once more the same, at the margin, in export and home industries (each being equal to the new money-wage rate).[1] But, from the point of view of Alpha consumers, an extra £100 earned in exports is worth more than an extra £100 earned in home industry, for £100 of exports exchanges for £100 of imports at world market prices, and for these goods consumers in Alpha are willing to pay an excess over £100 equal to the tax upon them. Thus the real productivity of resources in exports must be reckoned in terms of the purchasing power of money in world markets, and real productivity in home industry in terms of the purchasing power of money at home market prices. When money values of the two are equal, the real value of productivity in exports is greater than in home industry, and there has been a loss due to transferring labour (with the appropriate capital equipment and land) from export to home industry. Since productivities are equal at the margin in the first instance, the loss is insignificant for a small transfer, and it becomes progressively greater as the transfer is extended.[2]

[1] It is assumed for simplicity that cases of economies of large-scale industry, if any, are distributed equally between export and home production, so that losses due to the reduced scale of the one balance gains due to the increased scale of the other.
[2] The familiar index-number problem is here involved. The reduction in productivity is different from the point of view of different individuals, according to the extent to which they were accustomed, before the tariff, to purchase imports or home

In this sense, real productivity in Alpha is reduced by the tariff. But this is not sufficient to show that Alpha's real income has fallen, for the terms of trade have been turned in her favour. When the gain in the terms of trade outweighs the loss of real productivity, Alpha enjoys a larger share of a diminished total world real income.[1]

It is obvious that this must be the case where the rest of the world's demand for Alpha goods has an elasticity not greater than unity. If the elasticity of demand for Alpha exports over the relevant range is equal to one, the total value of Alpha's exports, and therefore both the value and the volume of her imports, is the same after the imposition of the tariff as before (though Alpha citizens are paying more for the imported goods which they buy) and the additional home product of labour released from export industries is a net gain. If elasticity of demand for Alpha's exports is less than unity, their value, and consequently the value and the volume of imports, actually rises, and Alpha enjoys additional imports as well as additional home output.

It may seem strange that a tariff should increase imports. The reason is that the rise in real income in Alpha due to improved terms of trade leads to an increase in demand for imports which more than offsets the relative disadvantage of imports in the home market imposed by the tariff. If the demand for imports in Alpha does not expand in this way, so as to offset a rise in the value of exports, the rise in money-wage rates in Alpha must continue until the demand for exports turns elastic and their total value falls. In that case the improvement in Alpha's terms of trade is so much the greater.

So long as the elasticity of demand for Alpha's exports is not greater than one, a tariff, however high, will increase Alpha's real income. Where the elasticity of demand for Alpha exports is greater than one, their value, in equilibrium, is less after the imposition of a tariff than before. In this case it is possible for a

goods for which the price is raised (relatively to home money-wage rates) by the operation of physical diminishing returns when the production of them is extended with resources transferred from export industries.

[1] The following argument is the same in substance as that of Edgeworth, *Papers Relating to Political Economy*, Vol. II, 'Bickerdike's Theory of Incipient Taxes'. See also Lerner, 'The Diagrammatical Representation of Demand Conditions in International Trade', *Economica*, August, 1934, p. 333; Scitovszky, 'A Reconsideration of the Theory of Tariffs', *Review of Economic Studies*, Vol. X, No. 2, 1942; and Kaldor, 'A Note on Tariffs and the Terms of Trade', *Economica*, November, 1940.

tariff to be so high as to reduce Alpha's real income, just as it is possible for a monopolist to reduce his profits below the competitive level by charging too high a price for his commodity. But provided the tariff is not too high, it can easily be seen that Alpha's real income is increased by it. Suppose a tariff calculated to bring about a small transfer of resources from export to home industries. Since productivity at the margin was initially the same in all industries, the real value of the output lost in exports is only slightly greater than the real value of the output gained in home industries. But the loss in total value of exports (which governs the value of imports) is appreciably less than the value of the output lost, since the price of the remaining exports is raised. Therefore the gain in volume of home output is greater than the loss of volume of imports, even if world prices of imported goods are unchanged. If the rest of the world's supply to Alpha is less than perfectly elastic, there is a further gain to Alpha, since a given reduction in value of imports then represents a smaller reduction in volume of imports.

If Alpha is a small country, both selling and buying in close rivalry with others, the elasticities of demand for her products and of supply to her of world products may be very high, but, taking transport costs into account, it is impossible for them to be infinite. There is, therefore, always some gain in real income to be made by a tariff, as compared to the position of equilibrium under free trade.

The gain to Alpha from a given tariff is greater: (1) the less the elasticity of demand for Alpha exports; (2) the less the elasticity of supply to Alpha of imports; (3) the greater the elasticity of Alpha's demand for imports; (4) the less rapid the fall in productivity as output expands in Alpha industries.

The advocates of free trade (apart from certain fanatics[1]) have generally admitted that one country can gain, at the expense of the rest of the world, by taxing imports. But they condemn such a policy on two grounds. The first is, that it is inexpedient for one country to introduce tariffs, as this will provoke other countries to do likewise. This argument would not apply if the relevant elasticities were such that Alpha stood to gain from her own tariffs more than she lost by those of other nations. It is possible (though certainly not generally probable) that the absolute

---

[1] See *Tariffs: the Case Examined*, p. 14 note.

amount of Alpha's share in world real income might be greater even when world real income is reduced by protection all round than it would be under universal free trade. Assuming, however, that Alpha stands to lose by all-round protection, the force of the argument depends upon Alpha's influence in the world. If Alpha's political influence is such that other countries follow her lead, or if her economic importance is so great that her resort to protection threatens the standard of life of the rest of the world and drives other countries to protection in self-defence, then the danger of starting the race is one which she would be unwise to challenge. But if the rest of the world would behave in the same way, whatever Alpha does, this argument has no force at all.

The second argument in favour of free trade is much more general. It is simply that it is immoral for one country to gain an advantage at the expense of the rest. When Alpha's economic situation under free trade is fairly comfortable, this argument has great weight. But let us glance back to the miserable situation of Beta, described above, when the establishment of equilibrium under classical free trade conditions requires an intolerable sacrifice in her terms of trade. If Beta had been in equilibrium at some time in the past, the fact that she is now suffering from a deficit indicates that she has lost some competitive advantage, and, whatever policy she pursues, it is likely that she will experience some reduction in consumption, as compared to the position while the deficit is running. But what we have to compare is her position if balance were restored by the classical mechanism of falling wage rates (or exchange depreciation) with her position if it were restored by means of a tariff. The dominant feature of the situation, which makes the classical solution onerous—a low elasticity of demand for Beta's exports—is one which also makes protection a promising alternative. And, in any case, the loss will be less, as we have seen (and may even be nil) if tariffs are used, than if classical equilibrium is reached. In such a case the purely moral claims of free trade cannot be urged to Beta's citizens with much hope of success.

IV

We have so far interpreted the classical model as applying to a world in which international lending is unknown. This is a severe restriction upon its usefulness. Let us now consider how it must be modified to apply to a world which forms a single capital market. It is not necessary to assume that the capital market is perfect. Owners of wealth may have preferences as between countries, on account of differences in risk. There will then be a certain pattern of national interest rates established in the world. But for simplicity of exposition we will assume an approximately perfect world market in capital, so that practically the same rate of interest rules everywhere.

To satisfy the condition of full employment in each country we must assume that the rate of interest always finds the level at which world investment absorbs the rate of saving corresponding to full employment for the world as a whole. Investment will take place in those countries where the prospects of profit are greatest, and if the rate of investment in any country is greater than the rate of saving corresponding to full employment in that country, the level of money wages there (relatively to the rest of the world) must be such as to cause a surplus of imports equal to the difference between the rate of investment taking place in that country and its home rate of saving. In any country where investment at home is less than the rate of saving corresponding to full employment, the level of money wages must be such as to cause a surplus of exports equal to the difference.

There is thus a unique equilibrium pattern of relative national wage rates corresponding to each pattern of world investment, but the position is continuously changing through time as the stock of capital in each country alters relatively to its opportunities for profitable investment.

To illustrate the mechanism of adjustment, starting for simplicity from a position in which trade happens to be balanced for each country, let us suppose that some fresh investment opportunities arise in Alpha. Investment in Alpha increases, her demand for imports rises, and a world boom sets in. According to our assumption, the rate of interest in the world is raised to the point at which home investment in the rest of the world is reduced to the same extent that it has increased in Alpha (assuming thriftiness unchanged).[1] Now, Alpha may be importing investment goods—say steel rails. Investment in other countries

---

[1] In so far as the rise in the rate of interest increases thriftiness, the total of world investment is increased. Part of the labour required for investment in Alpha is then released from consumption industries, in Alpha and in the rest of the world.

has fallen off, but exports to Alpha have increased. It may be that steel which was formerly going into investment in other countries is now shipped to Alpha. In so far as this is the case, readjustment takes place without any shift in employment (except into transport). A further part of the readjustment takes place by labour from home investment industries in other countries transferring to the production of investment goods for Alpha. In so far as this supplies the whole increase in Alpha's investment, no further readjustment is required.[1] But it is unlikely that the whole of Alpha's increased investment can be provided by importation of investment goods. Even if the rails are imported, Alphan navvies must build the embankments. There is, therefore, an excess demand for labour in Alpha, and Alpha money-wage rates rise. Alpha exports therefore fall off, and there is a transfer from home consumption to imports. The rise of wages goes to the point at which sufficient labour is released from export and home industry in Alpha to carry out the investment. For the rest of the world, employment in exporting to Alpha, and in making home goods in substitution for imports from Alpha, increases to the same extent that employment in home investment has fallen.

Now, consider the position of one country in the rest of the world, say Beta. The impact of the new situation upon Beta is that employment in home investment has fallen, as a result of the rise in the rate of interest, exports to Alpha have increased, and so has home production in substitution for imports from Alpha, but there is no reason why these movements should exactly balance. If the decline in employment exceeds the increase, money-wage rates fall. Imports then decline and exports increase (to the rest of the world in general, not only to Alpha) until full employment is restored. In another country, say Gamma, the increase in demand for exports to Alpha exceeds the decline in home investment. Money-wage rates then rise, checking the increase in exports to Alpha, reducing exports to other countries and increasing imports in substitution for home production. Finally, a position of equilibrium is reached in which relative wage levels are such that each country takes its share, directly and

---

[1] As a curiosity we may observe that if thriftiness in Alpha is increased by the rise in the rate of interest, while the whole value of her increased investment is imported, there will be an initial fall in employment in Alpha.

indirectly, in providing the excess of exports from the rest of the world to Alpha.

Those countries where this equilibrium involves a rise in money-wage rates, relatively to the rest of the world, enjoy improved terms of trade, so that their real income is increased, while for the others real income is reduced. Alpha will normally be amongst those countries whose terms of trade improve, but she will not necessarily experience the greatest rise. It might happen that the relative rise in wage rates necessary for equilibrium was greater in Gamma than in Alpha.

We must now consider the financial aspect of the readjustment. Since the boom was centred in Alpha we may suppose that the rate of interest in Alpha rises somewhat ahead of the world level. This may have the result that the whole of the finance for the new investment projects is raised abroad, where interest rates are relatively lower. Now, on our assumptions, Alpha's import surplus is equal to the increase in her investment. Thus, assuming the foreign loans are drawn upon *pari passu* with investment outlay, her balance of payments remains exactly in equilibrium. But the issues corresponding to the new investment may be partly subscribed by Alpha citizens. Alpha's foreign borrowing then initially falls short of her surplus of imports, and she loses gold. This leads to an additional rise in her rate of interest, relatively to the world level, which, to check the outflow of gold, must go to whatever extent is necessary to attract loans at the rate corresponding to her deficit. Equally it may happen that the initial relative rise in her interest rate attracts loans in excess of what is required to match her trade deficit. Alpha then gains gold until a relapse in her interest rate towards the world level chokes off redundant borrowing.

If the quantity of money in Alpha is strictly related to the quantity of gold in her central bank she will require a larger stock of gold to support her raised level of money incomes. In this case, at some stage during the transition to the new equilibrium, she must gain gold. This is brought about by keeping the relative rate of interest for a time at a level which induces lending by the rest of the world at a higher rate than corresponds to her surplus of imports. Once the gold is in, the rate of interest falls to the level which insures borrowing equal to the deficit.

There is no necessary connection between the source of Alpha's borrowing and the source of her imports. It may be that loans to Alpha come mainly from Beta, and exports to Alpha mainly from Gamma. In the first instance, then, Gamma's export surplus rises above her lending, she gains gold, and her interest rate lags behind the world level. Beta initially lends more than her surplus, loses gold, and raises her interest rate, relatively to the world level. If there are no other countries in the story, Gamma then lends to Beta the difference between Beta's loans to Alpha and Beta's export surplus.

We have assumed up to now a nearly perfect world market, so that very slight differences in relative interest rates are required to adjust lending and borrowing to surpluses and deficits. Gold movements are required, if at all, only to make minor adjustments. But even if the capital market is rather imperfect, there are nlikely to be great monetary strains in our imaginary full-employment world. The dominant cause of a trade deficit is a higher rate of investment than is taking place elsewhere in the world. Deficit countries are those with favourable profit opportunities, and are attractive to lenders. Surplus countries are those where the prospect of profit from investment at home is relatively poor, and where the owners of wealth are therefore likely to be favourably inclined to taking up foreign securities. Thus there is a broad tendency to harmony between the flow of lending and the pattern of surpluses and deficits, and gold movements do not have very much work to do to bring about an exact adjustment.

The difference between the above analysis and what has been called the 'neo-classical' account of capital movements (elaborated, for instance, by Taussig[1]) is that a different point of departure has been taken for the discussion. The neo-classical story begins with Beta lending to Alpha. Beta consequently loses gold, her interest rate rises, prices fall (which may be interpreted to mean that the fall in home investment due to the higher interest rate causes unemployment and brings about a fall in money-wage rates), and so Beta squeezes out a surplus of exports. Meanwhile the gain of gold to Alpha raises prices in Alpha and so leads to an import surplus, while the fall in her interest rate, due to the inflow of gold, stimulates investment. There is nothing incompatible with this in the foregoing argument, but the case in which the initiating cause of capital movements is a difference

[1] *International Trade*, p. 232.

in the profitability of investment in different countries seems to have a wider application (at least in nineteenth-century conditions, with which the neo-classical analysis was concerned) than the case in which the initiating cause is a change in lending by the citizens of one country to another.

The foregoing adaptation of the classical analysis to a world with international investment enables us to describe a pattern of trade which gives equilibrium for the world (though the equilibrium position is continuously moving through time). But the whole analysis is based upon the arbitrary assumption that world full employment is always preserved. When that assumption is not fulfilled there is no one pattern of tiade which can be described as equilibrium. If there was ample unemployment in Alpha when investment increased, there is no guarantee that money wages will rise to the point at which her surplus of imports offsets the increase in investment. All we can say is, that if wages in Alpha rise (or her exchange is appreciated) employment in Alpha will increase by less, and in Gamma and Beta by more, than if they do not. There is no one distribution of employment between them which has any more claim than any other (within a wide range) to be called the equilibrium distribution.

Nor will the monetary mechanism work smoothly when there is unemployment (quite apart from the flights of money, which in recent times have wrecked it altogether). Relative national money-wage rates (or exchange rates) are not forced to the levels which offset competitive advantages in trade, and, as we saw earlier, a deficit may arise from a country being undersold by cheap labour abroad just as well as from a high rate of investment at home. Deficit countries are not necessarily the most attractive to lenders, and very large differences in relative interest rates may be necessary in order to adjust lending and borrowing to surpluses and deficits.

But in a country which is losing gold, because of an import surplus not fully covered by borrowing, the monetary authorities are reluctant to make unemployment still worse by restricting credit and raising interest rates; while the countries which are gaining gold may be relatively prosperous, and their authorities have little motive, and may, in fact, not have the power, to bring about such a fall in interest rates as would induce their wealthy citizens to lend abroad on a scale corresponding to the country's trade surplus.

Thus balances of payments may remain out of equilibrium for long periods (indeed, the whole international monetary system may be disrupted before they are restored) and monetary strains further bedevil the confusion of trade. It seems, then, that as soon as the assumption of full employment is removed, the classical model for the analysis of international trade is reduced to wreckage (the removal of the assumptions of perfect mobility and perfect competition would blast it afresh).

On the other hand, if full employment is established by national policies, each country has a range of choice between home investment (or measures to promote home consumption) and an export surplus, as a means of securing it.

The more a country makes use of home investment (or reduced thriftiness) the smaller its surplus of exports (or the greater its deficit) and the more it helps to provide employment in other countries. The more it makes use of wage-cutting (or exchange depreciation) or of protection, the harder is employment to maintain in the rest of the world. The situation of each country is affected by the policies of the rest, and any number of permutations and combinations are possible.

In short, the notion of a unique natural position of equilibrium is a mirage, and, for better or worse, international trade must be directed by conscious policy.

THE UNITED STATES IN THE WORLD ECONOMY

THE Department of Commerce report gives a detailed account of the U.S. balance of payments from 1919 to 1939, and, incidentally, provides what is probably the clearest and most penetrating analysis that has yet appeared of the whole history of international trade in that period.

The narrative is conducted in terms of the world supply and demand for dollars. Its central episode is the fall in supply of dollars with the onset of the great slump. This is dramatically shown in the following table:

	1929	1932	Percentage Decrease
	\$ millions		
Dollars supplied by U.S. through purchases of goods and services and new investments abroad	7,400	2,400	68
Dollars required to meet fixed debt service payments to U.S.A., assuming no defaults or readjustments	900	900	—
Remainder available to foreign countries for other purposes	6,500	1,500	77

The fall in supply of dollars was due to the cessation of foreign lending, and to the fall in U.S. purchases on income account. The report emphasizes the great weight of U.S.A. in the world economy. Her national income, in money terms, was equal in 1929 to the combined total for the twenty-three other largest capitalist countries. Her industrial production was nearly half that of the entire world. Her consumption of the principal raw materials and foodstuffs was 39 per cent of the total for the fifteen greatest commercial nations. This predominance is important because the American economy is less stable than that of the rest

Economic Journal, December, 1944. A review of: *The United States in the World Economy*. Prepared in the International Economies and Statistics Unit of the Bureau of Foreign and Domestic Commerce, U.S. Department of Commerce. By Hal. B. Larry and Associates; with a foreword by Wayne C. Taylor, Under-Secretary of Commerce.

of the capitalist world. In 1920–21 the decline and recovery in U.S.A. was sharper than in any other country. In the great slump, U.S. industrial production fell by almost 50 per cent, while in other countries (excluding U.S.S.R.) the decline was 25 per cent. In 1937 a swing of Government policy towards 'sound' finance precipitated a fall in industrial production of more than 20 per cent in a single year.

The variability in U.S. production is reproduced with more than proportionate violence in her purchases from the rest of the world. Partly because of her high protective tariff, but perhaps more because of her superior productivity in manufacture, U.S. physical imports consist mainly of industrial raw materials. The volume of these imports moves almost exactly with industrial production, so that their volume falls sharply in a slump. As the U.S.A. market is a substantial proportion of the world market, and as the commodities in question have in general an inelastic supply, a reduction in the volume purchased in U.S.A. leads to a sharp fall in their prices. The value of imports therefore falls more than in proportion to the decline in home activity in U.S.A. Nor do other types of imports come to the rescue. The small trickle of luxury imports which comes in over the tariff shrinks when the wealthy classes are suffering from the financial consequences of the slump. Foreign travel, which provides a substantial volume of invisible imports in boom periods, falls sharply for the same reason. Family remittances to relatives abroad fall off with the growth of unemployment in U.S., and foreign missions and other charitable institutions curtail remittances when their subscribers are hit by the slump. After 1921 U.S.A. was a net importer of shipping services, and payments under this head also fall sharply with the decline in passenger and freight traffic due to the slump. Total payments on income account fell from $6,361 million in 1929 to $2,322 million in 1932. Thus a decline in national income to about half of the boom level reduced purchases from abroad to little more than a third.

The decline in the world supply of dollars on capital account preceded the fall on income account. The report gives a vivid account of the orgy of American foreign lending in the late 'twenties: 'Considerable importance must be assigned to the competition between investment banking firms for this business and the abuses engendered thereby. Enticed by the prospect of commissions much higher than those available on domestic issues, and faced with the necessity for a continuous flow of new securities to keep large staffs of bond salesmen employed, American investment bankers had their agents "sitting on the doorsteps" of prospective borrowers, as one observer put it, offering them money, and many times persuading them to borrow more than they actually needed. The bonds were widely distributed, in turn, to the American investing public, which was attracted by the high yields obtainable, and apparently willing to rely on the judgment of the selling bankers as to the safety of the loans'. In 1928 the great bull market in Wall Street, coinciding with a deterioration in activity abroad, particularly in Germany, reduced this business sharply, and the cessation of foreign lending, as a result of the slump which it helped to precipitate, became almost complete in 1931.

The fall in purchases on income account and in loans between them produced the cataclysmic decline in the world supply of dollars depicted above. How did the world react? The various elements cannot always be sharply distinguished in the figures, but the following factors can be seen at work:

1. There was a decline in demand for dollars which may be called coincidental with the fall in supply. There would have been some recession in activity in the rest of the world in 1929 even if U.S.A. had not fallen into the slump. This, so to say indigenous, decline in home incomes abroad reduced demand for dollars both because of falling consumption of U.S. goods and services along with goods and services in general, and because of a decline in dividends on U.S. foreign equity investments and in profits earned in U.S. concerns operating abroad.

2. More important than the coincidental decline in incomes abroad was the decline induced by the fall in American expenditure. The multiplier operating upon a fall of four milliard dollars in U.S. payments to the rest of the world, set the slump spinning on its downward spiral, reducing income abroad, and consequently consumption of U.S. goods and services (as well as dividend payments). This in turn deepened the slump in U.S.A. itself.

3. Defaults reduced fixed-interest payments to U.S., both on business and government account. (Service of war debts, which

bulked so large in contemporary discussions, was numerically a relatively small part of the whole.)

4. On top of the decline in foreign incomes directly induced by the fall in U.S. payments for visible and invisible imports, a further decline in incomes was indirectly induced, through the medium of deflationary policies adopted in many countries struggling with an adverse balance of payments (each country thereby increasing the difficulties of the rest).

5. As the slump wore on, deflationary pressure was somewhat relaxed as many countries sought an alternative in exchange depreciation and in various devices of economic nationalism. The appreciation of the dollar, brought about by the depreciation of sterling and allied currencies in 1931, was reversed in 1933. While it lasted it brought only slight relief. For the bulk of American imports, as the report clearly shows, price elasticity is zero. Depreciation of the suppliers' currency merely reduces the amount of dollars paid for imports. On the other hand, depreciation must have played some part in curtailing American exports, though it was less important than direct measures of protection. The scramble towards autarky which followed the onset of the slump, while it curtailed the foreign trade of each country relatively to its shrunken home income, curtailed imports from America relatively to imports in general. (This is shown in a particularly interesting series of tables in the report.) Thus in the end the world evolved for itself something like the scarce currency clause of the Bretton Woods proposals, and, after bitter struggles, partially solved the problem of the deficiency in the world supply of dollars by discriminating against imports from U.S.A.

The tone of the report is extremely sympathetic towards the troubles caused in the rest of the world by the instability of the American economy. The authors by no means subscribe to the view that economic nationalism helped to cause the slump, and that, if a regime of fixed exchanges and non-discriminatory trade could be re-established, all would be well. (Indeed, it is hard to understand how this view has succeeded in surviving at all in face of the evidence.) They hold that one reason why the rest of the world suffered more in the great slump than in 1920 or in 1937 was precisely because the gold standard was in operation in 1929. In the earlier slump drastic exchange depreciation enabled the rest of the world to some extent to insulate itself from U.S.A., and by 1937 it was partially cut off by protection, trade planning and 'multiple currency practices'. Mr. Wayne Taylor, in his admirable foreword, sums up: 'Unless the supply of dollars is more adequate to meet foreign requirements, other countries will assuredly insist on their rights to exercise a close selective control over the use of the amounts available and to promote more intensive relations with third countries under preferential trading arrangements. Unless dollars are made available with greater regularity than in the past, it would be both unjust and unwise to demand the removal of restraints and controls largely designed to protect the internal economies of other countries against external shock and pressure'.

If the rest of the world must blame the vagaries of *laissez-faire* in U.S.A. for much of its troubles, in one respect it has only itself to thank. Mr. Wayne Taylor continues: 'Serious difficulties also arose from the misuse of dollars by foreigners. This was notably true of the behaviour of foreign capital, which was especially attracted to the United States in time of distress and unrest abroad and of economic expansion in this country. Such shifts of capital, which went largely into speculative stock-market transactions and short-term balances, were of little or no benefit to this country and did positive damage to other countries. Unless brought under control in the future, capital movements of this nature might readily nullify other efforts to attain greater stability in international transactions and would decrease the amount of dollars available to foreigners for purchases of American goods and services'.

It is impossible to distinguish movements of 'hot money' sharply in the figures. In the early part of the period short-term capital movements are hard to trace. As the report says: 'It is a remarkable commentary on the complacent *laissez-faire* attitude that characterized the 'twenties that only the barest data were collected on the volume and composition of short-term funds'. After 1931 the data are more complete, but, even then, the type of asset acquired by a lender does not necessarily provide a clue to the nature of the transaction. Capital movements are analysed under the headings of new issues, direct investments, repayments, dealings in outstanding securities, and short-term capital transactions. The last two are the main vehicle for purely financial movements, induced by exchange speculation, stock-exchange speculation or political uncertainties and fears. The report does not attempt to provide an over-all figure for movements of this type, but it is clear that a great part of the suction which dried up the liquidity of the world, and forced her superfluous gold hoard upon U.S.A., came from this source.

This is most clearly seen in the latter part of the period. After 1934, American exports were kept in check by protective devices in other countries while internal production, and with it American imports, revived (mainly under the influence of deficit finance), so that from 1935 to 1937 U.S.A. had an adverse balance on current account (in million dollars, 1935, — 156; 1936, — 218; 1937, — 31), yet in these years there was a large net inflow of capital (1935, + 1,508; 1936, + 1,208; 1937, + 877) leading to an inflow of gold of more than a milliard dollars in each year. In 1939 the inflow of gold from the distracted world reached the fantastic level of three milliard dollars, while the surplus on current account was $732 million.

In the discussions leading up to the Bretton Woods proposals it has been recognized that this sort of thing cannot be allowed to continue. It is clear enough in principle that private owners of wealth have no right to the liberty to move funds around the world according to their private convenience, and it is clear that, in the uneasy conditions of modern times, no conceivable international currency system can survive for long if that liberty is granted. Admitting this principle involves a substantial departure from *laissez-faire* ideals. It entails that each country (or each group of countries joined in a currency union) must exercise control over its foreign exchange dealings, and permit no net outflow on capital account beyond the limits of the surplus on the national income account. This is not a simple matter, even for a relatively well-disciplined society like our own, provided with competent statisticians and incorruptible officials. But whatever difficulties and disagreeableness it may entail, it is clearly a *sine qua non* for the re-establishment of any reasonable international currency system.

It is interesting to observe that Article VI of the Bretton Woods document is drafted in such a way as to leave U.S.A. free from any inducement to control capital transfers. In itself, this is not of much importance. A flight *from* the dollar if it occurred (for instance, in the interval between a new slump and a new New Deal) would merely bring about a welcome redistribution of gold around the world. But it seems rather unlikely that there would be any eligible place for American capital to fly to, since other nations would be free to prevent the retransfer of the capital once lodged with them. The drafting of this article has, however, wider implications. It is symptomatic of the fact that the U.S. authorities have no intention of exercising control over capital movements of any kind, so that the adjustment of new lending to the balance on income account is to be left as heretofore to the chances of *laissez-faire*. Even if the 'hot money' nuisance were kept within bounds by controls in the deficit countries, the major problem of international lending would still remain to be solved.

It is laid down in the Bretton Woods proposals that when a currency threatens to become scarce, the International Monetary Fund may issue a report 'setting forth the causes of the scarcity and containing recommendations designed to bring it to an end'. At the onset of the next American depression a report such as this Department of Commerce document—enlightened, lucid, sober, based on indisputable evidence—might have a great influence in educating the capitalist world. But, at best, what could it recommend? It could call for the cessation of a perverse capital movement from deficit to surplus countries, if this was still persisting; it could instruct the Fund to provide liquidity, so as to check the secondary deflation in deficit countries attempting to defend their balances of payments; it could give its blessing to policies of mutual support among deficit countries attempting to counteract the fall in their own home activity. But the hard core of the problem—the fall in American purchases from the world—would still remain. An appreciation of the dollar, or the enforcement of the scarce currency clause, would check American exports, and throw back some of the secondary consequences of the slump on to the United States, making unemployment some-what worse there and somewhat less outside. But this at best would be only a partial remedy for the rest of the world, and for the world as a whole, including U.S.A., it would be no remedy at all. Nothing but a recovery of outlay by U.S.A. could provide a genuine solution.

Mr. Wayne Taylor and his colleagues tentatively favour the maintenance of U.S. national income by means of a large surplus of exports matched by foreign lending; since they are shy of discussing inter-government loans, and since the sale of foreign bonds to the U.S. public has such a dismal history, they lay the main emphasis on direct investments in countries requiring development. Yet it is scarcely plausible to suppose that direct investments, commercially profitable, can be found on a sufficient scale to maintain a high level of employment in U.S.A. for long. And, if found, it is very doubtful how far they would be welcomed by the countries in which it was proposed to situate them. (The report suggests that the association of local with American business interests serves to ' "nationalize" enterprises financed by alien capital', but this scarcely seems sugar enough to get the undeveloped countries to swallow the pill of dollar imperialism.) Nor is there any reason to suppose that a boom based on such investments would not lead to a slump, when the cream had been skimmed, which would face the world with the old problem in a slightly new form. But what are the alternatives? Investment planning inside U.S.A.? Perpetual deficits? A redistribution of income that would cut at the root of the excessive American propensity to save? We could scarcely expect the Fund, reporting on a scarcity of dollar exchange, to recommend a revolution in the United States.

The conclusions of the Department of Commerce report are its weakest point. Yet it is scarcely a reproach to the authors to say so. It is just because they see the problem clearly that they find it baffling.

EXCHANGE EQUILIBRIUM

THE phrase 'a fundamental disequilibrium' occurs in the Bretton Woods Final Act. 'A member shall not propose a change in the par value of its currency except to correct a fundamental disequilibrium'. Since this is part of a solemn international agreement, it is a matter of considerable importance to know what it means. But so far as I know, no definition which will hold water has ever been proposed.

The word 'disequilibrium' implies that there is some state of affairs which can properly be described as equilibrium. The question we have to discuss is 'What is a condition of equilibrium in international trade?'

Exchange rates have no meaning apart from the relative levels of costs in the various countries concerned. Broadly speaking, the effect upon trade of an all round rise in money-wage rates in one country is equivalent to the effect of an equal proportional appreciation in the exchange rate of that country; and the effect of a fall in wage rates is equivalent to a depreciation in the exchange rate. To simplify the discussion I will at first assume that the level of money wages in every country is fixed. This is, of course, quite arbitrary, and the assumption is made purely for convenience in conducting the argument.

Before going further with the discussion, it is necessary to clear up some verbal points. We must distinguish, in a country's external receipts and payments, between the income account and the capital account. The income account covers payments for imports and exports, including 'invisible' items such as shipping services and tourist expenditure, which make up the balance of trade, and other income payments, such as interest on foreign capital. The income account is balanced when, over any period, say a year, a surplus on the balance of trade offsets interest payments, or a deficit is offset by receipts.

The balance of payments covers capital movements as well as the income account. The balance of payments is in equilibrium when no net gain or loss is taking place in a country's monetary reserves—that is, in its gold, foreign exchange or rights of drawing on the Fund. Equilibrium in this sense exists when capital movements are offsetting any discrepancy in a country's income account—a surplus on income account being matched by an equal rate of lending abroad, or a deficit being matched by borrowing. Equilibrium in the balance of payments is not easy to define precisely, for it is not always possible to draw a quite clear-cut line between movements of monetary reserves and capital movements, but this is a minor complication, which we need not go into now.

Equilibrium in the balance of payments is of the greatest importance, especially in connection with the monetary position of a country—its liquid reserves—but it is clearly not the criterion of equilibrium which we are looking for. A discrepancy between the income account and capital movements must normally be dealt with by altering the capital movements, not by altering the exchange rate. Moreover, equilibrium in the balance of payments may be equilibrium only in a very superficial sense. Most of the western European countries are at present matching a surplus of imports by drawing on Marshall Aid, which diminishes or prevents monetary disequilibrium. But the balance is temporary and precarious. No one would say that Western Europe is in a position of equilibrium, though disequilibrium does not show itself in the balance of payments.

If the balance of payments is not the criterion, should we take the balance of income account? Should we say that there is equilibrium when the value of imports (say, over a year) is equal to the value of exports (for simplicity, including in those terms all income items)?

At first sight this seems reasonable enough. But, in fact, it is of very little use. There is no one unique position of equilibrium with balanced trade, for the amount of imports, and to a less extent the amount of exports, depend upon the level of activity in the country. When employment and income are high, the demand for imports is high. A surplus of imports can be corrected by a fall in home employment. Any value of exports, within wide limits, will be matched by an equal value of imports at some level of home income. This was the basis of the so-called 'natural' mechanism of a *laissez-faire* system. A fall in exports causes unemployment and depression in the home country and so reduces the consumption of imports. The consumption of imports will not of itself fall to just the right extent to balance the fall in exports. According to the old orthodox monetary policy, a further fall in home income had to be brought about by raising interest rates and restricting credit. Balance between imports and exports is restored, without any change in exchange rate, when national income has fallen low enough. For instance, if one quarter of marginal income is spent upon imports, the fall in national income required to restore balance is four times the initial fall in exports. This is an exceedingly cruel and wasteful way of restoring equilibrium, as many nations found to their cost in the inter-war period. But it does establish equilibrium, if by equilibrium we merely mean imports equal to exports.

Then should we take as our criterion a position in which equilibrium is established without a fall in employment—or, in the words of Bretton Woods, 'without resort to measures destructive of national or international prosperity'?

This also fails to provide any unique solution. If we started out from an ideal position of equilibrium in which every country had full employment (not at the peak of a boom, but as a continuous state of affairs), then we might talk of a set of exchange rates which would preserve that equilibrium. But, unfortunately, the world (outside the economic text-books) never has been in that ideal state. The idea of a position of equilibrium, to be maintained, or restored after it has been lost, is merely an economist's version of the myth of the Golden Age.

So long as world unemployment exists, there is no one position of equilibrium. Any country with a lower exchange rate (relative to its home costs) can secure for itself a larger share of the given total of world employment, at the expense of increasing unemployment in other countries. In 1931 the depreciation of sterling gave Great Britain an advantage over U.S.A. and France. In 1933 the dollar snatched back the advantage from the pound, leaving the franc and other gold bloc countries to suffer. In 1936 the franc followed the pound and the dollar, and everyone was back where they started from.

It is precisely this kind of thing that the Bretton Woods system is designed to avoid. It is now accepted that no country should indulge in purely competitive depreciation. But when is depreciation 'purely competitive'? Unless we have an ideal position to start with there is no particular advantage in preserving whatever happens to be the *status quo*. There is no meaning in the conception of an equilibrium distribution of unemployment between the nations of the world.

Should we then take as our criterion of equilibrium a position in which there is both full employment in each country and balanced trade? Does this provide the ideal position that we are searching for? I do not think that it does. First, it does not really provide a unique solution of the problems of exchanges. Full employment in each country can be preserved only by conscious policy, and there is an infinite variety of patterns of trade compatible with full employment, corresponding to various employment policies. (It is the matter of the highest importance that the plans which are being made in various countries at the present time should be designed to fit each other—but that is a point by the way.)

The second objection to this criterion is that it is purely ideal. Must we wait for universal and successful employment policies before we can begin to discuss the problem of exchanges? The world we are living in is far from ideal, and if some major nations are not in fact planning for full employment, or are not succeeding in their plans, what becomes of our criterion?

The third objection is of a different kind. Why should we regard balanced trade for each country as the ideal for a full employment world? If each country is to maintain full employment with balanced trade, it means that each country must absorb its own savings in home investment, and each country's investment must be limited by its own savings. The habit of thinking nationally has become so ingrained that this does not sound unreasonable. But looked at from the point of view of the world as a whole it is far from reasonable. It means that accumulation of real capital must go on rapidly in wealthy countries where capital is already plentiful, and slowly in poor countries where needs are great. The breakdown of international investment may be going to drive the world near to this position, but it is certainly one which cannot be regarded as ideal.

It should be the object of policy to keep international lending alive as far as possible, rather than to set up a system where every country's trade is balanced and no lending whatever takes place. The old orthodox *laissez-faire* ideal was quite different from a system of balanced trade. Under pure *laissez-faire* in the ideal system of economic liberalism, capital is continually flowing to the point where prospective profits are greatest. Wealthy countries carry out their investment abroad, and run a surplus on income account equated to their rate of lending. Countries with favourable opportunities for investment run a deficit on income account —that is, a surplus of imports—and borrow at a corresponding rate. Exchange rates then have to be such as to permit the deficits and surpluses in the balances of trade to the various countries to correspond to the international flow of capital. This liberal ideal requires sufficient international confidence to make the whole world a single capital market, and it requires that world investment is always sufficient to provide full employment for each country. The first condition is certainly not fulfilled to-day, and the second was never fulfilled even in the most prosperous and successful period of liberal capitalism. Indeed, the whole picture of harmonious world development is little more than an economist's opium dream; we certainly cannot find in it a secure foundation for our standard of exchange policy.

The free flow of capital, in the inter-war period, degenerated into flights of 'refugee money', and nowadays national control of capital movements is generally agreed to be a *sine qua non* of any international monetary system, so that the rate of lending becomes a matter of more or less conscious policy. The actual position must be something between a state of affairs in which each country's trade is balanced, and a state of affairs where balances are dictated by a free flow of capital seeking to find its own level in the economic contours of the world.

In this intermediate region there is no one pattern of trade which has any claim to be considered the equilibrium. Currency stability requires that, whatever balances may be, lending and borrowing shall be compatible with them—otherwise some countries are losing monetary reserves and a breakdown will occur. But there are any number of possible positions of purely monetary equilibrium, with more or less lending going on, and we cannot pick out any one of the possible positions for the honour of representing 'fundamental equilibrium'.

If I am right in the foregoing argument, there is no one meaning for 'equilibrium' and therefore no clear standard for 'fundamental disequilibrium'. It seems that any country which wishes to alter its exchange rate can find plenty of arguments to show that it is in fundamental disequilibrium, in one sense or another, and equally the managers of the Fund can always find plenty of arguments to show that it is not. Perhaps we may guess that the architects of Bretton Woods were not so naïve as their phraseology suggests, and that their conception was that under cover of their mystic formula, a system of 'case law' would gradually be built up, on the basis of precedents. It is certainly a more useful approach to the problem, instead of looking for a general principle of equilibrium, to consider particular cases, and to see what rules might reasonably be applied to each one, but, even then, the notion of an equilibrium exchange rate begs all the questions.

The case which is most obviously pertinent to discuss at the present time is the deficit of the rest of the capitalist world with the United States.

Europeans are apt to develop an ambivalent attitude to the United States. We regard her economy as a great benefactor to the world, and at the same time as a menace. The menace consists in two things—first, a tendency to develop an export surplus of huge dimensions; and secondly, the extreme instability of the United States economy. For the moment we are concerned with the first aspect of the menace—a continuous surplus in income account.

A surplus of exports not matched by an equal rate of lending is a menace to world stability in an obvious sense. It sucks up the liquid reserves of other countries, and creates a monetary crisis for them. The United States has sometimes been accused of sucking up the world's gold reserve in this way in the pre-war years. This accusation, in the main, is false. The great inflow of gold into the United States, which reached its peak of three milliard dollars in 1939, occurred when the surplus was only seven hundred million. The flight of capital to seek refuge from the troubles of Europe was the main cause of that influx of gold, and such flights in the future will presumably be checked. But if the United States has been falsely accused in the past, the danger still remains for the future.

So long as the surplus country is lending at the appropriate rate, equilibrium is preserved in the purely monetary sense. The balance of payments is not disturbed. But the surplus country may still be creating a problem for the rest of the world. It may be taking advantage of a strong competitive position to keep up employment at home while causing unemployment abroad. Thus the merely monetary criterion is not sufficient to show that nothing is amiss.

At the same time, a surplus, as I have already argued, is not necessarily disadvantageous to the rest of the world, and, indeed, may be of very great benefit. A surplus is beneficial to the world when the lending which accompanies it is making investment possible in other countries which would not be possible without it, or where relief payments are raising the level of consumption. Lending which is matched by new real investment or consumption in the world is raising the whole level of world income. The employment generated in the lending industry by its surplus of exports is then not at the expense of employment anywhere else, and the surplus is beneficial all round. This may be clear enough as a theoretical distinction. But it will always be hard in actual cases to distinguish between a 'good' surplus which is benefiting the world as a whole and a 'bad' surplus which is exporting unemployment from the lending country to the rest of the world. Probably in the main the British surplus in the nineteenth century was a 'good' surplus in this sense. It permitted development in the New World which would not have been possible without it, and helped to maintain world prosperity. Equally, the American surplus from the end of the war to the present time has undoubtedly been mainly a 'good' surplus. The world, until recently, was not suffering from unemployment so much as from the reverse evil—a pressure towards inflation—and relief payments and reconstruction loans have been of the greatest benefit to the world as a whole. This is true even of loans which are 'tied' to dollars. Each country much prefers loans made by U.S.A. to others to be free, for then they have a chance of getting some dollars by exporting to the borrowers. Borrowers also would prefer free loans. But tied loans are a great deal better than none in a period of reconstruction. So long as the American surplus is covered by lending, and so long as the lending is contributing to world recovery, we have no reason to regard it as a menace, and every reason to welcome it.

But the period of post-war reconstruction is highly abnormal. If American lending and gifts could continue indefinitely, well and good. But if they do not, the American surplus cannot continue without causing disturbance to the rest of the world. It may be difficult to distinguish in practice between a 'good' surplus and a 'bad' when lending matches the surplus, but there is no doubt at all that a surplus which is not matched by lending cannot be allowed to persist.

The rules of good neighbourly behaviour in international trade require that a country should have a surplus no larger than its continuous lending can cover. What policies are appropriate to wipe out an undesired surplus?

First, without interference with the relative prices of home-produced and imported goods, the total of imports can be increased by increasing total national income. Every country normally imports more in a boom than in a slump, and it may be that the establishment of full employment in the surplus country would be sufficient by itself to wipe out the surplus.

Second, if the surplus country has been restricting imports by tariffs and other means, imports at a given level of national income can be increased by removing the restrictions.

Third, imports may be increased, and at the same time exports reduced by an appreciation of the exchange rate (or, removing for the moment my initial assumption, by an all-round rise in money-wage rates).

The last two measures reduce the level of employment in the surplus country. The best policy, from the employment point of view is to combine measures which increase imports and reduce exports relatively to a given level of national income, while at the same time maintaining or increasing the total level of income by promoting investment or consumption at home.

An alternative is to reduce hours of work, without reducing weekly money wages. This has the same effect as exchange appreciation in making production in the surplus country more expensive, relative to world prices, and so restricting exports and increasing imports, and at the same time it substitutes leisure for unemployment.

Any of these measures, carried far enough, will wipe out an undesired surplus, but they are by no means all alike from the point of view of the outside world, for they have very different effects upon the terms of trade, and therefore upon the real income of the outside world. An increase of imports into the surplus country brought about by an increase in its level of activity, and

still more one brought about by lowering of tariffs, will (except
in very peculiar cases) raise the prices which it pays for the goods
it imports relatively to the prices of its exports; whereas an
appreciation of its exchange rate is very likely to have the reverse
effect. The recognition of this difference, as we shall see in a
moment, lies behind the famous 'scarce currency clause' of
Bretton Woods.

In so far as the surplus country fails to take measures to reduce
its surpluses to the dimensions of its continuous lending, the
outside world must perforce take measures to lop the surplus off.
Broadly, the world has three choices, to go into a sufficiently deep
slump to cut its imports to the extent necessary to restore balance,
to appreciate the surplus currency by devaluing its own currencies, or to cut down imports from the surplus country by tariffs
or direct controls. The Bretton Woods scheme deprecates the
first, and offers a choice of the other two. The fact that it offers
a choice and does not merely insist on the adjustment being made
solely by altering exchange rates, was due to a recognition (perhaps not very consciously formulated) that adjustment by means
of exchange rates may be so exceedingly onerous for the deficit
countries (because of the cataclysmic effect upon the terms of
trade of a depreciation large enough to meet the case) as to be
quite impracticable. In such a situation the process of lopping
off the surplus must take the form of discriminatory exclusion of
imports from the surplus country, development of alternative
supplies, and all the devices of 'dollar saving' with which we are
only too sadly familiar.

The choice between the two methods (exchange depreciation
and 'dollar saving') must be a matter of judgment for the deficit
country—a judgment which has to be made very much in the
dark, since most of the information necessary for a wise decision
is not available. Bretton Woods purported to give a mechanical
criterion—when a currency becomes 'scarce' discrimination
against it is permitted. But this scarcity is not a world-wide
scarcity of dollars such as we are experiencing now; it is a purely
technical scarcity within the Fund, which is neither here nor there.
The spirit of the scarce currency clause was far-sighted indeed,
but its actual form has not been of the slightest use.

What is needed now is not a mechanical scheme derived from
the mythology of 'equilibrium', but a code of good neighbourly

conduct which ensures that the deficit countries, each endeavouring to economize imports and push exports in the struggle to balance their trade, should help one another, and each try to find means of solving its own problem without making the problem harder for others. Bitter experience is beginning to teach us this lesson. But many minds are bemused by the *fata morgana* of 'equilibrium exchange rates' which, they still believe, could be achieved if only all nations would trust themselves to the 'free play of economic forces' and allow exchange rates to find their 'natural' level.

The second menace which the United States' economy holds for the rest of the capitalist world is its instability. Even if balance is somehow or other established with the United States in a high level of activity, the American surplus would be bound to emerge again if the United States fell into a slump.

When United States activity declines, other countries find their exports fall off. They are then faced with the problem of finding alternative uses for the labour dismissed from export industries. To discuss this problem would take us too far afield; for the purpose of the present discussion we will assume that they are reasonably successful in doing so. Then their imports, in the first instance, will fall, if at all, by much less than exports, and there will be a deficit on current account to be financed. It might be that the countries in question had ample reserves, which they were willing to lose. Or the American genius for improvisation might throw up some new 'point' or 'plan'[1] by which sufficient dollars are lent to finance the rest of the world's deficit. If neither of these ways of fending off the problem is available, the deficit countries are brought up once more against the necessity to balance their trade either by depreciation or by import restriction. It has been specifically declared that a deficit due to maintaining employment in face of a slump elsewhere enables a country to plead 'fundamental disequilibrium' under Bretton Woods. But there is nothing to show whether depreciation is a desirable course. Any one country might be able to defend its full employment policy and secure balanced trade by depreciating, but it can only do so by making the situation worse for the rest. If a number of countries depreciate, in effect the dollar is appreciated and the

---

[1] For instance, the one suggested in the United Nations' report on *National and International Measures for Full Employment*.

slump in the United States is made all the deeper. Equally, if the deficit countries reduce imports by tariffs or direct controls, they make the situation in the United States worse (and incidentally may damage each other considerably in the process). Either way, the onus of restoring equilibrium is thrown back upon the United States. Thus our argument comes full circle. The policies which restore equilibrium 'without resort to measures destructive of national or international prosperity' are policies which surplus countries, not deficit countries, can pursue.

The deficit countries are necessarily in a weak economic and political position. It seems a little absurd for us all to stand around wringing our hands and begging the United States to save us by destroying her own competitive superiority. But at least we are better off if we understand our own position clearly, and do not allow ourselves to be deceived by hollow phrases such as 'fundamental equilibrium'.

One final point: I assumed at the beginning that money wage rates were fixed in each country. In reality, of course, relative wages, especially relative efficiency wages, are highly variable. When a country's trade is thrown out of balance by a rise in its money wages, then exchange depreciation can save it from the necessity for undertaking the wasteful and painful process of lowering home money-costs. This is a proper and useful function for exchange policy. The main reason for making exchange rates variable is not to correct the deep-seated causes of disequilibrium, for which, I have argued, more far-reaching policies are required, but simply to offset differences in the cost structure of various countries. When Lord Keynes used to maintain that Bretton Woods was not the gold standard, but just the opposite, it was this that he had mainly in mind. The fact that we now have a system which does not periodically require a cruel and barbarous deflation is at least so much to the good.

But by solving one set of problems this creates other difficulties —for theory: how to define an 'equilibrium' movement of money-wage rates—for policy: how to combine the inflationary tendencies of a successful full-employment policy with reasonable stability in the value of money. On both levels, these problems are still unsolved.

PART V

BEAUTY AND THE BEAST

ONCE upon a time there was a great and successful merchant who lived in the prosperous commercial state of Urbania. He filled with success the role of trader and organizer of production, for he invariably dealt thoughtfully with the difficult and vital problems of his business, studying the broader movements of the markets, the yet undeveloped results of current events at home and abroad, and contriving to improve the organization of the internal and external relations of his business. By his bold and tireless enterprise, he had reaped a rich harvest of that material reward which is the steadiest motive to ordinary business work. Yet in the accumulation of his wealth he was, like many traders, often stimulated more by the hope of victory over his rivals than by the desire to add something to his fortune; moreover, like everyone who is worth anything, he carried his higher nature with him into business, and there, as elsewhere, he was influenced by his personal affections, by his conceptions of duty, and his reverence for high ideals.

The business to which he had devoted so much toil, energy and foresight, was located in the capital of Urbania, but the growth of facilities for living far from the centres of industry and commerce had enabled him to take up his residence in a suburb, where an excellent system of drainage, water supply and lighting, together with good schools, and opportunities for open-air play, afforded conditions at least as conducive to vigour as are to be found in the country.

These considerations had been of particular importance to him, as he was the parent of a family of three daughters. This number may appear unduly small, but although in early days he had often reflected that members of a large family are more genial and bright, and often more vigorous in every way than members of a small family, it was yet true that the additional benefit which

---

This paper was compiled in my undergraduate days, in collaboration with Dorothea Morison (afterwards Mrs. R. B. Braithwaite).

a person derives from a given stock of a thing diminishes with
every increase in the stock which he already has. That is to say,
that the marginal utility decreases, and the merchant had
observed that the marginal utility of daughters decreases with
surprising rapidity.

To the education of these three daughters he had always
devoted the utmost personal attention, for whereas he himself
was brought up by parents of strong, earnest character, and was
educated by their personal influence and by struggle with difficulties, he was anxious lest his children, who were born after he
became rich, might be left too much to the care of domestic
servants, who were unlikely to be of the same strong fibre as the
parents by whose influence he was educated; for he was conscious
that though there are many fine natures among domestic servants,
those who live in very rich houses are apt to get self-indulgent
habits, to over-estimate the importance of wealth and generally
put the lower aims of life above the higher. The company in
which the children of some of our best houses spend much of their
time is less ennobling than that of the average cottage, yet in
these very houses no servant who is not specially qualified is
allowed to take charge of a young retriever or a young horse.

In the determination that his household should not be such as
this, he had been careful so to regulate his business that he was
able to spend his leisure hours amongst his family, and by example
and precept to build up a strong and righteous character in his
children.

A time came, however, when his daughters were approaching
maturity, and it became apparent to him that an opportunity
offered for pushing his trade into new and more profitable
channels; for, taking account of his own means, he had already
pushed the investment of capital in the home trade until what
appeared to his judgment to be the outer limit or margin of
profitableness had been reached, that is, the gains resulting from
any further investment in that particular direction would not
compensate him for his outlay.

In other words, the principle of substitution prompted him to
invest capital and personal effort in pushing the sale of his goods
into a field where the reward seemed to him greater than that
which he would receive by any enlargement of the particular
branch of trade in which he was at that moment engaged.

He therefore called his daughters together, and communicating to them his intentions, he addressed them as follows. 'My children, as a merchant I have pursued my own interests, but I have generally benefited my country; my personal connections, as well as my patriotism, have hitherto inclined me to give a preference to home goods, other things being nearly equal. A promising opportunity has now presented itself, and I propose to go myself to Baghdad, there to superintend the expansion of my business.

'In view of this new venture, I would have you remember that business men in the past who have pioneered new paths have often conferred on society benefits out of all proportion to their own gains, even though they have died millionaires. A close and careful watching of the advantages and disadvantages of different courses of conduct has led me to anticipate considerable profit from the adventure upon which I am now embarked, but as it has never been my custom to allow the exigencies of commerce to override the dictates of my higher nature, I intend to purchase for each of you a gift, and this I am the more willing to do when I reflect that the sacrifice will be relatively small owing to the decrease in the marginal utility of money which will attend upon the increase in my income.

'I will therefore ask you to inform me after due reflection the nature of the presents which you desire'.

He then departed to make preparations for his journey, and his daughters were left to the discussion of their momentous choice.

The decision of the first daughter was influenced by the knowledge that total satisfaction is maximized when marginal utilities are equal, and her choice fell upon jewellery, for she was animated by that desire for display which is enhanced among the upper classes by custom and emulation, and though jewellery may be considered a luxury, the demand for it among such persons tends to be strong.

But the second daughter, casting an eye upon her existing stock of possessions, concluded that a more urgent need in her case was for clothing, and that the marginal utility of jewellery would therefore be less for her than that of clothes. Consequently she decided to ask for a beautiful and serviceable gown. We may also assume from this that she discounted the future at a higher rate than her elder sister, for it will be generally admitted that the income of satisfaction to be derived from a gown will be yielded over a shorter period of time than that to be anticipated from jewellery.

When the turn of the third daughter came round, she considered various gratifications which she might obtain for herself, and her desires turned now towards one and now towards another; but she remembered after a time that gifts on so lavish a scale would be likely to reduce her father's stock of available purchasing power, and she realized that her choice lay between personal satisfaction and obedience to the dictates of filial affection. We may here note that the economist does not claim to measure any affection of the mind in itself or directly, but only indirectly through its effects, and he studies mental states rather through their manifestations than in themselves, he does not attempt to weigh the higher affections of our nature against those of our lower, he does not balance the love of virtue against the desire for agreeable possessions, he can only estimate their incentives to action by their effects.

When, therefore, the youngest daughter finally chose not such extravagant gifts as her sisters, but a simple rose, we are justified in assuming that she estimated her father's well-being of higher account than any possible gratification which she might obtain for herself.

The choice of all three being thus determined, the merchant set out to pioneer the way for his new markets in the Orient, taking advantage of that growing rapidity and comfort of foreign travel which has induced so many business men and skilled artisans to carry their skill near to the consumers who will purchase their wares. Let it suffice to say that his efforts were amply repaid, for his rare ability and rare good fortune, both in the particular incidents of speculative enterprise and in meeting with a favourable opportunity for the general development of his business, led him to succeed abundantly. Not only did his commerce afford him that increment on his capital which would just have induced him to continue in business, but over and above this, brought in a surplus which he regarded as a payment for the bearing of risks and the earnings of exceptional ability. On the return journey, not unmindful of the claims of family affection in the midst of the manifold cares of commercial enterprise, he sought for the most suitable market in which to purchase for his daughters the presents which they had desired him to bring home.

He was able, on the further side of the Mediterranean, to find jewellery for his first and garments for his second daughter, at a price which, having regard to the undertaking which he had made and his present income, did not appear to him excessive. But in regard to the rose for his third daughter, he had in mind not only the preference due to home products (other things being nearly equal), but to the difficulties and cost involved in the transport of perishable goods.

Therefore it was not until he arrived at the shores of Urbania that he commenced to entertain serious thoughts of his purchase. Upon inquiry, he discovered that the production of roses was subject to seasonal fluctuations, and that during the current month, although employment was provided in certain preparatory processes, the final product was unprocurable. In the commercial papers, roses were quoted at a scarcity price, but the figure was merely nominal, as there were, in fact, no roses on the market. In view of the dissatisfaction (to him) which would attend his failure to procure a rose, he would have been willing not only to offer a very considerable price, but to undergo a certain amount of fatigue in the search for the desired article. In this sense the disutility of labour may be regarded as entering into the price that he would be willing to pay.

Doubting whether the rose market was so highly organized that communication between the surrounding localities was complete, he set out in the hope of finding some secluded market to which the scarcity demand for roses had not yet been transmitted. In this, however, he was not successful, finding that in those few cases where a small number of roses had been produced at this season, the producers had been able speedily to profit by the high prices ruling elsewhere. Eventually, however, he arrived at a locality where intelligence reached him of a certain landowner who was in possession of a garden of roses. He proceeded thither, and his observation confirmed his information with regard to roses.

He was contemplating the respective quality of various blooms, when the owner of the garden appeared. His aspect was unusual, as he bore the semblance of a beast. The merchant became conscious that he was committing an act of trespass, and attempted to mollify the indignation manifested by the owner by inquiring the price of roses. The beast, knowing that he was in the position of a monopolist, thereupon took unusual steps in maximizing a monopoly profit. Instead of asking a high money price, as might have been expected in the circumstances, he demanded that the merchant, in exchange for the rose, should yield him whatever object first met his view on returning home. The merchant, conscious that his demand for the rose was unusually rigid, and his bargaining position weak, thereupon accepted the somewhat unusual offer. Trained in the course of his business to judge cautiously and take risks boldly, he determined that the certain reward was not out-balanced by a loss which might prove negligible. In this, he displayed that courage and confidence which has by degrees established an upright and honourable tradition in the conduct of business throughout the civilized world; but it must be remembered that while some men make their way by the use of none but noble qualities, others owe their prosperity to qualities in which there is very little which is really admirable except sagacity and strength of purpose. Of such a nature was the beast, who, unknown to the merchant, was in possession of a detailed knowledge of the future, and did not scruple to reap a reward which he had earned neither by constructive work, nor by that function of risk bearing which is the characteristic of speculative activity. For it has been well observed that the speculator who by intelligent foresight anticipates the future, and who makes his gains by shrewd purchases and sales, renders thereby a public service of no small importance, but when to a normal degree of foresight is added supernatural information, the speculator is in a position to enhance his own gains at the expense of less enlightened members of the community. Such malignant forms of speculation are a grievous hindrance to progress.

The merchant, however, was unconscious of the special circumstances which rendered the case a somewhat unusual example of speculative activity, and thereupon concluded the bargain, and entered into immediate possession of the rose. Having thus acquired the object which had caused him such great expense of energy and labour, he proceeded homeward along a route made expeditious and convenient by modern developments of communication.

His arrival in his own city inspired the merchant with that sensation of pleasure which all men of fine feeling must experience after a prolonged absence from the familiar surroundings of their native land, and he looked forward with pleasurable anticipation to those comforts and luxuries of home life which brighten men's lives and stimulate their thoughts.

A certain anxiety which he experienced as to the possible issue of his most recent speculation detracted somewhat from his sense of satisfaction, but he reflected that great progress can be attained only by bold daring, and security may be purchased at too high a price.

As he approached his home, however, this feeling of anxiety gave place to one of positive alarm when he perceived his youngest and best-loved daughter issuing from the house to meet him. He was not slow to realize that this was the price which he would be required to pay for the rose, in fulfilment of the contract which he had made with the foreign landowner. He had never been accustomed to regard his daughters either as capital or as stock-in-trade, and this payment would be in every way as unusual as it was exorbitant. He was therefore for a moment in some doubt as to the advisability of repudiating his obligations—but, reared in that school of honourable tradition which has peopled the world with merchants distinguished for upright dealing and the strictest integrity, he reflected that the structure of modern industry could only be maintained by that rigid observance of contracts which is the essential basis for all commercial progress; for he had always been of opinion that the marvellous growth in recent times of a spirit of honesty and uprightness in commercial matters and the progress of trade morality had been achieved, and could only be maintained, by the scrupulous integrity with which every member of the business community must refrain from yielding to the vast temptations to fraud which lie in his way. But the evils of reckless trading are always apt to spread far beyond the persons directly concerned, and this truth was immediately realized by his youngest daughter when the merchant revealed to her the part which she was called upon to play in the consummation of the transaction which, in obedience to the dictates of his higher nature, he felt himself compelled to fulfil.

With that courage and cheerful determination which had been so carefully inculcated in her by the discipline of a truly liberal education, she instantly proceeded to consider her situation. After much careful thought, an analysis of the position revealed that the disutility of the labour she was called upon to perform was hardly outweighed by the satisfaction of assisting her parent, which would be her reward. For the discommodity of labour may arise from bodily or mental fatigue or from its being carried on in unhealthy surroundings or with unwelcome associates, and the employment which she was contemplating presented undoubtedly the latter, with possibilities of the former characteristics.

Indeed, connubial relations with the beast appeared to her employment of so unpleasant and distasteful a nature that the satisfaction of filial affection hardly appeared to her sufficient remuneration to represent an effective supply price. For the price which is sufficiently attractive to call forth a given expenditure of effort is the effective supply price for that amount of effort, and in the case of employments which are degrading, distasteful, or irksome, the number of persons who are willing to enter them may be so small that a low price is often inadequate to induce the exertion required.

The issue, therefore, seemed to depend on the degree of undesirability represented by the employment under consideration, and she ended her reflections with the following inquiry:

'Father, did you ascertain whether the beast was hairy?'

The merchant, who had always cultivated the faculties of observation and memorization to a high degree, was able to assure her that the degree of hairiness was not above the normal for that class of person.

Quickly balancing the factors relevant to the situation in the light of this additional information, she finally replied: 'In these circumstances, I am just willing to accept the bargain'. At this moment they realized simultaneously that she was on the margin, for they did not omit to notice that an additional (small) increment of disutility would have outweighed the satisfaction to be obtained from obedience to filial duty.

The contract was thus ratified by all parties concerned, and when the day of maturity arrived, the daughter of the merchant presented herself punctually at the residence of the beast. As he came forward to meet her, she compelled herself boldly to face the stern fact that she was about to enter into the service of an employer who was likely to prove both harsh and exacting. No sooner, however, had he taken her by the hand than he became transformed into a beautiful prince.

Such sudden transitions are rare in nature, and though she had been accustomed to the contemplation of the astounding progress of scientific achievement and the innumerable marvels which human invention have rendered possible, she yet was filled with astonishment at such an unusual phenomenon. It became instantly apparent to her that the bargain, far from being the marginal transaction which she had supposed it to be, was one from which she would reap a large producers' surplus. The situation was, indeed, exceptional, for the disutility of labour had now sunk to a negative quantity. It was, indeed, a case parallel to that of intellectual pursuits, where, after the painful effort involved in starting has been overcome, the pleasure and excitement, after they have once set in, often go on increasing until progress is stopped, either by necessity or prudence.

With mutual pleasure, they then proceeded to discuss the bargain which had yielded to both of them so large a degree of satisfaction; for he entered into the enjoyment of a large consumer's surplus by the acquisition of a beautiful and useful wife at the price of a single rose, while she, at the cost of an effort which now promised to be pleasurable, had secured a prize for the attainment of which she would have been willing to undergo irksome and unpleasant labour.

With this happy union of producer's and consumer's surplus, they then lived happily ever after, constantly keeping in mind their higher ideals and maximizing their satisfaction by equalizing the marginal utility of each object of expenditure.